FINAL
REPORTS

By Richard Rovere

ARRIVALS AND DEPARTURES:
 A Journalist's Memoirs

WAIST DEEP IN THE BIG MUDDY

MACARTHUR CONTROVERSY & AMERICAN FOREIGN POLICY

THE GOLDWATER CAPER

AMERICAN ESTABLISHMENT & OTHER REPORTS,
 OPINIONS AND SPECULATIONS

SENATOR JOE MCCARTHY

AFFAIRS OF STATE:
 The Eisenhower Years

THE GENERAL AND THE PRESIDENT
 (Coauthored by Arthur Schlesinger)

HOWE & HUMMEL:
 Their True and Scandalous History

FINAL REPORTS

*Personal Reflections on Politics
and History in Our Time*

RICHARD ROVERE

Doubleday & Co., Inc.
Garden City, New York
1984

Library of Congress Cataloging in Publication Data
Rovere, Richard Halworth, 1915–79
Final reports.
Includes index.
1. Rovere, Richard Halworth, 1915–79.
2. Journalists—United States—Biography.   I. Title.
PN4874.R7A296   1984   070'.92'4 [B]
ISBN: 0-385-13600-5
Library of Congress Catalog Card Number 81–43263

FOREWORD

Richard Rovere, the reader will find, doubted that my critical judgment of friends was to be trusted, and I fear that he was right. However, even while recognizing his point, I continue to regard him as one of the remarkable men of my generation—the generation that was born during the First World War, came of age during the Great Depression, survived the Second World War, and coped in the years thereafter with the vicissitudes of national vainglory and disillusion. He was, in his own phrase, one of the "1915 people," along with his friends Theodore White, James Wechsler, John Bartlow Martin, Alfred Kazin. We all (I am one of the "1917 people") lived through a chaotic era, punctuated by historic illuminations that never fade in memory. Richard Rovere was fourteen when Wall Street laid its egg, seventeen when Franklin Roosevelt told us we had nothing to fear but fear itself, twenty-six when the Japanese struck at Pearl Harbor, twenty-nine when FDR died in Warm Springs, forty-eight when John Kennedy was killed in Dallas. He was sixty-four when he himself died, in Poughkeepsie, New York. He was always deeply interested in public events, yet managed to stand coolly apart from them. I don't think that any one of the writers of my generation recorded the dying fall of history with such verve and at the same time reflected on it with such dispassion and elegance.

The older one gets, the more baffled one becomes by the chemistry of human lives: what makes people what they are, what gives them their peculiar qualities, what leads differing backgrounds and preparations to produce affinities of temperament and taste. From the moment I met Dick Rovere, in the late 1940s, I recognized a man whose values, purposes, and very rhythms of wit and life were deeply sympathetic. But it remained a puzzle how the boy who idly repeated his first grade at school and was soon consigned to a class for the retarded, the young man who had joined the Communist movement and worked for *New Masses,* had grown into the astute, disciplined, and greatly admired journalist. Perhaps it was a puzzle for him, too. In any event, though diffident as a man and impersonal as an observer, he could not bear to leave his own life unexamined. This volume and its predecessor, *Arrivals and Departures* (1976), represent his quest for self-knowledge. He did not live to complete *Final Reports.* But he worked away at it periodically for several years, and we owe a great deal to Jeannette Hopkins for skillfully joining the diverse pieces into a coherent narrative, and to Gardner Botsford for editing the resulting manuscript.

What must be understood about Richard Rovere is that he was first of all a writer. In his college years, he recalls, he fell in love with the English language. This romance survived his passage with the Communists and came to fulfillment when he joined *The New Yorker* in 1944. Harold Ross, the great editor, believed above all in the dignity of words—"single, holy words." Working for Ross confirmed Rovere's dedication. Precision in the use of language became a moral as well as an aesthetic duty—moral, because for Rovere, as for all truly committed writers, the awful discipline of putting words on paper was the only reliable means of ascertaining what one really believed; as Dean Acheson used to remark, "How do I know what I think until I hear what I say?" Rovere became an artist among journalists. His prose has a grace, fastidiousness, and lucidity matched during this century in the American trade only by Walter Lippmann. (Mencken remains in a class by himself.)

In the spring of 1951, when President Truman fired General MacArthur, Rovere and I decided to write a book on that momentarily sensational affair. *The General and the President* was the product of the most agreeable and satisfying of collaborations. I learned a good deal from Rovere in the process. In journal notes after Harold Ross's death in 1951, Dick listed me, quite accurately, among writers who he felt had "suffered from the loss of the sense of the single word." Bernard De Voto had, in fact, instructed me thoroughly in the sanctity of the word years before at Harvard, but writing propaganda during the war and political speeches afterward had nourished in me a fatal addiction to rhetoric. Collaboration with Rovere on the MacArthur book and, later, the merciless criticism to which he (and also Mary McCarthy) subjected the first draft of *The Crisis of the Old Order* brought me back—partway, at least—to first principles.

As a writer of excessively long books, I looked with special envy at Rovere's talent for distillation. It must be said that he looked with equal wonder at the ability of long-distance writers to go on piling up chapter after chapter. He forever brooded about his own alleged low productivity, though he was in truth highly productive. The number of holy words he put in print was formidable, and, reading this book, I was astonished at the further amount he had written which, for one reason or another, he never published. He used to kid about that unfortunate phrase "trained historian," saying that exhaustive studies and a parade of footnotes were not for him. Still, he said everything that a trained historian might want to say about Joe McCarthy in a dazzling book of two hundred pages. Journalists writing on politics in the 1980s seem to publish their raw notes in articles that wander on interminably. Rovere preferred to think about what he was saying and to turn out shapely, searching, pointed pieces, characterized by incisiveness and wit. Contemporary journalists too often give us an endless procession of facts. Rovere gave us the sense of a mind playing acutely upon the facts.

He was, in addition, a very funny writer. His irony was incorrigible and sometimes took in literal-minded readers. Not since Mencken's bathtub hoax has any flight of satiric fancy provoked such solemn discussion as Rovere on the American Establishment. Complaints from scholars that they could not find works cited in the footnotes—Hilary Masters's *Establishment Watering Places* (Shekomeko Press, 1957), Keith E. D. Smith-Kyle's *America in the Round* (Polter & Polter, Ltd., 1956), not to mention the weighty discussions reported in the *Proceedings of the Edgewater Institute, 1961*—gave him considerable bemused pleasure. "The American

Establishment" was a spoof of the kind of portentous conspiracy theory expounded by C. Wright Mills, the sociologist, in his briefly influential book *The Power Elite*—a work that Rovere, in a more serious vein, demolished in a thoughtful review entitled "The Interlocking Overlappers—and Some Further Thoughts on the 'Power Situation.' "

His sensitivity to language led him to begin as a poet, and he was always much drawn to literary criticism. His introduction to the Modern Library edition of Faulkner's *Light in August* was a significant document in the rehabilitation of Faulkner in the 1940s, and his introduction to *The Orwell Reader* (1956) is one of the best essays anywhere on Orwell. Throughout his life Rovere was fascinated by writing and by writers—much more than by politics and politicians. Saul Bellow, Bernard Malamud, Gore Vidal, Mary McCarthy, and Elizabeth Hardwick were close friends. He roamed widely as a reader and found a favorite refuge in the eighteenth century. Dr. Johnson, he has written, was "more alive in my imagination than any other British writer." Among Americans, he discovered special comfort in Oliver Wendell Holmes, partly because of his antimetaphysical bent of mind, his reliance on the "can't helps," but as much because of his style, on which Dick bestowed his ultimate accolade: "There is a liveliness and tension and rub about the briefest of Holmes' letters and the least controversial of his opinions from the bench. He never spoke or wrote except crisply. He never committed a soggy sentence."

"Nobody will believe me when I say that I'm really not especially interested in politics," Rovere wrote in his journal in 1948, "but it's true. . . . My interest in politics is probably equivalent to Lippmann's interest in literary criticism. My interest in criticism is probably equivalent to his in politics." He was, of course, more interested in politics than such disclaimers suggest. But I know what he meant. I remember another politically knowledgeable writer—Edwin O'Connor, of *The Last Hurrah*—protesting that he couldn't care less about politics. For Rovere, as for O'Connor, politics had less interest *per se* than, on one level, as a stage for picturesque personalities and, on another, as an expression of a democratic culture.

In his youth, Rovere had written about politics for *New Masses,* *The Nation,* and *Common Sense,* but he began to develop his distinctive voice—dispassionate, analytical, slightly satiric—in 1944 pieces for *Harper's* on Vito Marcantonio, the left-wing New York congressman, and on Governor Thomas E. Dewey. His early *New Yorker* assignments were mostly nonpolitical until, in 1948, he persuaded William Shawn, Ross's deputy, to let him cover the Truman-Dewey election. The success of Rovere's campaign dispatches led Ross and Shawn to approach him with an idea *The New Yorker* had been resisting for years—a periodic Washington letter, to be written by a disinterested observer who would not be seen as selling the reader a bill of political goods.

Detachment came easily to Rovere. For all his rather definite private feelings, he had an impressive ability to distance himself from the passions and personalities of his time. The Communist experience unquestionably reminded him never to surrender independence to anybody. But he really knew that anyway. He was, he believed, a naysayer by temperament, and he must have been a most implausible Communist, except insofar as that involved saying nay to a broken-down capitalist system. Before he was thirty, he had concluded that writers ought not to try to combine observation with participation. He liked, as he said, a ringside seat when he could get one, but he did not want to be in the ring or in anyone's corner.

His idea in writing the Letter from Washington was to review Washington as dramatic critics reviewed the Broadway theater— describing the play and the performers, extracting all possible fun from the spectacle, seeking what meaning might be found in it, striving always (here he characteristically quoted Matthew Arnold) "to see the object as in itself it really is." Later he decided that the comparison with literary and dramatic criticism might be fallacious. A novel or play is aesthetically complete; the political process infre-

quently reaches well-defined conclusions. Nevertheless, he brought
to politics the sensibility of a literary critic.

Rovere started the Letter from Washington in December 1948
and continued it until his final illness, thirty years later. "We are
very quiet there," Holmes once said of the Supreme Court, "but it is
the quiet of a storm center." This was the particular charm of his
reports from the capital. The lightning flashed and the thunder
crashed, but his remained the unperturbed voice of quizzical rationality. In time, he visited Washington less and less. That made no
difference. His Letters from Washington continued as well informed
as ever and were considerably more reasoned in analysis and urbane
in judgment than anything produced on the scene. The prophetic
afflatus never descended on him. His stance remained that of the
critic who never forgot that the contemporary comedy is played out
in the context of a longer past and a longer future.

He was endlessly amused by the roguery of politics, as he had
been by the roguery of lawyers in his delicious *Howe & Hummel:
Their True and Scandalous History*. Characters like Arthur Vandenberg delighted him. Still, he never forgot that politicians were engaged in serious business. This saved him from an easy Menckenian
dismissal of the whole scene as gaudy nonsense. His book *Senator
Joe McCarthy* kept in marvelous balance his relish of McCarthy as a
super con man and his very real concern over the damage that
McCarthyism was doing to the republic. Basically, he respected the
hard work, the close judgments, and the inevitable frustrations that
marked the lives of serious politicians. His portrait of Robert Taft is
notably appreciative, especially given his disagreement with most of
Taft's views. Nothing better has been written about John Kennedy
than Rovere's discerning sketch in this volume.

Politics entertained him, but in the end depressed him. Through
most of the 1950s and 1960s, he generally separated his preferences
from his commentary. Only in extreme cases did he let himself go—
as in *Waist Deep in the Big Muddy*, his essay in controlled disgust
over the American adventure in Vietnam. "We are," he concluded,

"in a war that threatens all mankind, that can liberate no one, that is irrelevant to our proper concerns as a nation among nations, that acts as an acid on the ties that bind us as a people. . . . Going on with it becomes daily more unconscionable." By this time, the American condition deeply disturbed him—the brutal war and the apocalyptic passions the war bred among the young. Democracy, in his view, depended on civility, on law, on mutual respect and mutual tolerance. It offered not perfection but hope, and violence destroyed the democratic hope. Rovere had liked Kennedy most of all for the young President's conviction that we could create in the United States not only a good society but a good civilization. The emotions unleashed by Vietnam now seemed a reversion to barbarism. "Violence and terror in this country in the foreseeable future will lead away from, not toward, a more humane society."

Dick Rovere himself was preeminently a civilized man—decent, fair-minded, responsible, skeptical, honorable. He was blessed with a marriage of singular felicity. The Roveres adored Manhattan, Key West, travel abroad, but were most at home in the Hudson Valley, where they lived in a succession of venerable houses for a third of a century. They delighted in displaying the river's beauties and recounting its lore to newcomers, and their hospitality was boundless.

His *oeuvre* as a whole describes the journey of an observant and reflective man through the intellectual and political history of America from the 1930s to the 1970s. This last book is a kind of scrupulous meditation on the meaning of the strange and difficult years through which he lived. It will be of enduring interest for its vivid evocation of the atmosphere and mood of the mid-twentieth century. More than that, it embodies a quest, akin to that pursued by Henry Adams the century before, for an education that might equip modern man to face modern reality. Rovere sought meaning for his country, and for himself. Years before, when everyone was turning Donne's mighty line into a cliché, he had written: "I happen not to share the view that no man is an island. I think that every man is an island in the only sense that matters." The individual remained the ultimate mystery. I have said that he was a humane and judicious man. He was also a very brave man. In 1973 a surgeon cut through muscles to remove a malignancy from his neck. Dick lived the rest of his life in unceasing, racking, accelerating pain. He endured this agony with entire fortitude and stoicism. I saw him regularly in these years. His discomfort could not be concealed, but he admitted to his condition only in response to direct questions, and never complained about the constancy of pain or about the unlucky surgical decision. He was a man of courage, of profound and equable honesty, and of absolute integrity.

Reading *Final Reports,* I could not but recall Rovere's own sentence about Orwell: "One feels oneself always in the presence of a writer who is fully alive and has eyes and an intellect and a vibrant character of his own." Readers and friends alike, for a long time to come, will miss Dick Rovere's quirky independence of mind, his sharp and funny insights into a troubled age, and his unalterable devotion to justice and truth.

—ARTHUR M. SCHLESINGER, JR.

AUTHOR'S PREFACE

Just as I was settling down to this work, with a sense of impending adventure, accompanied by a certain trepidation, I came upon a rather intimidating essay by the British critic John Russell. Autobiography nowadays, he wrote, is not so much a distinctive genre as a growth industry. For the elderly, it is, like whittling or needlepoint, "part of the ritual of retirement: a slow fandango to the music of time." One draws one's pension, signs up for Medicare, moves to a warmer climate, and composes one's memoirs. For the indecently young, it is often part of the ritual of success, as in the case of record-breaking athletes, movie stars, astronauts, affluent call girls, youths who have triumphed over drugs or the stock market or spectacularly wretched childhoods. Russell claims to know of one "eminent international publisher who cannot talk to a pretty woman for ten minutes without offering her a contract for her autobiography." (Considering how many such women an "eminent international publisher" is likely to sit next to in the course of a year, I would not like to be on that man's list of authors; he is headed straight for bankruptcy.) That autobiography still has possibilities Russell does not deny—as modern exemplars, he cites Jean-Paul Sartre, Vladimir Nabokov, and Henry Green—but anyone hoping to claim the time of a discriminating reader should, Russell says, be aware that "it is one of the most demanding forms of literary expression." Among other things, the autobiographer "should write as if a complete society had somehow to be reconstructed on the basis of his testimony alone." In short, one needs the gifts of a Dickens, a Balzac, or a Faulkner: "If an autobiography is not a work of art, it is no more than a balance sheet that will never go up to the auditors." However, Russell notes, most great writers have, wisely, eschewed the form. There is something almost ludicrous in the thought of an autobiography by Proust or Joyce, men who poured all of themselves and their knowledge of the world into their monumental fiction. Russell ridicules Thomas Carlyle for having expressed, in 1828, regret over the fact that we have no life of Shakespeare from Shakespeare's hand. The concept of autobiography did not exist in English letters in Shakespeare's time, and even if it had, "we can be quite sure that [that] gigantic nature would never have embarked" on so mundane an enterprise. Yet of the mundane, Russell demands the sublime—art, novelty, the reconstruction of a complete society, "energy, hard work, an excellent memory, a sense of history, exceptional powers of evocation, and an inability to be boring."

Had it not been for the last phrase, I might have found Russell's words not only cautionary but almost unmanning. Has there ever been á writer who was *never* boring, who lacked even the *ability* to glaze a reader's eyes and send his thoughts elsewhere? No doubt it is my fault that I have nodded over Shakespeare, that I have skipped over much of *Moby Dick*, that I have never finished *Don Quixote* and probably never will, that I have wearied of Joyce's word games. My education has been spotty, my tastes are in many ways uncultivated, and I am at times too indolent to meet the demands that great writers make of readers. But I am on turf I know when I consider the case of Sartre, whom Russell hails as a masterly contemporary autobiographer. Sartre is a courageous man and a brilliant and versatile writer, but he is also a man whose capacity for being tedious is as well developed as his gift for the outrageous; he can belabor the obvious in one passage and affront the intelligence in the next. It may be that my energy, already diminishing, will fail to sustain me in the effort I have embarked on here, and that my memory will prove too fallible to be relied upon. But I will not be put off by anyone who tells me that an ability to be tiresome disqualifies me. That I have such an ability can be attested to by family and friends; the point is to avoid exercising it. A large part of any writer's work is editorial; much time and thought must go into spotting and striking the trivial, the bromidic, the repetitious, the irrelevant. But there are pitfalls even in this. "Crispness is all," Russell writes. But Hemingway was crisp, and Dickens, a meanderer who wrote at space rates, was not. Who would call Hemingway the greater of the two? The writer—not just the autobiographer—must also bear in mind that truisms tend to be true, that relevance is relative, and that the irrelevant is not necessarily pointless.

But enough of that.

Who, what, when, where, why—these are the questions that editors and college professors instruct aspiring reporters to try to answer in every story, preferably in the first paragraph.

> At 4 P.M. yesterday, John Doe, of Smithville, pleaded guilty before the justice of the peace, Richard Roe, to a charge of shoplifting in Brown's Bakery, 427 South Main Street, on March 18th. "I just couldn't resist those buns," Doe, a 27-year-old plumber said. "I've always had a sweet tooth." Justice Roe set sentencing for April 1st.

No self-respecting psychologist—indeed, no self-respecting justice of the peace—would accept Doe's explanation of his misbehavior. It is far too simple. A sweet tooth doesn't come from nowhere. What kind of childhood did Doe have? Was there a dietary deficiency? Was there some insecurity that those buns gratified? Plumbers are well paid. What was the nature of the compulsion that led him to steal the sweetmeats? Was there a Jane Doe in his life? Was he, perhaps, a kleptomaniac who would walk off with anything not nailed down? Was there a history of such behavior in the Doe family? Or did Doe see Brown's Bakery as a symbol of an exploitative system? The "why" of the formula is the most vulnerable part, and as an autobiographer I do not expect to do very well with it. Except that I am antideterminist, I have no particular philosophy of history. I tend to believe that, in the final analysis, there is no final analysis. Since I am seldom able to explain my own behavior to my own satisfaction, I have no confidence in being able to explain the behavior of other individuals, let alone of great collectivities such as nations and races and religious movements. But I have some confidence, shaken but not destroyed by Mr. Russell, that I can deal with the who and the what and the when and the where, and that in doing so I can perhaps uncover at least part of the truth.

RICHARD ROVERE,
Key West, 1979

FINAL
REPORTS

1
Who Am I?

I

"Who am I? What have I done?" Stendhal once asked himself. And answered tentatively, "If I write it all down, I may find out." It is in somewhat this questing spirit that I begin. I do not wish to leave my life—or, more important, the time in which I have lived—unexamined. The only way I have of going about this is by writing; for me, as apparently for Stendhal, mere contemplation yields almost nothing. I am the kind of writer, as apparently Stendhal was, who is not quite sure of what he thinks or feels until he sees how it all works out on paper.

To me, at my stage of life, Stendhal's second question is more interesting, more in need of response than the first. I have a literal, reportorial, essentially unmetaphysical mind. A rose is a rose is a rose. I am what I see in the mirror—the stubborn, disorderly, hopeful creature I confront each morning and must contend with throughout the day. The mirror shows only a shell—a husk, a chassis—with perhaps a clue or two (in the eyes, the mouth, the bearing) of what the shell holds. By this I do not mean to say that I think self-knowledge is a simple matter or that it is easily come by. On the contrary, it comes slowly and painfully, in random, ill-fitting bits and pieces, and—at least in my experience—with few dazzling illuminations: merely some shafts of shadowy light now and then, dispelling, sometimes only momentarily, innumerable patches of darkness. And what I mean by self-knowledge is something quite different from what people nowadays mean when they speak of "identity." As I understand it (and I may not understand it very well), identity is established by acts of will, by affirmations, by acceptance and love of self. Self-knowledge, on the other hand, is the quarry of a search, and death comes with the search still in progress. Rembrandt was still seeking a true likeness when he did his last self-portrait; the greatest of literary self-portraits—Montaigne's—was still being re-written, edited, and amended when the author died. Perhaps I labor these distinctions because, though I write forty years after Freud's death, I am more pre-Freudian than Stendhal, who died fourteen years before Freud was born. It is no dishonor to Freud that I have not learned much from him. If I ever experienced an identity crisis, it either passed quickly and quietly, or, as is entirely possible, I have driven away all memory of it. Today, I am content to settle the matter with vital statistics—name, rank, serial number, a bit more:

> Rovere, Richard [Halworth]. Off-white American male. Born May 5, 1915, only child of Louis Halworth and Ethel Roberts Rovere, immigrants. Husband of Eleanor, née Burgess; father of Ann, Mark, Elizabeth. Failed athlete, failed poet. Jack-of-all-trades journalist, 1937– . Mostly seen in New York City and northern exurbs, and, in recent years, Key West, Florida. Conservative by temperament, radical by conviction, liberal by compromise. Astigmatic, arthritic, tendency toward hyperthyroidism. Drinks and smokes too much. No felony convictions. Etc., etc.

But what have I done? Was it worth doing? What have I learned and what, like Henry Adams, have I had to unlearn? When the poet Louise Bogan was about my age—approaching sixty-three—she wrote: "One should set oneself the task, in full maturity, to fix on paper the bizarre, disordered, ungainly, furtive, and mixed elements in one's life." Though I do not have her sense of obligation, I share her need to fix on paper.

I sometimes think of myself as one who has for more than forty years been taking courses and doing field work in what the universities now call American Studies: American society, American politics, American government, American literature, American business, American crime, American justice and injustice—American life in all its wonder and looniness. And, for purposes of comparison, I have observed and tried to understand other societies, their institutions, their people, their particular brands of looniness. In the line of duty, at times disagreeable, I have encountered many of the movers and shakers and many, many more of those who have been moved and shaken, at times beyond endurance. I have been a nonresident Washington correspondent for *The New Yorker* for more than thirty years, an occasional foreign correspondent for that magazine, and a United States correspondent for European journals. My work has ranged from the shamelessly frivolous to the shamefully ponderous and portentous. There have been millions of words—too many by far, and many that I know I would regret if I steeled myself to review them all again. And for me, as for most twentieth-century Americans, work has been mainly a series of interludes—son, husband, father, traveler, wage earner, victim, victimizer, buyer, seller, trader, citizen.

II

My formative years were the 1930s. Depression and unemployment, violence in the mines and mills, dust and devastation on the plains and prairies. Hoovervilles in the cities. Roosevelt and the New Deal. Hitler and the Gestapo. Stalin and the Moscow trials. War in China, war in Ethiopia, war in Spain, eventually war everywhere. The decade was half over before I was touched by much of this, or even aware of it. I was in school and college in quiet, rural settings, remote from breadlines and picket lines. I never worked in a mill, never saw a prairie. I experienced none of the suffering (except vicariously), was witness to none of the killing. When war came, I was deferred because of blindness (with which I was born) in one eye and not very good vision in the other. Nevertheless, I was shaped—perhaps in some ways frozen—in that period. My mind bears its stamp, as vivid, I often think, as a tattoo on a sailor's arm.

When the decade began, I was fourteen and in the second of Shakespeare's seven ages—"creeping like snail unwillingly to school." Most snaillike, most unwillingly. I had spent two years in first grade, and in fourth and fifth was in a section for slow learners. There were many times when teachers advised my father that I might be ineducable. In 1929 I managed to complete the course at a public elementary school (P.S. 9) in Brooklyn, and in the fall, just before disaster struck on Wall Street, I was packed off to a Long Island boarding school (from which I eventually graduated second or third from the bottom of an undistinguished class). I was sent to boarding school because my mother was British, or thought she was, or because she was colonial, which is something rather different. In my luggage when I left Brooklyn were, along with much winter underwear and cod-liver oil, my baseball autographed by Babe Ruth, my Boy Scout uniform, my scalloped-felt skullcap, made from my father's old hat and festooned with gaudy political buttons, and also, I imagine, the latest in the Tom Swift series. My mind then must have been a jumble of batting averages and lineups: funny-paper characters like Happy Hooligan, Fritzie Ritz, Moon Mullins, and the denizens of Gasoline Alley; mythical figures from the recent past like Eddie Rickenbacker, Barney Oldfield, Jim Thorpe, and Jess Willard; pop tunes I had heard on the radio from Ukelele Ike, the Happiness Boys, the Mills Brothers, and the A&P Gypsies; stirring scenes from countless movies; shiny images of automobiles of various makes, models, and vintages—and, no doubt, even shinier images of girls of various makes and models. In that autumn of 1929, Theodore White, my junior by exactly one day, was hawking newspapers on the streets of Boston, speaking Hebrew as well as English and Yiddish, studying French and German and Latin, and dreaming of some day becoming a professor. My proudest attainment then was my ability to spot almost any car (Reo, Maxwell, Hupmobile, Willys) at a hundred yards or so and give its name and year of manufacture. And my dream was of the day when I could own and drive one—preferably, I am sure, in a coonskin coat. I was getting ready for the Jazz Age just as it was ending. Those were the boundaries of my universe when the 1930s began.

When the thirties ended, I was in another universe. I had fallen in love with the English language and was a writer, or called myself one. I was two years out of college, where I had edited the student newspaper and literary journal, and I had published some pretentious poems and criticism in pretentious little magazines. I was supporting myself, after a fashion, by hack work of various kinds. I wrote advertising copy for a man in the pet-food business. I rewrote fairy tales for a physiotherapist named Henrik Hulander, who thought that he was Sweden's answer to Hans Christian Andersen. And I wrote a good deal for magazines that featured "true" accounts of notorious and freakish crimes—"Solving Baltimore's Bloody Enigma of the Bludgeoned Brunettes," "April 1938—the Cruelest Month in Colorado," "Mayhem in Mackinaw, Michigan." For these, I was sometimes Carson Hammond, veteran private investigator, or Stephen Peabody, noted criminologist. I was also doing occasional articles and reviews for *The Nation*, whose staff I was to join in 1940; for *The New Republic*; and for the New York *Herald Tribune*. And this was after I had spent four years in the world of radical politics—organizing workers in upstate New York, raising funds for the Spanish Loyalists, writing left-wing tracts and speeches for left-wing politicians. For a year and a half, I had been on the staff of *New Masses*, a Communist weekly from which I resigned after the Soviet-Nazi nonaggression pact. In August of 1939, I was a Stalinist, in September an ex-Stalinist, in October a vehement anti-Stalinist. My mind was a jumble: Trotsky, Zinoviev, Kamenev, Bakunin, Tukhachevsky, Vishinsky, Radek—and T. S. Eliot, Aldous Huxley, Bertrand Russell, John Dewey, the Arthur Koestler of *Darkness at Noon*, the Edmund Wilson of *To the Finland Station*. I was, politically and intellectually, a displaced person.

III

I was displaced (or misplaced or unplaced) in several other ways—ways to which, through most of my life, I gave little thought and only now begin to deal with as I sort out the furtive and mixed elements.

Sometime in the spring of 1915, my parents moved across the Hudson River, from Washington Heights, in Manhattan, to Jersey City, New Jersey, a grimy, ramshackle industrial town, whose waterfront commands a splendid view of New York Harbor and of the backside of the Statue of Liberty. There they shared expenses and a small apartment with a friend, and there, soon after, on May 5, I was born. A few weeks later, my parents packed up again and returned to Washington Heights, the first of many New York neighborhoods in which I spent my childhood and adolescence.

Both my parents were born abroad and came to New York close to the turn of the century, but neither was part of any of the great immigration waves of the period. My ancestry is so elusive that, in an age of high ethnic consciousness, I am part of no ethnic tradition —or part of so many that I can identify with none. I assume—but only assume—that I am on my father's side French. But I may well be Italian or a mixture of both, and perhaps of several other strains as well. I know that on my mother's side I am British, Scotch, Welsh, and Scandinavian. It is possible that I am also part black, and perhaps part Spanish and Portuguese.

My father had always seemed to me a rather unimaginative man, but for reasons I despair of understanding he created for himself an almost wholly fictitious past. He said that he had been born in New York City in 1888, the only child of Genevieve and Henry Rovere, an importer of chinaware. Rovere, he said, was an Anglo-Saxon name; it had earlier been Rover, but since that had once been a common name for dogs, the terminal *e* had been added to discourage bad jokes. He said that he had spent several years at a boarding school in Switzerland; his mother had gone there for a cure of some kind, had taken him with her, and had died there about 1900. After that, he said, he had gone to Culver Military Academy, in Indiana, before entering Columbia University's School of Mines and Engineering in 1905. His father had died in the fire after the San Francisco earthquake in 1906. There were no living relatives.

The only truth in all this is that he *did* enter Columbia in 1905. I could not, however, have said so until after his death, in 1975, when I was sixty, though I had long been skeptical of much of his account. It is possible that he was born in 1888, though some documents show 1886 and others 1887. The story about our name had a fishy sound, and indeed it turned out to be a fishy story. I had noticed that he sometimes wrote his first name as Lewis, sometimes as Louis. He could not explain this, nor could he explain the origin of the strange middle name—Halworth—he bore and had given me. When asked for details about his early years, he said he could recall almost none. What sort of people were Henry and Genevieve? He had hardly known them, he said, having lived apart from them for so many years. Where in New York had they lived? Where in Switzerland was the school he attended? It was all so long ago, he said, and he simply couldn't recall. But it wasn't all that long ago, and it was inconceivable that this man (he was an electrical engineer with the Western Union Telegraph Company) who could store so much technical data in his mind could have forgotten almost two decades of his life. I did not press him much, for I felt that behind his reluctance to talk there must have been some great pain. If he wanted to bury the past, that was his right. But when he died I wanted to unlock as many of the mysteries as I could. It came to me that some twenty years earlier, one Ernest Rovere, a professional bridge player and the author of a column on contract bridge for a

San Francisco newspaper, had told a mutual acquaintance that he
thought he and I might be related. Though I considered this unlikely—I had believed my father when he had said there were no
relatives alive—I tried to get in touch with Ernest at the time and
failed. But a week or so after my father's death I tried again, and this
time I reached him without difficulty. We quickly established that
he was my father's half brother—some seventeen or eighteen years
younger—and thus my uncle. From him and from a number of leads
he gave me, I learned some, though by no means all, of the truth.[1]

My father was born not in New York—not even in this country—
but in France, in Lyons. My grandfather's name was not Henry but
Leo—in some listings Léon. He and his son, Louis—no Genevieve
in the party—arrived here not later than 1900 and probably a year
or two earlier. They may have been illegal aliens. Leo was not an
importer but a real-estate dealer—a rather shady one, Ernest recalled. In 1904, Genevieve still being absent, Leo married Rae
Bloomfield, a New York schoolteacher, and Ernest was born the
following year. About five years later, after some kind of blowup in
the family, my father, then about twenty-one, left home and was
never again seen by his younger brother. Ernest's memories of my
grandfather seemed anything but fond. In the family, Leo was a
martinet. No one seems to have trusted him. Rae Bloomfield's family had hired private investigators to make certain that the wedding,
which Leo had arranged and which took place in the old Waldorf-
Astoria, was on the level, and that the bridegroom was not a biga-
mist; presumably, no trace of Genevieve turned up. I discovered
later that Leo was listed in the City Directory as a real-estate dealer,
but the Real Estate Board has no record of his operations. He had a
partner who did time in Sing Sing.

Leo died not in 1906 in San Francisco but in 1930 in New York,
not far from where we were living; I was fifteen at the time, Ernest
twenty-five, and my father about forty-two. Of my grandmother, I

[1] For a fuller account of what I learned and how I learned it, see Chapter 11 of my
book *Arrivals and Departures* (New York: Macmillan, 1976).

have learned nothing—not even if her name was really Genevieve. There are indications that she may have been a prostitute, which would explain the fact that her child was put in the custody of the father rather than of the natural mother. "My father never spoke of her or of anything that happened before he got to this country," Ernest said.

As for *my* father, he went to school not in Switzerland or in Indiana but (presumably) in Lyons and later in Manhattan, at St. Ann's Academy, a Roman Catholic institution with many French-speaking students. He graduated with honors in 1905 and entered Columbia. He did badly there and was not allowed to return in 1906. As an engineer—much equipment currently in use is patented in his name—he must have been self-taught; he was quite respected in his profession.

Ernest said he thought that Leo was French, and I have no evidence that he was not. But "Rovere" is a distinctly Italian name—a *rovere* is an oak tree—and "Léon," which seems to have been an afterthought, is commonly a French variant of the Italian "Leo." All the Roveres I know anything about have been Italian—including another Richard Rovere, also born in Jersey City. A "bloke with papal name," Ezra Pound once called me when bringing my attention to what he considered an error in something I had written about him. Sixtus IV (1471–84) was a Rovere, as was one of his nephews, Julius II (1503–13), who laid the cornerstone of St. Peter's, commissioned Michelangelo's frescoes in the Sistine Chapel, and lies beneath a tomb of Michelangelo's design. Mussolini had a henchman named Bruno Rovere, and *Generale della Rovere* was a film about a quintessential Italian con artist. It is conceivable that someone—my father or my grandfather—was trying to conceal Italian origins. In the New York in which I grew up, Italians were considered an inferior breed, much given to crime: e.g., Al Capone, Lucky Luciano, Thomas Lucchese, and Tough Tony Bastoni, a nightmarish figure in Brooklyn until someone had the notion of embedding him in the Pulaski Skyway. In 1973 Richard Nixon explained to a White House aide that Italians were "different from us." He did not mean that they were more virtuous.

Or it may be, as I sometimes suspected, that my father, or his father, was concealing Jewish origins. Ernest's mother was Jewish, and Ernest was brought up as a Jew; Leo, upon his marriage, announced that he had been "converted" to Judaism. As for my nameless grandmother, she was probably French, but she could as well have been Swiss or German or Italian or Belgian or Algerian or Eurasian. I suppose I could learn about her by going to Lyons and burrowing in the archives there, but I have neither the strength nor the appetite for such an enterprise; I have puzzles enough on this side of the ocean.

For one, why, why did my father do what he did? I will, of course, never know. My childhood memory is of a decent, truthful, generally unremarkable man—intelligent, industrious, considerate, responsible, conventional, conservative. I do not recall ever thinking of him as anything but a good and dutiful father. After I left home, after college, I came to know my father—by then separated from my mother—more intimately than I had before, and I grew much fonder of him. In time I came to realize that he had had a deeper influence on me than I had understood. We cared about different things, but we were alike—as my mother and I were not—in being skeptical about most things and suspicious of all certitudes. I began to remember his persistent way of asking me, when I made some broad assertion of what I regarded as truth, what my evidence was, where I had got the opinion I expressed, and if I had considered all other possibilities. To almost every declaration I made, he asked, "Why?," and I became grateful to him for this corrective intervention. And in spite of the question of his identity, I shall continue to think of him as an honorable man. Except about what happened before I was born, he never, as far as I can recall, told me a lie. And he was always kind and generous to those around him—to me, to my wife and our children, and to my mother, even years after they had separated and he had remarried.

Of my mother's family more is known, but much is, and will remain, uncertain. She was born Ethel Josephine Roberts in 1888 in Kingston, Jamaica, in what was then the British West Indies, to a colonial family. My grandfather Roberts, then an Anglican priest, was mostly Welsh, my grandmother mostly British and Scotch. But from the family history, chiefly oral, many chapters are missing. Illegitimacy and miscegenation were rampant. Early in the last century and late in the preceding one, the custom was for young Britons to go to the colonies in their early twenties and spend at least a decade, often two, cultivating the land and getting ready to receive, almost as if by mail order, a suitable bride from home. While waiting, few were celibate and childless. In the British West Indies, most were planters—sugar, coffee, pimento, bananas—or breeders of horses and cattle. Others were soldiers, traders, or civil servants, and underlying both groups, of course, was a fair sprinkling of losers, idlers, and colonial ne'er-do-wells. Among the latter was my grandfather Roberts, an erudite drifter and dreamer saddled with the first names Adolphus Sigismund—no doubt after some dashing Swedish figure in a Gothic romance. At twenty or so, Adolphus Sigismund had gone to Canton from Jamaica and spent twelve years doing something—I cannot imagine what—in the silk trade while living with a Chinese concubine, who may have provided my cousins and me with some Chinese uncles and aunts. Back in Jamaica in his thirties, he attended a theological seminary in Kingston and was soon chaplain to a British regiment garrisoned there. He did this, my mother told me, because a girl named Josephine Napier had decided that if she ever mated it would be to a clergyman. This may be so. I suspect that he also found the vocation attractive because the duties were light and mostly liturgical, leaving plenty of time for reading, drinking, and philandering—activities to which he seems to have devoted himself with uncharacteristic diligence.

The Robertses were less settled and respectable and more widely scattered over Jamaica and the empire than the Napier tribe, which was clustered around the Jamaican town of Mandeville, in the Blue

Hills—today the preserve of multinational corporations mining bauxite for aluminum mills. Adolphus Sigismund Roberts and Josephine Napier had two sons, the first of whom died, and two daughters, of whom the older was my mother, Ethel. Adolphus fathered a third girl by the daughter of the overseer on one of the Napier plantations, but his marriage to Josephine was in disrepair even before that: about ten years after his ordination, he was defrocked—not, as my mother liked to believe, for some sort of heresy, but for drunkenness. Liberated from the church, he spent most of his days tutoring his children, none of whom had had so much as a day of formal schooling, and he did, on the whole, a splendid job of it. All three children spoke almost flawless English, had a good knowledge of French, and were firmly founded in English history and literature. To the end of her days, my mother kept in her mind great swatches of English poetry—not the best but far from the worst. (She was partial to the late Victorians—Swinburne, Henley, Dowson, Thompson, Kipling—and she formed in me a taste for them, so that I, too, can render many of them by the running yard.) After a brief journalistic apprenticeship in Kingston, the surviving son, Walter, my uncle, came to this country in his late teens and began a career as a reporter, historian, magazine editor, and journeyman novelist and poet—he signed himself "W. Adolphe Roberts" and was, before the First World War and for several years after it, an interesting though peripheral figure in the literary and intellectual life of the period. (Much of what I know about my Jamaica background comes from his unpublished autobiography, completed shortly before his death, in 1962.) Walter took up residence in Greenwich Village and became a thoroughgoing Bohemian. In 1910 my mother joined him there, and she, too, enjoyed the heady life of the Village's cafés and salons, bewitched by the thought of associating with poets and artists. (I have a lovely sketch of her made on a restaurant menu by J. B. Yeats, the poet's father.) She and Louis Rovere were married in 1913, and she left the Village for a series of middle- and lower-middle-class neighborhoods, in which they were to spend the next twenty-five years together.

My mother was, not only in my memory but in surviving photographs, a woman of considerable beauty. Like her father and her brother, she was a romantic, a dreamer, an idealist. She lived into her nineties, and my present memory is so strong of a person of ravaging senility, accompanied by a terrible anger—at me, at my father, at life, at everything—that I find it difficult now to picture her in earlier years. But I recall a woman of quite high intelligence—articulate, stubborn, and self-willed, and combining a mixture of nineteenth-century British liberalism and (a heritage from my grandfather, I imagine) nineteenth-century British prejudices.[2]

In time, my grandmother Josephine and her other daughter, Ivy, also settled in New York. As for Adolphus Sigismund, he, enchanted by something he had read about the natural beauties of Oregon and the rewards of growing apples there, set out for the West Coast by way of Panama; he got as far as northern California, where disenchantment prevailed, and returned to Jamaica, to take up residence with a black woman, who bore him still another daughter. He died in 1926. I went to Jamaica twice as a small child, but all that I recall of my grandfather is a wispy moustache and bony knees. I made an extended visit to the island with my mother and my Uncle Walter in 1939. By then, there were no more Robertses. There were two legitimate Napiers—a great-aunt named Lucy and a great-uncle Charles, feeble-minded since birth. There were also two illegitimate but recognized mulatto great-aunts—Margaret, aged 107, and Nora, not much younger.

[2] When I was ready to enter grammar school, in 1921, my mother would not have me attend the public school (P.S. 28) in Richmond, Staten Island, where we then were living, because one of the four teachers was a black. I went instead to a Roman Catholic school (as, indeed, my father had), my mother's racial prejudice being stronger than her religious prejudice. But that, too, displeased her Anglican sensibilities, and though I remember the school with some affection (I was devoted to the mother superior and to my teacher, Sister Irene), I failed first grade. The following year, I entered public school and eventually became a student of the black teacher's.

So much, then, for my tangled, speculative roots. "Embrace your ethnicity, man," a character in a John Updike story admonishes the Jewish writer Henry Bech, who thought he was doing exactly that. I regret having only ethnic spooks and fantasies to embrace. I envy the pleasure and pride and humor that other writers have got from racial and national backgrounds—Saul Bellow and Bernard Malamud from their Jewishness, James Baldwin and Ralph Ellison from their blackness, John Cheever from his Waspness. I, an ethnic alloy, am deprived thereby, I think, of a strand of self-knowledge; my work is uninformed by a kind of passion I find in many of my contemporaries. No ethnicity to embrace, no tradition to reject. But there it is. Until I was nearly grown and was developing doubts about my father's origins, I took it more or less for granted that I belonged to the community of white Anglo-Saxon Protestants. The cultural ambience in a Presbyterian boarding school and a predominantly Episcopalian college was certainly that. But a boy spotting cars on the Jericho Turnpike doesn't think about cultural ambiences, and the young revolutionary I was to become embraced all mankind —except, of course, the property-owning exploiters. Had I known the truth about my father then, it would, I am sure, have made a difference in my life and his. Knowing him to be a liar would probably have destroyed what was a close, affectionate relationship. Or if he had given me some insight into the agony that led him to lie, it might have had the opposite effect. In any case, I would have wanted to know whether he was French or Italian or Jewish or whatever. But now he is several years dead, and I have seen the last of middle age, and the matter seems almost academic. If I were to learn now that I am in fact half Jewish or half Italian or half something I had not previously suspected, it would, I think, be rather like receiving from a hospital laboratory a report that my blood is type O rather than, as I had been led to believe, type A—information for a medical file.

I do, though, find some irony and amusement in the situation.

The thought that I am, as likely as not, half French is to me an odd one, and in a way unsettling. I can think of nothing about my mind and temperament that is in any way Gallic. Paris is a city in which I have often been ill at ease. I find its elegance, its beauty, its self-assurance a bit intimidating. It is no one's fault but my own that I speak such execrable French, but I resent having my syntax mocked and corrected by Parisian taxi-drivers; I would not think of correcting New York drivers, whose English is often as bad as my French. As for my being Jewish or Italian, that would be rather a good joke on those who once admitted me to their company because they assumed, as I did, that I was Anglo-Saxon, or at least Gentile. And a good joke, too, on those Jews in the radical movement in the 1930s who were suspicious of any goy in their midst.

I feel some affinity for the Jamaican side. I like the lilting English of the West Indies. The class system of my mother's day was an ugly thing, but less so, I think, than this country's in the same period. The house in which my mother grew up, Berry Hill, was passed on to a succession of mulatto heirs until after Great-Aunt Nora died, when my mother, quite late in her life, inherited it. I am attracted by what I know of my grandfather Roberts, a rather weak and shiftless character but with a stout and independent mind. He, however, was not greatly attracted to Jamaica or to England. He taught his children that the Chinese had created the greatest of civilizations. In the Boer War, he thought the British cause unjust. Like most colonials, the Robertses and the Napiers did not much like the colonies. They fled them when they could. The Napiers I knew were caricature Britons, and I think it was only the press of circumstance that led my grandmother to spend her last quarter century in New York rather than in England. My most lasting memory of that lugubrious old lady, who cultivated in dress and manner a slight resemblance to Queen Victoria, is of her sitting, in black, as if in mourning, in a dank, dark room over a cigar-and-candy store owned and managed by her youngest,[3] on Hylan Boulevard—a dis-

[3] Ivy had married a Pennsylvania pharmacist.

mal thoroughfare that cuts across the wasteland of Staten Island—
and lecturing her bored grandchildren on the wonders of an England she had not seen since she spent a year or so at a boarding
school there almost three quarters of a century earlier. She died in
1936.

IV

As a sometime biographer (several of my books and at least a
hundred articles fall loosely into the category), I have serious misgivings about the genre, and the most serious of these has to do with
the way that biographers—especially those who try to employ psychoanalytic theory—treat childhood and adolescence. I would not
for a moment deny the crucial importance of the early years. Of
course the boy is father to the man, and of course the tree inclines as
the twig is bent. But the problem with the metaphor—apart from
the fact that it is a metaphor and partakes a bit of the pathetic
fallacy—is that little of the bending occurs on sunlit days in the
presence of reliable witnesses. Much of it, indeed, occurs before the
twig is even a twig and is exposed to the elements. The boy who
fathers the man dies in the process of gestation, rather as the cater-
pillar dies in becoming a butterfly. There are, of course, techniques
for resurrection. A man begets not only his natural offspring but the
child he once was, or thinks he was, fashioning this creature from a
memory that is often revisionist. So if it is always true that the boy is
father to the man, it is also true that the man often begets the boy
who was, and the biographer begets both. All the books I have read
about Richard Nixon, including his own, draw on precisely the same
material—there is not much of it, and he is the source of most of
the information about his childhood. The books written after the
fall have little difficulty in finding the Nixon of Watergate in the
Nixon of Yorba Linda and of Whittier, California. Those written
earlier, including a few whose authors approached him with some

animosity, could find almost nothing in the past that might account for the future.[4]

When I was gathering materials for my book *Senator Joe McCarthy,* I found that a good many reporters had spent considerable time in and around Grand Chute, Wisconsin, McCarthy's birthplace and early home, in search of clues that might help explain the man who left so large and ugly a stamp on American life in the middle of this century. They talked with people who had known him as a child—members of the family, neighbors, teachers, employers, friends, enemies. They searched all available public records. I think I can sum up their findings in a sentence. The fifth of nine children born to a poor farm family—Irish in background, Roman Catholic by religion—McCarthy was a physically unattractive boy and something of a bully, but nevertheless a reasonably bright, ambitious, and industrious one. Nothing in that sentence helps explain the emergence of Joe McCarthy, the most formidable and gifted American demagogue of the century. Given these facts, I wrote, the Grand Chute boy might have become "an Outagamie County farmer like his father, a respectable dentist in Appleton, a priest, a Communist functionary, a burglar, a respected public servant in the great Wisconsin tradition, or Joe McCarthy"—the last seeming perhaps the least likely of all. The child of Grand Chute was surely the father of

[4] A post-Watergate biographer, David Abrahamsen—a New York psychoanalyst with impressive connections and credentials (Bellevue and Columbia in New York, the Menninger Clinic in Kansas, St. Elizabeth's in Washington, D.C.)—learned from a strongly pro-Nixon biography published in 1959 that Nixon's mother had described her son as a helpful boy around the house, particularly when it came to mashing potatoes. "He was the best potato-masher one could hope for," Hannah Nixon said. "He never left any lumps. He used the whipping motion instead of going up and down the way the other boys did." Dr. Abrahamsen found this a telling bit of information. "Nixon's fascination with potato-mashing," he wrote, "has psychoanalytic implication. What is unusual in Richard is that he chose to release his energy through potato-mashing. The extent and intensity of this activity might suggest that [it] was a form of aggression against an inanimate object which was a substitute for people. Potato-mashing apparently allowed this tense and moody child to express his unconscious anger." Perhaps, but it makes one wonder what kind of unconscious anger Abraham Lincoln was working off when he was putting the axe to all those trees in Illinois. Was the rail-splitter getting ready to split the Union?

the McCarthy of McCarthyism, but there was no way in which this could be established in a literary paternity suit.

The Freudians claim to have a better way—in fact, a science—of summoning hidden memory, but while their long, difficult, and mysterious procedures may dredge up the sources of a crippling neurosis and in so doing liberate the sufferer, the being that emerges is often unrecognizable to the man who was the child, and I do not think that these procedures yield much of value to biographers. They cannot uncover the roots of greatness or, for that matter, malevolence. Analysts have much to say about guilt but little about innocence.

The historical past is almost always an invention of the present, and most biography is of necessity extrapolation. In general, though, what research can turn up about childhood is very little and rarely to be taken at face value. There are children—princes and prodigies, the offspring of the very famous and the very infamous—whose early lives are studiously observed, whose development is monitored by people outside the family circle, some of whom may be relatively disinterested and qualified to provide useful evidence. And there are a few transcendent figures whose lives are of such compelling interest that they attract the most sensitive and devoted of scholars, some of them ready to spend a lifetime getting at and judiciously interpreting every slight bit of information that investigation can provide. Samuel Johnson would be a case in point, and we have, from Boswell to W. Jackson Bate, a record so meticulously compiled, so carefully screened and scrutinized by the finest of critical minds, that we can accept it almost as we might accept an X-ray or a high-quality tape recording. But there have been few Dr. Johnsons (in fact, only one), and with most subjects we have only the testimony of parents, siblings, a few friends, a few teachers, and the subjects themselves—in short, the very witnesses least to be relied upon.

All of which is a rather roundabout way of getting to the point that I do not believe the autobiographer is, on many matters, any more to be relied upon than the biographer. Indeed, the biographer probably has the edge, for while he lacks the advantage of memory and experience, he stands at a distance from his subject. *The Education of Henry Adams*—autobiography in the form of biography—is in many ways a great book, but I think it tells us less about Adams than the studies of him by others. As for me, I cannot with any assurance identify or isolate the forces and experiences that shaped me intellectually. I have what I think is a reasonably good memory; as a reporter, I have seldom been let down by it. I can recall almost every step of every journey I have ever made, and when there are records to be checked against, they generally bear me out. But a long journey backward in time is different in kind from any other. I have never known anyone who has not remarked on the miragelike quality of childhood scenes revisited. The territory and the artifacts may be physically unchanged, but when seen through adult eyes they bear a different look. What once seemed beautiful may now seem drab; what once seemed uninteresting and commonplace may now seem enchanting. When, as a boy, I played in Prospect Park in Brooklyn, I no doubt thought of it mostly as open space—a lot of grass, a lot of trees, a lot of squirrels and pigeons, some paths on which to ride bicycles, some slopes on which to sled. Not until long after I had used it as a playground did I see it as an exquisitely planned and planted landscape, a great product not only of nature but of the human imagination, a work of art. As a rule, the sizes and shapes of places we knew as children turn out in fact to be smaller and shorter than we had remembered them; but the Prospect Park I recalled seemed epic in its proportions—almost a wilderness—when in truth, as I later learned, this was all an illusion, a bit of magic from the drafting board of Frederick Law Olmsted. And what, I have asked myself, does the memory do with things that have no measurable dimensions—with events, with attitudes, with ideas? And with loves and hates?

What, indeed, does the memory *do?* Since writing all that precedes this paragraph—and much that is to follow—I have made, quite by accident, a discovery which forces me to question many things about my own life that for years I have taken for granted. I must pause to explain. It was part of my intention to deal at some point in this book with racism—particularly with anti-Semitism. Had I not made the discovery of which I speak, I would almost certainly have treated the matter lightly, even blithely. Yes (I would have written), both my mother and my father—my mysterious and perhaps Jewish father—were anti-Semitic, and so, naturally, was their son. In their case, I would have explained, it was an attitude common at the time among people of their class and kind, and this I would have documented. It was not, as my memory had it, racism of the virulent kind. It came up only occasionally and was without consequence in their day-to-day lives. My own anti-Semitism, I planned to explain, was a mild infection from which I made a speedy recovery—it was all theory and no practice. After all, in the many places in which we lived in New York, I would have been a very lonely boy if I had had no Jewish friends. For my purchase of Tom Swift books, Mr. Horowitz, who stocked them in his stationery store on Underhill Avenue, was an indulgent creditor and a valued confidant. And the girl I hoped against hope would smile at me as I looked at her across Mrs. Greenbaum's eighth-grade classroom at P.S. 9 was Ruth Moscowitz.

Not an altogether unpretty picture: a mild and inoperable bigotry overcome by love and friendship. Alas, it could not be more false. The memory of which I have so often boasted was serving my moral comfort, covering up something that was repellent to what I think of as my liberal conscience. For in 1978, not long after I had started writing this book, I came upon a letter to my parents—undated but clearly written in the autumn of 1933, when I was eighteen—in which I write of disliking "filthy Jews," "cringing, yet loudmouthed Jews." This in, of all years, A.D. 1933! The Weimar Republic dead, Hitler in power, pogroms under way. And I was eighteen, no child, old enough to serve as an SS man, writing my parents in Brooklyn about "filthy Jews."

And who were these Jews I was writing about? I am not sure there were any. The letter was written from the Connecticut state college, in Storrs, which I attended for the first semester of my freshman year. It had earlier been planned that I would go to some tonier college—Amherst, if it would have had me with my dismal record, and in 1933 it probably would have had me. But my father had taken several salary cuts and was very short of cash. At the time, he owned a summer cottage on half an acre or so of Connecticut woodland, and I was thus entitled to free tuition at the state college. Snob that I was, I disliked the place intensely and was bringing to bear all the pressure I could to get out. Until that year, what is now the University of Connecticut was Connecticut Agricultural College, and it was still, in the main, a school for farmers. I was a member of the first liberal-arts class; nearly all the sophomores, juniors, and seniors were agricultural students, and so were many of my fellow freshmen. Now, I do not think there were many Jews in Connecticut at the time, and there certainly weren't many Jewish farmers. I cannot recall a single Jewish name, though I do remember that Polish and Italian ones were common. The only students I knew well were the three with whom I roomed and a fourth—as it happened, an Amherst graduate—who had decided to become a farmer and was taking some advanced courses. One of my roommates was the son of a minister in, I think, Milford. Another was the son of a professional motorboat racer in New Haven. The third was a hulking Norwegian from Winsted who seemed to be majoring in castration; each morning before the sun was up, he would go out to the sheep barn to neuter several rams. I disliked him and almost everything else about the place, especially the compulsory military training, which I somehow hadn't bargained on when I enrolled. I was fitted for a uniform but flunked ROTC deliberately. None of this was what I told my parents—far from it. I wrote them that I was unhappy because there were "so many filthy Jews," knowing that this would win sympathy, as indeed it did. In short, I was using Jews —phantom Jews in this case—as Hitler did, as scapegoats. In January 1934, I transferred to Bard College, at Annandale-on-Hudson,

New York. The atmosphere there was more that of a seminary than of a cow-and-sheep college. A few months later, I was denouncing Hitler and was well on my way to becoming a Stalinist, but that is another story.

The young man who could have written such a letter in 1933 would not have been in this book at all if I had not come upon him in 1978 in the course of clearing out some old papers. And when I did meet this revolting stranger, I did not know what to do with him. Obviously, if I was going to write an honest book, he would have to be part of it. But I kept him to myself for several days, wondering how best to handle him. I said nothing to my wife, not wanting her to meet him any sooner than she had to. Finally, I told her. And Eleanor said, "Well, you know, there's something I never told *you.*" In 1934, when she was seventeen, she went to a hospital in Springfield, Massachusetts, for an appendectomy. She was in a ward, and in the bed next to hers was a black woman. They were separated by a glass partition—no chance of contamination—but Eleanor wanted to be in a private room. To effect the desired change, she had only to call her mother's attention to the black woman in the nearby cubicle: "Look who's in the next bed there! Get me out of here!" That did it; she knew her mother well. Her case differed from mine, though, in that the woman was real, and in that she had concealed the memory from me but not from herself. As for me, I had driven that Dick Rovere so far from memory that he is a complete stranger to me now. Yet, although the language of hatred is part of that penciled scrawl, I do not believe I would have gone beyond language. I do not believe I would have deliberately hurt any Jew. I brought my Jewish friends—including Robert Shaplen, my colleague at *The New Yorker,* then a next-door neighbor on St. John's Place—to my home, and they invited me to theirs. Some months after I had come across my anti-Semitic letter, I happened to be talking with Bob Shaplen about our memories of Brooklyn, and Bob said to me, "How many other Jewish kids besides us were there on that block?" And I said, "I'm not sure I was Jewish—

I'm not sure what I am—I may be Jewish, but it's news to me if I am." He had simply assumed it. When I was twelve, a Jewish boy named Nathan Davis and I were almost inseparable for a year or so. We were both collectors—of matchbooks, of bottle caps, of Lindbergh mementos, of Brooklyn Dodgers scorecards. And I like to think—I do think—that I would have done battle against anyone who hurled racist epithets at the lovely Ruth Moscowitz, the girl I dreamed of when I should have been working on the principal cities and major products of Indiana. Or at Nathan Davis or Arthur Onitz or Robert Shaplen. And yet . . . and yet . . .

Is it any easier to go beyond the child and find the young man who is father to the old one? For many of us, I think it is. Ever-larger circles surround the small circle of childhood. Friends, acquaintances, observers grow more numerous. Records begin to proliferate. The free-form existence of childhood vanishes, and life becomes a progression of jobs, of loves, of places, of experiences. And it is a fact—often a troublesome one—that writers make permanent, unalterable records of themselves. When I began to write, I began creating a record that will endure, at least in my lifetime. I was committing my thoughts, my observations, my interpretations to print—first in college publications, then in newspapers and magazines, and then in books. I was sometimes anonymous, as in editorials, and sometimes pseudonymous, as in the hack work I did for some of those crime magazines, but my name is on nearly everything I ever wrote, and I can't begin to estimate how many square miles of print, how many million words are under that name. My growth or my lack of growth can easily be documented. I have fixed it on paper.

I've been shuffling what are known as my "papers," so that I may turn them over to Mr. Leslie Fishel, of the State Historical Society of Wisconsin, when he comes here—I hope in a truck

—next Tuesday.* The universities of this country are going through a form of madness known as "collecting." They pursue all kinds of people and ask them to ransack their offices and studies and homes for manuscripts, correspondence. People agree, partly, I suspect, from an urge for immortality, partly for tax purposes. Anyway, I was suddenly in demand—by Syracuse University, Boston University, the Library of Congress, the Eisenhower Library, the nonexistent JFK library, and maybe one or two others. Wisconsin was highly recommended by Herman Kahn, my old and dear friend at the National Archives, and by others. Also, it specializes in people like me—people in "communications" and "media"—and Mr. Fishel came to see me and was most agreeable and, perhaps most important of all, agreed to take from my hands the whole problem of getting the damned stuff from here to there. I have always been one with Smith—Sydney or Logan Pearsall, I can't remember which, though more likely the latter—who said, "I would gladly lay down my life for a friend, but I'll be damned if I'll do up a bundle for him." Amen. I hate to wrap and mail things. Mr. Fishel got me out of it, but not, I find, as completely out as I thought. Sorting things, stuffing them in folders or envelopes, and then labeling and describing the contents is almost as bad. Driven from my study by the clutter there, I now sit in the dining room surrounded by stuffed and labeled manila envelopes and folders.

All this week I've been at it. It's rather like death and resurrection combined. I'm sending part of me to a mausoleum. But I'm also bringing back to life and memory many forgotten parts of the past. Sometimes it's creepy. For instance, I just came on a long essay called "Conservatism"—evidently written about 1956, a mere decade ago. I have absolutely no memory of writing it, yet surely I did. I know I never published it or tried to

* EDITOR'S NOTE: This is an excerpt from a memorandum Rovere wrote in 1966, presumably as an entry for his journal.

have it published, for I have a good memory for that sort of thing and fairly good records. And it is so uncharacteristic of a lazy hack like me to write anything that some editor hasn't said he'll pay for. But there it is. And so much else. No one could have convinced me that I once carried on a long, solemn correspondence with my brother-in-law [Clifford Burgess, Rovere's roommate at Bard] for years before and a few years after I married his sister. Had I ever received a letter from William Faulkner? Of course not. I wrote an introduction to the Modern Library edition of *Light in August*, in 1950, but I always supposed that he'd thought ill of it (if, indeed, he ever read it). But here we are, Oct. 11, 1956, on Random House stationery: "Dear Mr. Rovere"—apropos of politics, not very interesting. Out of an ancient folder marked "Personal" comes one of those little envelopes in which safe-deposit-box keys are kept. I open it and find a wad of paper that, when unfolded, tells me in an archaic hand, brown ink on wax paper, "This is to certify that according to Entry No. 2572 in the Baptism Register of Bethabara Church on the Island of Jamaica, British West Indies, Richard Halworth, the son of Lewis and Ethel Rovere of New York, United States of America, was born on the 5th day of May 1915 and baptized on the 26th of April 1917. The officiating minister, F. P. Wilde." I had knowledge of the event (on a trip to Mandeville, Mother had me baptized by the nearest divine, a Moravian, because my aunts were scandalized to learn it had not yet been done), but not of the papers. Yet as recently as twenty years ago I must have gone to the trouble of stuffing the certificate in a key envelope and putting that in a folder. . . .

V

I am, without any doubt or qualifications, a New Yorker. Of myself I have written that for my first thirty years New York City was "the center of my entire life," and I went on to say, "I become keenly aware of this when I am flying into or out of the city, for there comes a moment when, clouds and smog permitting, I can see framed in the window nearest me all the places in which I have lived, studied, or worked for any length of time." I can see all of the city in which I lived and went to public school; the Long Island town of Stony Brook, in which I spent four years in preparatory school; the Connecticut village of Rowayton, in which we spent several summers; and the Dutchess County communities in which I went to college and in which Eleanor and I and our children have lived since 1946. I would amend this now by saying that, with the children gone, we spend part of the year in Key West, Florida, but I take New York there, as I have taken it to wherever I have gone abroad. I am a product of New York's urban culture and of the rural culture of its outlying counties, and I am more than content to be. Rhinebeck, the Hudson River town that was our primary residence for a number of years, is in many respects like other small towns, but its life would not be what it is (for me, at least) if its distance from New York—a bit less than one hundred miles—were much greater.

When I married, at twenty-six, I made a list of all the places I had lived, most of them in the city—Manhattan, Brooklyn, Staten Island—and my calculation showed that we had moved on an average of slightly more than once a year. From Jersey City on, the Roveres were upwardly mobile in a modest way, and this was accompanied by a lateral mobility that gave a nomadic quality to our lives. We pulled up stakes for gains in space or convenience that were seldom perceptible to me. Moving was a very casual business in New York in those days; if one's apartment didn't seem right for a coveted piece of furniture, one found a more suitable place. There was a great building boom in the city, and landlords competed with one another in offering rent concessions or some other enticement, like a new electric stove. As I think back on it now, it must have been, for my parents, a rather bleak existence. Going from one part of the city to another meant giving up one set of friends and finding others, establishing new relationships with tradesmen, doctors, and the like—all for the sake of more closets or less antiquated gadgets. I often pleaded with my parents not to make a contemplated move. Most of the neighborhoods we lived in I recall with some fondness, and I liked them well enough to resent, with the resistance to change that seems much stronger in children than in adults, each summons to move on, to be displaced or *re*placed. But making new friends is easier for children than for their parents, and I cannot remember any setting I actively disliked, even though I never formed for any of the neighborhoods I lived in the sort of passionate attachment that Alfred Kazin, who was also born in 1915, felt for the steaming, suffering Brownsville ghetto in which he lived while I was growing up elsewhere in Brooklyn. He says he can still smell the wares on the pushcarts and in the shops. He can hear the rhythm of the treadle on his dressmaker mother's sewing machine, feel the texture of the paint on his father's overalls. He can taste what was brewed in the kitchen, recapture the talk of the old men, the gossip of the old women, the insults the children hurled at one another. He has rich folk memories of the Russia he never saw until, decades later, he saw the other Russia—Soviet Russia—as a visiting American writer. He can re-create for us his painful sense of what it meant to be a Jewish boy in Brownsville, with a great fear of the Gentile world that lay beyond it—a fear accompanied by, almost contradictorily, the hope of some day escaping Brownsville, whose children seemed destined to become either criminals or, like him, men of learning. He hated the place, he loved it. Part of him—the richest, most poetic part— lives there still.

My memories of Prospect Heights are vivid, but I could not make poetry of them. I remember best and with the most warmth the thirty or forty blocks near the main entrance to Prospect Park. We lived in that area for several years at several addresses—Park Place, Vanderbilt Avenue, Lincoln Place, St. John's Place, Eastern Parkway. I think of it as a kind of square, bounded on one side by the park, on a second side by an Italian section near the tracks of the

Long Island Rail Road, on the third and the fourth sides by two commercial thoroughfares, Flatbush and Washington avenues. Inside the square were solid blocks of solid old brownstones, even then past their days of glory, and streets lined with nondescript four- and five-story apartment houses, built, I think, early in this century. The brownstone people were property owners and thus more stable, less footloose than apartment dwellers like us. Sometimes the brownstones housed extended families, with grandparents, maiden schoolteachers, bachelor police officers, and other relatives, either dotty or drunk, sequestered in hall bedrooms on the upper floors. Our apartment-house neighbors were bookkeepers, small contractors, seamstresses, clerks, lower-level managers, technicians like my father. The apartments were not spacious enough for extended families, but to me the accommodations seemed pleasant enough; I was an only child, and I was never without a room of my own. And, except for being uprooted more than I liked, it was a good life for a boy in that time. Prospect Park, one of the noblest pieces of landscape architecture, was a rural retreat never more than a few minutes away. There was always a vacant lot for baseball games or an urban campground; now and then we pitched tents and built fires to cook hot dogs and roast potatoes. The apartment-house rooftops were available to those who wanted not to be seen smoking cigarettes or heard discussing sex. Though I regarded school as a rude intrusion on my life, I did learn a few things, and the two schools I attended—P.S. 111 and P.S. 9—were said to be among the best in the city, and this at a time when New York's public schools were among the best in the country. For several years, I was an enthusiastic Boy Scout and worked for my scoutmaster harder than I worked for any teacher, avidly acquiring a variety of merit badges and skills—mapmaking, cooking, carpentry, animal husbandry—that I was never to put to much use. In time, I became a Star Scout—two steps from Eagle, which I might have made if my interests hadn't broadened to include girls and sports.

I had a friend whose father was a sports reporter, and he managed to get us free tickets to Ebbets Field, the home grounds of the Brooklyn Dodgers and an easy walk from where we then lived. I think I must have been eighteen before I set foot in a New York theater, but there were movies all around us, including an open-air one on a Flatbush Avenue rooftop. It was almost obligatory to attend at least one movie a week, usually on Saturday afternoon, when the chief attraction was the serial. I can even now envision scenes from *The Fighting Marine,* an all but interminable sequence of episodes in which the boxer Gene Tunney played himself in what purported to be his life story. I count it as no deprivation that the time I might have put in reading books worthier than Tom Swift, Zane Grey, and Don Sturdy were spent instead at three movie houses—the Bunny, the Carlton, and the Savoy—that sometimes offered a bonus of vaudeville; I found time for reading later. I saw my first play with live actors when I was about twelve and we were spending a few days in Hartford, on one of my father's business trips. My parents' principal recreation was an occasional evening of bridge; on my father's vacations, we toured the countryside, and for a time, when something like affluence struck, we went boating on Long Island Sound in a small cabin cruiser we owned for a couple of years. We lived with a rootlessness and a lack of continuity, yet also with a lack of variety that I, in my own adult years, would have found oppressive. Though my wife and I have moved twice in the last thirty years, we have stayed within a relatively small part of northern Dutchess County, and we are still very close to friends we have known nearly all our thirty-five years of marriage, and to quite a few whom both of us knew before we knew each other. Our children, now in their twenties and thirties, still see friends they have known almost from infancy. (By contrast, and almost by accident, the only person I now know whom I knew as a boy is Robert Shaplen, but until we found ourselves working for the same magazine we had not met for twenty years or more.)

My mother's brother Walter, she has told me, asked her often how she could stand the boredom and respectability of the kind of life she and my father were leading. But it was not until I was leading a quite different kind of existence myself that *I* ever thought of their life in those terms, and if *she* ever did at the time, she never told me about it. My memory of my parents as husband and wife is of two rather conventional people sharing life together with no discomfort that I could notice. Perhaps my mother's earlier Bohemianism was only an interlude in the life of a woman whose fundamental values were Victorian and middle class. How much and how long my parents loved each other during their quarter of a century together I do not know. Until I was fifteen or so, I thought it was a perfect marriage. Though they separated with very little acrimony, it is plain to me that they were temperamentally incompatible from the start.

VI

In Spanish, I have learned, there is a word with a lovely sound, *querencia*, which means a kind of fitting, affectionate feeling for a particular environment, for a place—or it may be a community—that gives one nurture. It is not patriotism (nowadays a suspect emotion, and always a rather grandiose one), nor is it love of country, though that can be a part of it; *querencia* applies to something smaller than a nation—smaller, certainly, than this one. It refers to a spot of earth that holds one's love and loyalty even though one may not have seen it in many years—even, in some cases to a place one has never seen but knows from folk history. Despite the you-can't-go-home-again literary exiles, this is a place to which one can return for further nurture. Or, the world being what it is, it may be a place one loves but to which one is forbidden to return, like Aleksandr Solzhenitsyn's Russian villages. It is a place one understands, in which one feels understood. It may be a place of pain and suffering, even a place one would wish out of existence, as one wishes a slum out of existence, yet, like James Baldwin's Harlem, it is a natural and appropriate setting for memories and fears and hopes. There are places I love and feel very much at home in, but I have no *querencia* for them, at least as I understand the word. I have lived in and around New York City all my life, and there is a part of it—a very small part, measurable in acres—to which I go whenever I can. It is a hundred miles down the Hudson from my river home—a section of Manhattan that to me is the capital of the republic of letters, or at least of the division of it in which I claim citizenship. In it are *The New Yorker* offices, the New York Public Library, the seedy old hotel in which Eleanor and I have kept an apartment for twelve years, and the Century Association, a gathering place of countless old friends. But this is a place I did not know until I was grown up and working in it. It is the place where my friends and colleagues— many of them with *querencias* for other parts of the country and of the world—happen to meet, and if it were to be picked up and moved to the mountains, to the plains, or to the desert, I would seek it out when the spirit moved me. It is not a community; no one lives in it except, as we do part of the time, in a hotel; children and animals are rarely seen in it. And though I love New York very much, even in the kind of maudlin way that makes me offended when the Yankees—as grubby a commercial enterprise as a used-car lot in Calumet City, Illinois—fail to win a pennant, I realize it will not do to speak of it as the object of my *querencia*. Except as a geographical and political entity, New York is an abstraction. To the man I may stand next to in an elevator, my "New York" is a remote, unexplored territory, and his New York may be a place I have never known at all.

From time to time, in my middle and later years, it has occurred to me that my lack of *querencia* and the fact that I am ethnically such a mixed bag may account for much about my life and work, both good and bad. The good is, I think, that I can move quite comfortably from one environment to another. The past does not tug at me as it does at those who are preoccupied with establishing their relationship to it. As my mother and her brother Walter grew older, they felt a powerful *querencia* for the Blue Hills of Jamaica. In

Walter's case, it led him to write some good books, but in my mother's case it led to misery. She was a dreamy sort, and had impossible ideas about life and marriage. She decided that life in New York had treated her very badly, and that it had been a dreadful mistake to leave those mountains. She wrote a few lyrical short stories about them, but they were the tall and verdant mountains of an old woman's fantasy, not the hills with their crumbling plantations she had been eager to leave as a young girl. I have visited those hills and admired them much as I admire the Green Mountains of Vermont, but I never had a feeling that I belonged there. I saw a peasant society liberating itself from colonialism and moving to an independence that might offer more in dignity and at the same time, perhaps, more in suffering. That was decades ago, and I think my detachment provided a clearer view.

But there is more to a journalist's life than detachment. My lack of *querencia* may account for what I feel is a certain thinness in my work, a certain choppiness, a reluctance to take on and see to completion any work that will take more than a few days or a few weeks to finish.† My past is strewn with abandoned projects and plans for journeys never made. The books I have started and put aside far outnumber those I have completed. This is true of many writers, perhaps of most. Visions that take radiant shape in the darkness have a way of fading in daylight. It is almost in the nature of enthusiasms that they become wasting assets. But I think that this has happened with me more often than with most. For one thing, working journalists regularly chase wild geese. Like firemen, they answer alarms, many of them false; not their own passions but those of others determine much of what they do. Self-pity is an occupational disease, sometimes disabling, and I have spent God knows how many unproductive hours asking myself if I was really put on this

---

† EDITOR'S NOTE: In a letter to Arthur Schlesinger, commenting on one of Schlesinger's manuscripts, Rovere wrote: "I of course have never attempted—and surely never will attempt—anything on this scale. Simply holding, feeling the thickness of a wad of your manuscript produces in me a response similar to that of the washerwoman looking at Niagara Falls."

earth to write about the likes of Richard Nixon and Joe McCarthy, to spend years chronicling the madness of our war in Vietnam. To feel thus ill-used is, of course, unworthy, but though eight books bear my name I cannot deny that I have wasted much time thinking about how much time I was wasting, and I have explored many a mare's nest in search of a solid structure. I have consoled myself with the thought that some runners, I among them, are sprinters, and that some run the marathon, and that both are valued in their own contests. And with the saying—I think it comes from the Reverend Sydney Smith—"Give me a short book on an inescapable subject."

2

From Hedgehog to Fox

I

I am not by temperament a philosopher. I do not respond to the image of the thinker in the sculpture by Rodin—the solitary figure, naked, chin in hand, drawing wisdom from his inner depths as water is drawn from a well. When I assume that posture, I can almost feel spiders weaving cobwebs in my brain. But when I write, I often find fallacy where I thought there was truth and, on occasion, truth in what I had thought was fallacy. For me, writing—writing of any sort —is in some ways like a laboratory experiment. If I can make a proposition work on paper, I tend to take this as prima facie evidence of its soundness. My rule, for better or for worse, is that there is probably something unsound in any proposition that I cannot find words to defend, and, vice versa, that what makes sense as I set it down is likely to be close to the truth.

I know this to be defective, even dangerous logic. Many illuminations can be found in awkward, groping prose. What is precious in a writer like Aleksandr Solzhenitsyn is not his command of language or his command of history (I think him quite vulnerable on that score), but his majestic rage, his sense of the vastness and the evil of suffering and torment. And many fallacies have been decked out in beguiling prose; among moderns, George Santayana comes to mind. But for me, in my kind of enterprise, the rule of thumb has more often than not been useful. Most of what I have scrapped deserved to be. And I am not displeased with most of what has survived my testing process.

In *The Hedgehog and the Fox*, a work that has meant much to me over many years, Isaiah Berlin holds that most writers are either one or the other of these creatures. The zoological metaphor comes from the Greek poet Archilocus, who writes: "The fox knows many things, but the hedgehog knows one big thing." I am surely no hedgehog; I like to think of myself as somehow related to the fox. The great hedgehogs, from Plato to Marx and Freud, had large, unified, unitary visions. They were determinists who saw the world whole and history as a continuum. Hedgehogs tell us why man behaves as he does, why civilizations rise and fall, why wars are won or lost, why life is sweet and beautiful or brutish and ugly. They know what is cause and what is effect. They find order in what the world perceives as chaos. The great foxes, from Aristotle to Balzac and Tolstoi, whose work is the subject of Berlin's book, may make high art of chaos, as the two great novelists did, but they do not find order or system in it. They know what takes place in wars, but not why wars take place. Tolstoi, according to Berlin, was a mighty fox who yearned to be a mighty hedgehog. He wanted order and certitude, but in *War and Peace,* he created a great canvas of human disarray, of effects without causes and causes without effects, of wheels within wheels, of hubbub and tumult, of the turmoil and pandemonium of history. He did not become a hedgehog until his later years, after his greatest works, and he was never a very convincing one.

In my youth, I wanted to be a hedgehog. I suppose that everyone does in one way or another. The hedgehog finds direction and purpose in life more easily than does the fox. In my teens, I had a heady fling at a hedgehog religion—fundamentalist Calvinism. I was saved, born again, filled with the Holy Spirit and the missionary spirit. That lasted for about two years and was followed by four as a Marxist of the Leninist persuasion—from redemption to revolution almost overnight, as it were. At the time, I thought it a move from pole to pole; it seems to me now a short and rather logical step—a move from one evangelical church to another. By the time I was done with Lenin, I knew that I was no predestinarian or determinist of any sort. I am as much in debt to the great hedgehogs as to the great foxes, but I am so addicted to speculation that I cannot bear to have it foreclosed at any point. I often wish it were otherwise. I am at one with Mr. Justice Holmes in affirming that "all I mean by truth is what I can't help thinking," but to have that strong sense of limitations—as against a stronger sense of possibilities—is to accept one's fate as what Holmes called "a retail dealer in notions," rather than as the "originator of large ideas." At the same time, I observe that more discernible harm has been done in the world by those with an unbounded sense of possibilities than by those of more limited perspectives. I have often been chastised for having written, many years ago: "I happen not to share the view that no man is an island. I think that every man is an island in the only sense that matters." This was contrary to the social gospel, but it was not the social gospel that I had in mind. (Nor do I think it was what John Donne had in mind.) I was saying that since my knowledge of myself is so incomplete—we all live without much knowledge of ourselves—I do not believe that I can go very far in explaining myself to others or explaining others to myself. I went further, to say that I thought Sigmund Freud had similar disabilities. I was writing in 1954 about a poor Italian girl—a waif from a war-ravaged village near Salerno—who was briefly part of our lives and who ended her own life with her head in a gas oven. I asked, "How could I conceivably presume to know anything of what this child from a countryside that Christ Himself is said to have found impenetrable, this wasted and pathetic disaster of war who came to find herself in

Babylon [Cannes, France, 1953], felt or thought, or felt she thought, or thought she felt, assuming that thought or feeling had anything to do with it? I knew only what events took place and what I made of some of them."

And that, as a rule, is about as far as I can go: I know what events took place in my time and what I made of them. I know, or I think I know, my way through the chaos of experience. To have any sense of where one is going it is surely necessary to know where one has been.

When Sigmund Freud died, in London in 1939, I wrote a brief obituary in *New Masses*, for which I was then a very junior editor, calling the founder of psychoanalysis a "towering genius." I was twenty-four at the time and given to oracular phrases. It tells me something about myself that I wrote of Freud as I did, and that what I wrote appeared in that particular and long since defunct semiofficial Communist periodical. In those days, Freud and his followers were held in low esteem by Marxists. The Freudian view of life, with its stress on inner tensions rather than on the tides of history, was seen as a threat to the Marxist certitudes; preoccupation with the subconscious militated against the development of class consciousness and was, by definition, escapist. It was not Freud the genius but Freud the famous Jewish refugee, the victim of Hitlerism, of whom the Communists took benevolent notice in death, and to acknowledge, as my article did, his importance in the history of Western thought was to border on heresy—and to lend a small touch of credibility to the magazine's generally bogus claim of independence from the movement it supported and was supported by. And I wonder now how I knew enough about Freud to have written about him at all. Marxism, after all, was a doctrine I had discovered and embraced only two or three years earlier. (At nineteen, I was not only a Calvinist but a Republican; at twenty-one a godless revolutionary; at twenty-four an ex-Communist—still a radical but, thanks to certain arrangements worked out by Stalin and Hitler a few weeks before Freud's death, a severely chastened one.) I had encountered Marx in a course in my second or third year in college, and I had at least a feeble grasp on dialectical materialism, but I do not recall hearing anything about the id, the ego, or the superego in the course of my formal education, such as it was. The only psychology I had been exposed to was a mix of physiology—"the brain has two lobes, left and right"—and philosophy of the William James–John Dewey dispensation. Although I recognize Freud as a giant, he has not meant much to me. Today, the people I know who have been in analysis may outnumber those who have not, but I must have been over thirty before I knew either an analysand or an analyst.

II

I cannot hope to uncover all, or even most, of the roots of my early involvements with radical social and political movements. Were I by nature a person with a strong ideological bent, I might be able to do so, but, though I have been caught up in ideology on occasion, I have always had a distrust for and dislike of it as such. Despite the lapses of my youth, I have rather consistently been a skeptic and an eclectic for as long as I have been anything, and I must add that I wasn't anything, intellectually, until I was twenty, when, almost overnight, I shucked my conservative heritage and moved to the left.

Before my third year at Stony Brook, I had no real interest in anything except myself, girls, and athletics. I had had little success with the second and almost none with the last, but in these matters, as in others, failure heightens the interest. Until I was in my late teens, my intellectual curiosity rose barely above zero. I either did not encounter or did not like the classical children's books, and have not to this day read through *Alice in Wonderland*. The only adult book that I read on my own was James Weldon Johnson's *The Autobiography of an Ex-Coloured Man*. It hit my eye on the shelf of the Stony Brook library and—perhaps because I had some instinctive feeling about the evil of racism—impressed me enough to cause me to remember it now. I suppose that I read some books assigned by my teachers, but I am sure that I read as few as I could get away with.

What changed me and perhaps set me on the road to revolution was an illness I had in the autumn of 1931. I was then a junior at Stony Brook, and I contracted some kind of neck injury that required surgery and several weeks in the hospital. (It was a mysterious ailment, and I never understood the doctors' explanations of it, but I believe it must have happened in football practice.) There was not much to do about either girls or sports in the hospital, and as a consequence I discovered reading and writing as serious pleasures.

I had inherited my father's politics unquestioningly. At Columbia, he had joined, he later told me, the Intercollegiate Socialist League, a student affiliate of the Socialist Party that had included among its Harvard members Walter Lippmann and John Reed. But that phase had not lasted long, and when I was a child he was an orthodox Republican—almost *de rigueur* in corporate circles in those days—differing from the party's leaders only on prohibition, which he opposed. I didn't much care about any of this, but I admired my father and thought he was right. Had I been asked, I would have said that Herbert Hoover—like my father, an engineer —was a great President. (I might also have said that Kaiser Wilhelm liked to wash down his sauerkraut with the blood of Allied soldiers and that I owed my carefree life to John J. Pershing and the American Expeditionary Force. I once believed that.) I made a speech for Hoover in a school symposium in 1932, and I still have a Coolidge-and-Dawes button my father gave me in the presidential campaign of 1924. My mother and my father took their responsibilities toward me as proper parents should. In terms of moral education, their aims seemed approximately the same; my mother, who had thought of herself as a flouter of convention, was just about as conventional in this respect as my father. Though neither was religious, both subscribed to the Protestant ethic and thought that more good than bad would come of my attending Sunday school, at least occasionally. When I went at all, it was invariably to the nearest church of whatever Protestant denomination. By training, my father was Roman Catholic, but the father I remember was agnostic, though in later life he became a Unitarian—largely, I imagine, because he thought Unitarians were worthy people and did many good works. When I moved left, he did not reprove me but moved in the same direction himself. When CIO organizers descended on Western Union, he was openly sympathetic, and once came home with a union button in his lapel. I told him that his support wouldn't help the union much—he was part of management and thus ineligible— and might cost him his job. He agreed and removed the button, but I liked the spirit that led him to put it on in the first place. He remained conservative in temperament, but in practice he became a conventional liberal, a New Dealer, a civil libertarian, and few things pleased him more than to learn, at eighty-five or thereabouts, that I had made Nixon's "enemies list."

I cannot with assurance trace my present view of life to anything I accepted or rebelled against in those days when I waited for three-o'clock deliverance from P.S. 9, but I do think that I know at least some of the steps that led to my becoming a radical at twenty. A couple of professors—one from Chicago, another from Baltimore— had something to do with it. So did some left-wing girls at Vassar. So did a visit, in the summer of 1934, to Brookwood Labor College, a school for trade unionists in Mount Kisco, New York. So did John Dos Passos and some of the other radical writers of the time— especially Granville Hicks, who was to become for me a mentor of sorts and a lifelong friend. But what of the soil in which the ideas took root? Little had grown in it earlier except a knowledge of Babe Ruth's orphan childhood, a fascination with the exploits of the Boy Allies, and the Kipling ballads I could not help memorizing because I heard them so often from my mother. Yet the soil could not have been altogether barren. At school in Stony Brook, when I was sixteen or thereabouts, it struck me that there was something rather jarring in the contrast between the strictness with which the students and teachers observed the Sabbath and the fact that the kitchen help, to provide the biggest meal of the week, worked harder on that day than on any other day. I was in most ways a dreadful little snob, and in no way a friend of the cooks and dishwashers. But I found myself proposing to someone—the headmaster? the student council?—that the people in the kitchen should have as much right to worship and contemplate their sins as any of the rest of us. I suggested to someone that a contingent of students could at least take over the dishwashing chores on Sundays. This was judged a fine, thoughtful idea. If I could find a couple of friends to work with me, I could initiate the custom. I found two to wash, and that Sunday I dried all the dishes.

For anyone of my background, becoming a Socialist, or even a Communist, in the 1930s meant that one had cast aside the most poisonous kind of bigotry and had joined a movement that one believed to be humane and fraternal. I have some apologies to make for that period, but not many. Better by far what I became than what I was; the radicals I knew at Bard were a generous lot, for the most part—hopeful, romantic in the Byronic sense, with a sharp sense of justice and an even sharper sense of injustice. Thank God, I went their way rather than the way in which that nasty young man at Storrs seemed headed. I see now that it may have been a very narrow escape. At Bard, the atmosphere, though much like that of an Anglican seminary, was liberal, and in some ways radical. (I seemed to hit colleges just as they were changing names and character. Until February of 1934—i.e., my freshman year—Bard had been St. Stephens, an out-of-town undergraduate division of Columbia University, a college, in the main, for young Episcopalians who planned to go into the ministry. In my day, there were still a good many preseminarians. The Columbia connection, which had started in 1928, ended during the Second World War, when, as a matter of survival, Bard became coeducational. Barnard College's contractual arrangement with Columbia specified that it was to be the only part of the university that could enroll undergraduate women.) The president of Bard until 1933 had been the Reverend Bernard Iddings Bell, a crusty and fiery churchman and a guild Socialist of the William Morris school—a quaint ideology long out of fashion even then. He had brought to the St. Stephens faculty a fellow clergyman, Lyford Edwards, who around the turn of the century had been associated with some of the founders of American sociology at the University of Chicago, and who, for his sympathy for the Russian revolution, had been dismissed from Rice Institute, in Texas. The faculty recruited by Columbia (more specifically, by Columbia's Teachers College, the liaison between Bard–St. Stephens and the university) was generally leftist in coloration. So I found myself in a place where fascism was regarded as a noxious thing. Since I so conveniently killed off the author of that anti-Semitic letter to my parents, I am unable to recall exactly when and under what circumstances I was reborn as the decent, compassionate young man that until recently I thought I had been well before 1933. I became an ardent Socialist, but I don't know what precisely did it, for up to then I was not interested in politics or economics, and studying the classic theorists put me to sleep. One large influence, I think, was reading of the tribulations of Eugene Victor Debs and listening to speeches by his successor, Norman Thomas. In my junior year, I decided to become a Communist, because the Communists seemed to me to be working harder than the Socialists, but although I called myself a Marxist, I was not serious enough to read Lenin; I was even more bored by him than by Marx and Engels. I wasn't much of an activist myself, but I admired those who were. Nor did I spend much time learning what Marxism was until much later, when I was let down by it and wanted to be sure what I had been let down by. I tried to join the Communist Party in Connecticut one summer, and I got far enough into it to know that it really wasn't for me. I was with it in spirit, but they held dreadful meetings, testing each other for ideological soundness. I never went back to that.* Now I am an

---

* EDITOR'S NOTE: In his journal for 1936, under the date June 15, Rovere wrote: "Joined Communist Party under assumed name of Dick Halworth—same as my *New*

ex-radical, but would gladly be rid of the "ex" if I thought American society had radical possibilities. Even after I stopped supporting the Communist Party, in 1939, I remained a Socialist for many years, and even today I would be some sort of Social Democrat if I lived in a country that had such a movement. But I long ago learned, much to my disappointment, that what I had thought of as settled Socialist doctrine—complete economic equality—had never been achieved in either theory or practice. For a few years, this seemed to me about the most attractive aspect of socialism, and though I realize what difficult problems economic equality could pose, I still cherish the thought and wish I lived in a world in which it might be given a chance. For I have never been able to see why a person with a gift that is found only rarely in the mass of humanity should on that account alone be more handsomely rewarded than persons no less meritorious in character but blessed only with everyday skills that qualify them to dig ditches or to scrub floors. "From each according to his abilities, to each according to his needs"—thus was the matter stated by Marx. In one form or another, it is central to every economic system. It makes good sense.

III

After graduation from Bard, in 1937, I sought work as a teacher and as an organizer for the American Labor Party, but had no encouragement on either score. Granville Hicks—whom I had got to know when I helped organize a political rally at Bard—had recommended me for an editorial job on *New Masses,*† but there were no

Masses name. I'm going on the soapbox for the C.P. in Stamford." And, under the date June 16: "Went to my first unit meeting and—quick like an arrow—gone was the sham and fourflushing, the hypocritical histrionics. It may sound sentimentally off-tune to say that I felt what Bergson must have meant by the _élan vital_ getting pumped into my heart with every word." The _élan vital_ was quick to evaporate.

† EDITOR'S NOTE: In a letter dated May 18, 1937, to Fred Dupee, then literary editor of _New Masses_ and later professor of English at Columbia University, Hicks wrote: "Richard H. Rovere, a senior. Very much interested in and writes well about modern poetry. Has handled publicity for the Youth Congress, and would be good for any-

openings and no assurance that if one turned up I would be asked to fill it. I had sold two articles to pulp magazines for a total of eighty-five dollars. I was doing occasional work for the Book-of-the-Month Club and the Literary Guild—preliminary reports on books submitted for selection—but the pay was five dollars for what was for me, a slow reader, two or three days' work. I happened to meet, in the house on Montague Street, in Brooklyn, where I was living at the time, a man who dreamed of getting rich by setting up a catering service for household pets; he asked me to write some promotion copy, and I did, but if I was paid for it at all I got only a few dollars, and the aspiring entrepreneur soon disappeared. At that rate, I could not pay the rent and feed and clothe myself. The prospects of employment were dim. I could, of course, have turned to my father for support, but that would have been hard on him and painful for me.

The problem was temporarily solved when, early in the autumn of 1937, Granville Hicks wrote to suggest that I spend the winter with him and his family in Grafton, New York, and, in exchange for room and board, devote part of each day to such chores as splitting wood for the stove and fireplace, shoveling snow, running the pump that moved water from the well to a storage tank, and driving their daughter, Stephanie, to and from school. (Granville's father, Frank, had handled many of these tasks until a year or so earlier, when he had been disabled by a heart ailment.) I accepted without hesitation and, before the first snow, moved from Brooklyn to Grafton—to a life quite different from anything I had known and to a house that Eleanor and I have come to know and love almost as if it were our own. It was the first really close family I had ever been in.

About a hundred and seventy miles north of New York City, Grafton is twenty miles east of the Hudson and ten miles west of the Massachusetts border, in the foothills of the Taconics. It was then a rural slum—a kind of Tobacco Road North. The climate is

thing on youth movements. Has taken a lot of economics, and might do less important books in the history of economics and economic theory. Rovere is unusually mature and could certainly be used."

harsh and the growing season short, and the stony land, never very fertile to begin with, was pretty well worked out before the century began. (The process began before the American Revolution, when New Englanders, moving west, were sharecroppers for the Dutch patroons.) The town center, on the road known as the Taconic Trail, running from Troy to Williamstown, consisted of a cluster of perhaps two dozen ramshackle and characterless buildings—two churches (Baptist and Methodist), an elementary school, a post office, a filling station, and some residences in varying states of disrepair. Grafton's few hundred people were scattered widely over the hilly countryside north and south of the east-west highway, most of them engaged in what might be called sub-subsistence farming. About half the farms that had once been worked were abandoned, the fields given over to woods and brush. Some of the people worked at logging and on town, county, and state road crews, and some worked in the grimy, mostly obsolete factories in Troy, a decaying city, as Grafton was a decaying village. And some of them, of course, in that year of recession in the midst of a depression, had no employment. The Hickses acquired their place as a summer house and weekend retreat in 1932, when Granville was teaching at Rensselaer Polytechnic Institute; they made it their permanent home two years later, when he was fired. It was two miles from the town center, on a dirt road that became a caldron of mud after a heavy rain or a thaw, and then, when it dried, was a network of ruts and exposed rock, which tested a driver as high seas test a skipper. It was a story-and-a-half house framed in clapboard and built around a central chimney, with a woodshed attached. (Its first owner had bought it in 1790 or thereabouts.) The style, typical of eastern New York, was simple and graceful, well suited to the environment, and Dorothy Hicks, with some assistance from the rest of the family, had surrounded it with shrubs, flowers, and a kitchen garden. When I arrived, there was no electricity, no central heating, no telephone, and only the most rudimentary plumbing. Electricity came one night that December—when the snow was high, the moon was full, and the air pulsing with the kind of excitement that occurs upon the birth of a new member of the family. (At first, it provided only light, replacing the kerosene lamps; for some years, the fuel for cooking and heating came out of the woodshed.)

It was an odd setting and an odd way of life for the country's best-known Communist man of letters. (Best-known, that is, of those actively engaged in Communist Party affairs. There were others—John Dos Passos, for example, and Malcolm Cowley—who were thought of as Communists, and who thought of themselves as such, but Granville was the only one who functioned within the Party structure, on occasion as a kind of official spokesman.) And he was an odd man to be such a Party man. An intellectual descendant of the Transcendentalists, he had embraced Marx and Lenin while teaching at Smith after training for the Unitarian ministry at the Harvard Divinity School. He was one part Marxist critic, insisting on history as class struggle and exhorting contemporary writers to champion the proletariat; and one part Yankee, who believed in and practiced self-reliance, loved the rural life, stayed away from cities as much as possible, and seemed to regret the course of history that had created the proletariat. And he was one part writer, who might spend the afternoon praising the work of Louis Aragon, Ilya Ehrenburg, Grace Lumpkin, and Clara Weatherwax and, in the evening, read his ten-year-old daughter to sleep with "The Song of Hiawatha" and Gilbert and Sullivan's librettos, many of which he knew from memory. As a polemicist, he could be vexingly dogmatic, but he never achieved the single-mindedness that is the mark of the true revolutionary. The irony of his expulsion from Rensselaer Polytechnic Institute—in a celebrated academic-freedom case—was that he was a Marxist who found it easy, proper, and natural to keep the political agitator out of the classroom. For many years before I met him, and for many years afterward, he earned his living reading manuscripts for his publisher, Macmillan. Granville knew that he was being paid not for his views on the organization of society, or even for his aesthetic judgments, but for his knowledge of the reading tastes and buying habits of the consuming public. Some of his Communist colleagues felt that what he did was, if not actually counterrevolutionary, something less than a contribution to the cause—that he was helping a capitalist enterprise pander to bourgeois tastes and provide escapist mechanisms for those who should have been facing the stern realities limned by Marx and Lenin. Given their premises, this was a sound enough judgment. But Granville did not see it that way. He had a family to support, and this was his first responsibility. The service he rendered was an honest and honorable one—a good deal more so than that of some of the Communist writers who earned huge fees for producing Hollywood shlock. It gave him time for his work as a Communist, and even left him with small sums to contribute to the Party. He did not feel corrupted.

During the winter when I hewed wood and drew water in Grafton, he was at work on a book he called *I Like America*—a salute to his country that almost smacked of chauvinism (he said he was reasonably sure that he "would not care to live in any country but the United States"), and at the same time a plea for a Communist restructuring of American life. This more or less fit the Party line at the time, when Earl Browder was saying that "Communism is twentieth-century Americanism" and the *Daily Worker* was telling its readers that "Daniel Boone belongs to us." (And this Party line, of course, made it easier for someone like Granville to be a Party member. He was a big catch for the Party: "Granville Hicks belongs to us.") It was rather a dry book, most of it the kind of lecture on economics and sociology that a New Deal supporter might have delivered. He managed to skirt such thorny questions as violence (in those Popular Front days, the Party had pretty much put the matter on ice) and human rights in the Soviet Union. He skirted some rather personal matters, too. In an early chapter, he recalled a talk in Grafton with a Party functionary from New York—a man who, as he looked out at the fields and mountains, at the scurrying rabbits and squirrels, at the gardens and henhouses, said, "A beautiful spot, comrade, but where is the class struggle?" which prompted the author to observe, "A stupid question. . . . Does one have to be in the trenches to know there is a war?"

But the question was not without its point. Wherever the class struggle may have been, it certainly wasn't in Grafton. The principal struggle there was against the intractable land, and the land was winning; there weren't even any landlords to blame, for the people who tried to work the soil owned it. There were some tussles among the town's Republicans (Democrats were about as scarce as Zen Buddhists) over who would get what jobs and contracts there were. Those who worked in Troy's factories resisted unionization as stubbornly as the Russian kulaks resisted collectivization. To meet with other Communists in the area—all five or six of them—Granville would go to Troy one night each week, where sessions were held in the dingy quarters of a Mr. Allen, a bookseller who lived above his shop. I now and then went with him; I recall the setting better than the participants, but they were a drab lot, who took part in no struggle but spent the evenings—as I had by now learned was characteristic of such meetings—drilling one another on the minutiae of Marxist theory. Granville's encounters with his near neighbors and townspeople were livelier, and in them he wisely made little effort to impart what he then regarded as received truth. When he saw his neighbors in the store, the post office, the filling station, or, on occasion, in the fields and the milking sheds, the talk was of the weather, of the crops or the lack of them, of the vagaries of the internal-combustion engine, of death and taxes, of course, and of who had been drinking too much, fornicating too promiscuously, or getting into trouble with the law.

Even in the Hicks household, there was little talk about the class struggle. Granville read about it and wrote about it in his upstairs study, while downstairs his parents, his wife, and his daughter occupied themselves in ways that a Communist critic would probably have regarded as retrograde. The sight that I recall most vividly, and always with much affection, was of his father at ease in a morris chair, his hair neatly parted in what used to be called a roach cut (it was a style most popular among bartenders at the turn of the century, though Frank Hicks, an abstainer, could never have emulated anyone in a saloon), with a book in hand and several more books piled on the table beside him. The books were hardly the sort his son would have recommended. In retirement, Frank Hicks seemed to be making a career of consuming the complete works of Zane Grey, Harold Bell Wright, Clarence Mulford, and any other writers of Western novels whose works Granville or I could find in the libraries of Troy and Albany. He was a crusty old Bostonian (I say "old," though he was probably then about the age I am now), who regarded his son's views and mine as being, if not criminal, misguided and perhaps unpatriotic. He was grateful to a system that had allowed him to rise from a blue- to a white-collar worker, despite the fact that, as Granville pointed out in *I Like America*, he had known harder times and greater insecurity as a clerk than he had as a foundry worker. But he had no sense of having been abused, and the only class struggle that interested him was between rustlers and sheriffs, cowboys and Indians.

If Central Casting had been looking for a woman to play the part of an idealized grandmother—kind, wise, doting, an ornament of the household—it would have been delighted with Carrie Hicks. She was just a trifle plump, bespectacled, dainty, with pink cheeks and hair just the right shade of gray. Her days were spent mostly in the kitchen—an ample room in which the Hickses dined and often entertained—either sewing in a rocker or bustling about preparing meals for the family, which, including me, numbered six. Neither she nor Frank thought much of the idea of having a young man like me in the house—particularly a Communist, and one from New York at that. His displeasure was clear (though not unkind; I could see that he disapproved of what he assumed I represented, and for this, even then, I could hardly fault him), but hers was artfully concealed. As for Granville's wife, Dorothy, Central Casting would have had no idea of what to do with her. One of a large family, she had been brought up on a farm in southern Maine. She had known great poverty and hardship, and had been struck down by polio and left partially crippled. She had developed a stubborn independence of mind and spirit and an ability to see through any pretense, any hypocrisy. I think she regarded Granville's Communist phase as something that was, like all else in life, bound to pass in time. As humane as anyone I have ever known, she had—she has—no very high opinion of humanity. Granville was a partially reconstructed New Englander; she was almost totally unreconstructed. She was a kind of instinctive Jeffersonian, disliking cities, even the smaller ones, and feeling that if there is a good life anywhere it is on the land, and the more remote and sparsely settled the better. She was not quite a Luddite—having no impulse to destroy anything—but her aversion to machines was not far short of total. She came to accept machines for washing clothes and dishes, but I think she would have considered it a better world if they had never been invented, and not long ago she was saying that a rather primitive electric toaster was more trouble than it was worth. Altogether, rather a quirky woman, especially to be the wife of a prophet of a new industrial order. But I have known few people who could store as much common sense and have as great a capacity for love, loyalty, and abiding friendship.

My stay with the Hickses did much, I think, to form the rest of my life. I had not lived with my parents for more than eight years, had never had a brother or sister or lived with a third generation. I had never done manual labor before, and have not done much since, but my hours on the woodpile and behind the snow shovel were tonic, and there was even a bit of what for me was adventure, as when, the roads being impassable one winter day, I got on skis for the first time and somehow made my way through the woods and fields to the post office. Stephanie Hicks was for me a surrogate younger sister, and although it was at times an awkward relationship —the gap between ten and twenty-two is a difficult one to bridge— my daily responsibility for her safety and well-being was one I rather

welcomed. I was not close to the elder Hickses, but I was charmed
by them, and I particularly relished the thought of the son manning
the literary barricades upstairs while downstairs the mother was bak-
ing cakes for a church supper and the father was fantasizing about
Hopalong Cassidy and life in the OK Corral. My chores left me
several hours a day for reading and writing. I turned out a few pieces
for the pulps, and reviewed a few books that Granville had persuaded *New Masses* to send to me. He and I talked less about
politics than about writing, and from him, as from George
Genzmer, I learned a great deal. Both were devotees of what Cyril
Connolly called the "common style" of English prose—the
unadorned style best suited for direct communication, the style that
achieves its effects mainly through the declarative sentence and the
simple colloquial rhythms. There can be interesting variations on it,
but it is, I think, best for most of the work I have done; in any case,
it is a style that every writer must master, just as a painter must
attain some proficiency as a draftsman before going on to other
things. And Granville strengthened my powers, such as they are, of
sequential thinking. Whatever the shortcomings of his critical
thinking, he knew how to marshal an argument, to construct a syllo-
gism, and to keep clutter out of his prose, and for a young writer—at
least of my sort—nothing is more important.‡

In early 1938, there was an opening on *New Masses*, Granville
recommended me for it, and I was hired.

---

‡ EDITOR'S NOTE: Rovere also credited a Stony Brook teacher, Pierson Curtis, for
shaping his prose style. Of him he once wrote: "He was the first person to give me
what is just about the most valuable thing a writer can have—an aversion to fattiness
in prose. He drilled it into us in school, and I remember an extra lick when I was
almost through college. I was the editor of the college paper, and he came to our
campus to visit, I think, one of his nephews. Anyway, he picked up a copy of the
paper I was editing, read some stuffy and didactic editorial of mine, put it down, and
said, 'There is no such word as "thusly." ' Not one syllable more than is needed—that
should be the first law. Incidentally, 'thusly' is recognized by the new Webster's, but
it shouldn't be."

IV

New Masses made a good deal of the fact that, unlike *The Daily Worker*, it was not an official organ of the Party. The distinction was all but meaningless. When the *Worker* used the editorial "we," it stood not for the editors but for the Communist Party itself; on *New Masses*, the conceit was that the opinions expressed in the editorials were views independently arrived at by the staff. But, of course, nothing that deviated from the Party line by as much as a hair ever saw print, and to make sure that this was the case an enforcer was always on the staff, put there by the Party leadership. In my day, it was A. B. Magil, a drab, bespectacled, unsmiling man who looked like a rather seedy small-town mortician. He would pore over every phrase and clause to see that it contained no hint of heresy; if he found a passage that in any way could be classified as what he called "incorrect," he would expunge it or rewrite it in his dreadful prose, which combined the worst elements of the bureaucratic style with the barbarism of Marxist-Leninist polemics. Sometimes he would find it necessary to appeal to a superior court. While still in Grafton, I had reviewed a life of Christ by a British Marxist who was an Anglican clergyman (I guess I thought my Stony Brook Bible studies qualified me for this endeavor), and it was not accepted until it had gone down to Party headquarters, on Thirteenth Street, to be checked for "correctness" by the chief cultural commissar, V. J. Jerome; the *New Masses* editors trusted their own judgment on political matters, but they needed a higher authority when it came to theology. The same thing happened when I wrote my editorial obituary of Freud, psychoanalysis apparently being regarded as akin to theology.

Still and all, the atmosphere at *New Masses* was less suffocating than it was at headquarters. We cultivated orthodoxy as much as anyone else, but we were less solemn about it. We weren't independent, but we often acted as if we were. We tried, as writers and artists, to rise above the dreariness and shrillness of the *Worker*, to assemble each week a magazine that was lively and entertaining as well as didactic and hortatory. And it was a lively and (except for Magil) a highly professional staff. The editor when I started work, Herman Michelson, was a huge, burly figure, much given to laughter, who had had many years of experience on New York newspapers in the 1920s and early 1930s and would not have been out of place as a tough, ribald, irreverent city editor in a Hecht-MacArthur movie. He knew good writing when he saw it, and he knew how to put some life into some of the soggy manuscripts our contributors often turned in. I have always wondered whether he was in fact a Party member or, like me, one who paid his respects to the church but never attended. I recall his saying—I think it was one evening at the Hickses'—that he had resisted joining the Party for several years and had not actually enrolled until a few months earlier, when he had signed up while on a visit to Moscow. It seemed to me an improbable story but a good cover; anything done in Moscow was unlikely to be questioned in New York. At any rate, he was one of my mentors, and from him I learned to be a fairly competent man on a rewrite desk.

Another editor for whom I had some affection was Joshua Kunitz, a stooped, sad-faced, brooding, and very gentle man—a Russian Jew who wrote movingly about the Soviet Union not so much as a Communist ideologue but as one who had a deep attachment for the land and the people. I had met him, too, at the Hickses', and he played something of an avuncular role in my life at *New Masses*. When I chafed under Magil's heavy-handed efforts to compel orthodoxy, Kunitz would explain sympathetically that discipline was a necessary evil and that while he and I might resent such a plodding time-server, we had to put up with him if we were to be politically effective. Michelson and Kunitz were of my parents' generation, and I was, I think, the youngest member of the staff—in any case, the greenest and least experienced—but there were others close to my age. There were James Dugan, a recent graduate of Penn State and the editor of its humor magazine, who wrote some amusing and literate movie criticism; Bruce Minton, a labor reporter, and, on and off, Minton's wife, Ruth McKenney, whose "My Sister Eileen" sketches in *The New Yorker* had been an immense success and were in the process of being adapted for Broadway and Hollywood; and Theodore Draper, the magazine's foreign editor, who in later, non-Marxist years was to become one of the most astute and respected writers on Vietnam and on American policy toward the Soviet Union. In many ways, the most talented member of the staff, who gave it much of what character it had, was David Leisk, who used the name "Crockett Johnson" on the masthead and on his drawings. He was a tall, very blond man—half Scotch and half Scandinavian, I believe—with the build of a linebacker and the mind of a Daumier. He was both art editor and makeup editor. He designed and redesigned the magazine each week, and in typography and layout it achieved a distinction that it often lacked editorially. And the artists he worked with were, on the whole, a more distinguished group than the writers Michelson edited. One of his cartoonists was Ad Reinhardt, later one of the admired painters of the New York school of the 1950s and 1960s. Three of the most gifted *New Yorker* artists— Mischa Richter, Sid Hoff, and Abe Birnbaum—were Dave's protégés. Dave was for a time a neighbor of mine on Brooklyn Heights and the one member of the staff I saw most often outside the office. Not long after I left, he began the syndicated comic strip "Barnaby," a charming kind of modern fairy tale that acquired a broad and literate following.

In the spring of 1938, when I came down from Grafton to work on the magazine, the offices were a cluster of cubbyholes in a grimy and dilapidated old building on East Twenty-seventh Street, and I shared a small one with a young woman named Barbara Giles, a frail young Southerner who functioned as I did—as a kind of utility infielder. I did a good deal of copy editing, rewriting, and, under Dave Leisk's supervision, some makeup. Once a week, Barbara and I would go to the printing plant, in Long Island City, to work on the foundry proofs and close the magazine. I wrote an occasional book review and some short articles and most of the promotion copy—house advertising and letters soliciting subscriptions and donations. (I don't know whether the magazine got any kind of subsidy from Moscow, but I do know that at times there wasn't enough cash to pay our salaries. Mine was twenty-five dollars a week, and I doubt if anyone got much more than that; we borrowed or went without until we could be paid. I had the impression that the chief source of funds was Hollywood, where a number of highly paid Communist writers—John Howard Lawson, Dalton Trumbo, Albert Maltz, and others—were regularly visited by emissaries from the magazine.) In the months before the fall of Czechoslovakia to the Nazis, I frequently wrote pseudonymously under a Prague dateline. Someone there regularly sent us packets of notes, newspaper clippings, copies of speeches by Communist leaders, and so forth, and I drew on these to make my stories read like on-the-scene reporting.

Not long after my arrival, we were told that a young man of enormous wealth—an heir to one of the great American fortunes—would soon join our group, and that his presence might bring an end to our payless weeks. The situation was to be handled with the utmost delicacy; not a word of it was to be spoken outside the office. Our benefactor was to be Huntington Hartford, of the Hartfords who founded the Great Atlantic and Pacific Tea Company and the A&P grocery stores. The story, as I later got it, was that young Hartford, after graduating from Harvard, had been given a position in the A&P accounting department—or perhaps it was purchasing or sales—in order to learn the family business. He was befriended there by a man, either a Party member or a fellow traveler, who quickly learned that Hartford did not relish the thought of a grocery career. What sort of career did he want? He would like to be a writer, the story went, and perhaps find work on some literary magazine. His leftist friend knew of a splendid literary magazine; he would introduce him to some of its writers and editors. He arranged a meeting with Michael Gold, the novelist and a man of considerable charm and social grace, who had been an editor of *The Liberator*, from which had sprung *New Masses*. I gather that little, if anything, was made of the fact that *New Masses*, though it might have had some claim to being a literary magazine, was primarily a Communist magazine. In any event, one day in the summer of 1938, Hartford was quietly installed in one of our dark and musty cubicles and assigned the task of reading unsolicited fiction and poetry. We junior editors were assigned the task of making life as pleasant as possible for him, in the office and out of it. Dave Leisk, Jim Dugan, and I were to offer ourselves as luncheon companions, tennis partners, whatever. Ruth McKenney and Bruce Minton, the most attractive as well as the most affluent young couple, were to entertain him at home and, occasionally, take him on one of their frequent out-of-state reporting assignments. I did my share of lunching, often paying the check, since, like so many of the rich, he seldom seemed to have any pocket money on him. I tried to draw him into conversation, but it proved to be an arduous task. I could not get him to talk much about literature—or about anything else I brought up. Had my instincts been sharper, I might have mentioned show business, and particularly show girls, in which, as his subsequent career showed, he had an absorbing interest. I recall Hartford now as a tall, almost strikingly handsome young man with a rather bored and decadent look. What he thought he was doing in that back room with those piles of dreadful poems and amateurish short stories I have no idea; I assume he scribbled his opinions of them, and perhaps he thought that this was the literary life. At any rate, he and we stuck it out for a few months, and then he left, soon to become a figure in gossip columns; the owner of Paradise Island, in Nassau; a celebrated hater of modern art who bought full-page newspaper ads to explain why Maxfield Parrish was superior to Picasso; the builder of the Gallery of Modern Art at Columbus Circle; the publisher of *Show* magazine; and, I learn from Who's Who in America, the author of *You Are What You Write*, a book I must someday read. *New Masses* got not one penny of the forty million dollars he was then said to be worth, and I estimate that he still owes me something in the neighborhood of twenty or twenty-five dollars, which compounded over forty years would be a respectable sum.

Changes in the magazine's staff were considerable, even in the year and a half I was there. Michelson was succeeded as editor by Joseph North, a very different sort—more a *Daily Worker* sort. Before he joined us, he had spent a year or so as the *Worker*'s correspondent in Spain, not only covering the war on the Loyalist side but taking part in it. He lacked Michelson's editorial skills and his wit and coolness. He was an odd combination of the political fanatic and the romantic journalist; he had been friendly in Madrid with Ernest Hemingway,[1] and had developed a reporting style that was in part a poor imitation of Hemingway's and in part the shrillest kind of Communist polemic. I was somewhat less at ease with him than I had been with Michelson, and I am sure that he, like Magil, distrusted me, a bourgeois kid and a friend of Granville's. But I liked working for the magazine, and I was getting some interesting reporting assignments. One in particular sticks in my mind, partly because, journalistically, nothing ever came of it. In New York in 1939, there was quite a bit of rowdy activity in the streets, incited by Fascist and anti-Semitic agitators. Rallies of one sort or another were being staged by Fritz Kuhn's German-American Bund, by Father Charles Coughlin's Social Justice movement, by a coalition of Fascist groups known as the Christian Front, and by a good many others. There was a particularly inflammatory rabble-rouser named Joe McWilliams, whose meetings had a way of turning into riots in

---

[1] He had an amusing Hemingway story that I do not believe has got into the hagiography. Once when he and the novelist and several others were in a truck just behind the front, Hemingway was observed pulling pieces of paper out of his pockets and ingesting them. "I thought he was crazy," Joe said. "Sticking thick wads of paper in his mouth and swallowing them. I asked him why he was doing it. 'Just practicing,' he said. 'Practicing what?' I asked. 'I'm practicing eating paper in case I get captured. I carry around a letter from Franklin Roosevelt saying that I'm his friend and deserve good treatment. If the Fascists found that, I'd be a goner. So I figured that if they got hold of me, I'd eat the letter and let it come out the other end. Now I'm building up a tolerance for paper.' "

which blood, generally Jewish, was sometimes spilled. North asked me to learn what I could about this hoodlum and his supporters. For a week or so, I kept track of McWilliams's appearances and made inquiries about his background, and in the course of this I met another reporter with a similar assignment. "Funny thing about Mc-Williams," this man said. "He used to be a Communist. Somewhere in Texas, I think." A Communist turned Fascist? This was incomprehensible to me—evidence, I suppose, of my political naiveté at the time. But I reported my finding to Joe North, who thought that I'd better get the facts straight before proceeding further. He made a call to Party headquarters, on Thirteenth Street, and then instructed me to go down there and tell my story to a man named Durba. Though I thought I knew the roster of Party functionaries fairly well, this was a new name to me. Durba was a huge, menacing man—a Latvian, I was later told—without a hair on his enormous head, and he spoke with an almost impenetrable accent. I told him what I had learned about McWilliams. Durba heard me out impassively, then went to a safe, pulled out an unwieldy ledger of the kind Bob Cratchit must have toiled over, locked the safe, and began to thumb through the ledger's large pages. In time, he came upon the name I had given him: a Joe McWilliams had indeed joined the Communist Party in Austin, Texas, just two or three years earlier. It was a common enough name, I pointed out—perhaps it was another man. Durba said nothing. He went back to the safe, replaced the ledger, and pulled out another, of similar bulk. He had not explained what the first volume was, but I had assumed it to be a roster of Party members. In the second, he seemed to find McWilliams listed again, and I assumed from this that it contained the names of defectors, of the Party's enemies, or perhaps of Party agents who had infiltrated other organizations. Whatever it was, he told me he thought I should drop the project until I got further word either from him or from North. I dropped it and heard nothing more from either of them.

It was an odd piece of business, and significant in a way I did not appreciate at the time. In later years, when the Party was being investigated by the FBI and a number of congressional committees, there was always, I learned, some mystification as to whether or not a master list of Party members had ever existed. It was assumed that somewhere there must be such a list, or must have been one, but none of the investigators—who were saying with great assurance that they knew who was and who was not a member—ever claimed access to hard documentary evidence. Once, sometime in the 1940s, I told the Durba story to Nelson Frank, a former Communist who was then the proprietor of a Fourth Avenue bookstore and later became a reporter specializing in anti-Communist exposés for the Scripps-Howard newspapers. I said that I thought I might be one of the few people who had ever seen a list (or at least a volume that appeared to contain one), and he asked me to write a memorandum, which I did. He later put a copy of it in the files of the House Committee on Un-American Activities, presumably for the guidance of its staff members in a search for the elusive master list. If they made such a search, they got nowhere. As for the mysterious Durba, I later learned from several sources that he was one of the top Soviet agents in the United States, one of those from whom William Z. Foster, Earl Browder, A. B. Magil, and Joe North took their orders. That is more than I ever learned about McWilliams. Was he a Fascist who infiltrated the Party? Was he a Party member raising hell on the streets of New York to discredit the Fascists? Was he a double agent? I don't know, and I don't think Durba knew either.

V

It is strange—or perhaps it is not—that I have so little memory, almost none, of August 24, 1939, the day the Soviet-Nazi nonaggression pact was made known to the world. In my life, this was an event as stunning and as consequential as Pearl Harbor. I know very well where I was and what I was doing on that first Sunday after-

noon in December two years later: I was in Wilbraham, Massachusetts, where Eleanor and I were working out the living arrangements
that would follow our marriage, which was to take place in two
weeks, and I hustled back to New York that evening on a train
jammed with excited, beer-drinking soldiers and sailors—the disaster
created a festive, almost Mardi Gras mood—and went to work on
Monday morning tearing up and reconstructing the editorial pages
of *The Nation*. I learned of Franklin Roosevelt's death while I was in
a dry-cleaning shop in Brooklyn Heights, and later joined the
hushed crowd in Times Square waiting for the details that were
flashing in bulletins from the old Times Tower. Hiroshima: I spent
the morning in my *New Yorker* office learning physics from the
newspapers—what is "fission"?—then kept a lunch date with a
friend, Morton Yarmon, in the Wigwam, a cheap bar-and-grill on
West Forty-fourth Street, where no one talked of anything else.
When John Kennedy was shot in Dallas, I was in my study in
Rhinebeck, writing about Barry Goldwater. Mark, in boarding
school, phoned and told me to turn on the news. By then the President had died; I caught the first train to New York, where I spent
the weekend—when not distracted by such spectacles as Jack Ruby's
televised gunning down of Lee Harvey Oswald—writing a long obituary for *The New Yorker*.

But August 24, 1939, is in my mind a blank, a nullity, a cavity in
time. So is the week or so before that date, when there were signs
that a deal was in the making, and so are the several days that
followed, with Ribbentrop in Moscow, Molotov in Berlin, and war
inevitable. I cannot recall what I did on that August day, much less
what I thought. Did I get the news by radio, by telephone, from a
newspaper? I don't remember. Come to think of it, I don't believe
that we had a radio or a phone. I assume that I got up that morning
and was alone in the Columbia Heights apartment that I shared
with Milton Meltzer; Milton, with multiple fractures caused by an
absurd accident, was either in the hospital or recuperating at his
mother's home, somewhere out near Coney Island. With or without

the news, I must have taken the Lexington IRT to Thirty-fourth Street, as was my custom, and headed for my desk in *New Masses*'s loftlike offices on Thirty-first Street. Surely by then I knew what had happened. Was I outraged? I would guess that I was more numbed than anything, which would explain my lack of memory. I don't recall what I said, or what anyone else said, or even whether anyone said anything. As a rule, the office was a noisy place, but on that day it may have been silent, and with reason. I imagine that at some point, perhaps on the next day or the one following, Magil—looking like an undertaker's assistant, his eyes impenetrable behind his thick lenses—must have appeared to tell us that what Stalin had done was manifestly "correct," that our comrades in Moscow had struck a mighty and decisive blow for peace and against the forces of fascism and imperialism. And he must have said—I can almost hear him saying it now—that we on the magazine must set about explaining this to our readers, some of whom may not have been "prepared" for this splendid turn of events.

My memory begins to return three or four days after the news, and it is largely a memory of walks—walks after lunch, long walks in the early evening, mostly down Fourth Avenue and around Greenwich Village. I knew I was going to quit the magazine, but I didn't know quite when, or how to go about it. We on the staff talked not so much about the accursed pact or what a betrayal it was or what it portended for the world as we talked about the effect it was having on us and what we were doing. I had been working on a series about the American Medical Association and how reactionary it was—how doctors got rich serving the affluent and neglecting the poor—and nothing about the pact changed that. Ruth McKenney was writing about the mines and mills in Pennsylvania, Bob Terrill about Henry Luce and his magazines, Jimmy Dugan about jazz. And now we were all required to defend Stalin's deal with Hitler. "It may be the greatest thing since Grant took Richmond," Kyle Crichton, who was also a *Collier's* editor, said, "but the dictionary I use doesn't have the words for it." I wasn't asked to find words for it, only to work over the lumpish Comintern prose that Magil wrote or brought up from the Little Kremlin on Thirteenth Street. (Delumping this stuff had always been one of my jobs. "Shrink this and English it," Herman Michelson would say, handing me a manuscript as if it were something unclean.)

In time, Granville Hicks, shattered, came down from Grafton; he told Earl Browder that he could stay in the Party only if it asked not for approval of the pact but simply for a suspension of judgment until the consequences were clear. (By then they were becoming quite clear.) Browder said that Granville might suspend judgment, as long as he did not do so publicly, but that the Party could not and would not. In mid-September, Granville formally resigned from the Party. Uncertain of my status in the Party—or whether in fact I had a status—I told Joe North that I was leaving the magazine. No effort was made to talk me out of it.

I was intellectually and politically displaced and disoriented, but for me I think the break was less wrenching than it was for many others. As far as I was concerned, it was not, as Arthur Koestler put it, that a god had failed—Marx, whose thought I never really absorbed, and Lenin, whose polemics bored me, had never been gods of mine, and Stalin had never been even a demigod. My emotional take had been small—for once my weakness of commitment had served me well—and my intellectual investment, unlike Granville's, had been meager. I think I felt mostly that I had made a fool of myself—a most unfunny and irresponsible fool. I had enlisted in an army led by mad generals and bloody-minded sergeants. At the start, four years earlier, I could have pleaded ignorance and innocence. By 1939, I knew that Stalin had liquidated millions of kulaks and was executing his former comrades. But I saw myself as an *American* radical, and my job, consequently, was to draw attention to brutality on *these* shores. The Communist Party seemed to me an effectively organized agency of change, and if it happened to have a corrupt affiliate in Moscow, that did not foreclose my working with it here. Good Christians—and there was still some of the good Christian in me—knew what crimes were being committed daily in the name of their faith (in Spain, for example, in that very year), but they did not on that account abandon their creed.

A thoroughly false analogy—the pact taught me this. American Christians were free to denounce Franco and his legions, even to fight against him with the Loyalists, but American Communists had to support—even acclaim—everything Stalin did. The truth hurt, but I took it as a revelation: never again! A new beginning of wisdom. (At twenty-four, one is able to think in terms of new beginnings.) And it was liberating to know that I would never again have to take Earl Browder seriously or have my copy examined for "correctness" by Magil or the asinine V. J. Jerome. I took many lessons from the event, the chief one being Don't surrender your independence to anybody. Still, it was a break in my life, a major one. I was fond of most of my *New Masses* colleagues, and I enjoyed life in the office. I liked the combination of radical élan and irreverence. I liked the sight of Herman frowning as he read some endless, cloddish polemic he was expected to print and groaning, "This is as long as the midsummer night's reverie of a very inexpensive prostitute." And his response when Sam Sillen would ask us all to patronize a nearby cafeteria whose owners were said to turn over all their profits to the Party: "I've taken my stand against the profit system, but I'm not sure I want a revolution if it means we're going to be eating sawdust hash with crankcase oil." Then he would lead a group of us to a Hungarian joint on Thirty-second Street whose owners, for all we knew, put their profits into U.S. Steel or General Motors. I knew that when I left that office I would not again be welcome in it. And I suspected that Milton Meltzer would not want to go on living with a defector. Without him and without a job, I would have to give up the apartment on Columbia Heights.

I was enamored then of one Sylvia Berger, a redheaded young divorcée and a researcher at *Time*, who was a firebrand in the Party faction of the American Newspaper Guild. A day or two after I made my decision, I had dinner with her at her mother's apartment, in a grimy, creaky tenement on the Lower East Side. Later, we took a subway to Union Square and strolled in the park. Expecting sympathy, if not approval (I had got that much at *New Masses*), I told her what I had done.

She wheeled on me. "Renegade! Turncoat! You're a baby—a spoiled baby! We're better off without you."

"But Sylvia, how the hell can any of us defend a pact with *Hitler?* Doesn't it make you sick?"

"You think you know better? You think you understand a revolution? You're afraid of it, that's what you are."

"Revolution," I said. "I haven't heard that word lately. The last I knew, we were talking about a popular front with Roosevelt, a united front against Hitler. Now you're in a united front *with* Hitler."

"Oh, shut up!"

We kept shouting at one another, and I proposed that we go across the square to the brownstone on West Sixteenth Street where my friends Goddard and Margaret Lieberson lived, and ask their opinion. I had never thought of them as dedicated Communists. Fellow travelers, yes, but probably not Party members—certainly not zealots. Goddard, who a few years later was to be the father of the long-playing phonograph record and a big-time entrepreneur in the music industry, was a composer—a very promising one, everyone said—and a witty observer of many things. At the time, he was trying to set to music some passages from "Anna Livia Plurabelle," a fragment of *Finnegans Wake* that had circulated in advance of the book. Margaret, a great beauty and a member of a wealthy clothing family, was pure aesthete, or so I thought. But the two of them gave me the business even before they'd heard me out. They quite agreed with Sylvia. Those two almost flawless members of the species looked me in the face and said I was nothing but a political dilettante. I sputtered a bit and stalked out. I did not see either of them again until the 1960s, by which time Goddard was the jovial, wealthy president of Columbia Records, parlaying Elvis Presley and

Stravinsky, and Margaret was the wife of the even wealthier A. N. Spanel, who was president of International Latex. (As for Sylvia, I never saw her again; she died in 1954.)

When I think of the mysteries of belief and commitment, my mind often goes back to that evening. In a sense, Sylvia and the Liebersons were right. If I wasn't then afraid of revolution, I was about to be. And I was more of a dilettante than any of them. I had approached the movement as an eclectic, thinking that I could take what I wanted and leave what I didn't. But the movement was totalitarian, in New York as well as in Moscow. I had no business defending it. It took me a long time to get that through my head. But it could have taken longer, and it could have hurt more, for I had not been a leader of any sort and had no followers to nag my conscience—either for having misled them in the first place or for having abandoned them later. And, I, at twenty-four, had no reputation as a writer or as anything else. I had nothing to lose, little to disown. All I had to repudiate, in case I was ever called upon to do so, were a few dozen easily forgotten articles—many of them, mercifully, anonymous or pseudonymous. For Granville, approaching forty, breaking with the Party meant the end of a career; he had a great deal to lose. It meant the repudiation of books he had written and the scrapping of books he was writing: ten years of honest, earnest work down the drain. He was giving up a following that was important to him, and he had invested great hopes in a doctrine that he had to disown. It took Granville two or three years to accept it all—to see that the pact wasn't just an abuse of power but a quite natural use of power by tyrants who saw it, however acquired, as an end justifying any means. It took him that long to admit that, rather than having been deceived by leaders he thought he had reason to trust, he had deceived himself when he first put his trust in them. And that long to acknowledge that the doctrines he had been preaching—and Granville, the ex-seminarian, was always a sermonizer—had been as ugly in their contempt for humanity as they had been human in their professed goals. In his twenties, he had been a dedicated teacher, a fine scholar, a critic of some talent; in his thirties, he had been less critic than publicist—a high-class producer of literary agitprop. Now he was faced with a big problem of professional rehabilitation, and he managed it in ways that, while altogether honorable, I sometimes found saddening. As a scourge of his non-Communist contemporaries, he had written—however wrongheadedly—with vigor and bite. When he called Faulkner a "Sax Rohmer for the sophisticated" (Rohmer was a prolific purveyor of the cheap baroque), he was, it seemed to me, more interesting than when, doing needless penance, he explicated the Master in the pedestrian columns of *The Saturday Review.* The acid went out of his style along with the Marxist certitudes, and he began atoning for the way he had treated many fine writers of his own generation by an easy acceptance of the young. Having yet to find a style, I had no such problem.

If the pact—or war—had come a year or two later, I might have found myself married to Sylvia Berger and settled into the extended family life of the Party. In New York at the time, the Party was more than a movement: it was a self-contained environment, almost an ecosystem. (It was appropriate that what Republicans and Democrats called "clubs" Communists called "cells" or "branches" or "units.") Party members married or lived with Party members, and children were reared in the culture of the tribe. Friends outside the Party were permitted, but not if they were "enemies of the people" —Trotskyites and the like—and they were not, as a rule, to be trusted. For most Communists, leaving the Party was a kind of death—a loss not only of faith but of vocation, of community, of *querencia.* But I had never really entered the community. Though Jimmy Leonard, my dearest friend in adolescence, was a Socialist, a pacifist, and a steadfast anti-Communist, he remained my best friend while I was on *New Masses;* when I left, after eighteen months on its staff, he said he had known all along that I would clear out sooner or later. I had kept in touch with my college friends, my Connecticut friends, and even with some friends I had made at

P.S. 9. And, of course, I had the company of Granville and others who had also broken. For a time, we organized ourselves as the nucleus of what we hoped would be a neo-Marxist movement, one not cursed by the incubus of Stalinist foreign policy. We called ourselves the Independent Left, and we met quite regularly in Max Lerner's apartment—Max, Granville, Crichton, Malcolm Cowley, I. F. Stone, Leo Huberman, and perhaps a half dozen others. But none of us was much of an organizer, and before long we began wondering whether we were really Marxists after all. After perhaps three months, we gave up and went our separate ways—some, like Huberman, back into the Stalinist fold, and some, like Crichton, swearing off politics altogether. My own instinct then was to do what I had almost done four years earlier: to join Norman Thomas's Socialist Party. In fact, I did, in a way, join it.* I wrote an article for *The Call*, the Socialist Party weekly, explaining why I had not done so before and how much I regretted my error. I think that at the time I was the only ex-Communist who claimed not that the Party had betrayed him but that he had failed to see it for what it always had been. The piece drew me to the attention of some veteran anti-Stalinists—particularly the novelist James T. Farrell, the critic Philip Rahv, and the poet Kenneth Rexroth. I saw a good deal of Farrell and Rahv, who were contemptuous of most of those who had recently broken with the Communists—especially Granville and Malcolm Cowley, with whom they still had many scores to settle. With Rexroth, who lived in San Francisco, I had for several months a lively, disputatious correspondence. Noting that I then lived at 143 Montague Street, in Brooklyn, Rexroth pointed out that I was a neighbor of Bertram D. Wolfe's, at 68 Montague. Wolfe, who Rexroth said had "more good sense and human decency than most any Communist I know," had been a founder of the Communist

* EDITOR'S NOTE: Rovere did in fact join it. He was notified of acceptance of his application for membership in the Socialist Party, Downtown Kings Branch, on January 6, 1940. In the covering letter, he was admonished that membership "is a serious matter" and that he was "expected to be an active and disciplined organizer and propagandist," with the usual three-month probation.

Party in this country and one of its leaders until 1929, when, after some stormy meetings with Stalin in Moscow, he and several of his confederates were expelled for, they were told, ideological "error." The error consisted of having questioned the proposition, then an article of faith in Moscow, that American capitalism was in its final crisis and would very shortly collapse.

VI

I had a curious and no doubt unworthy reaction to the fall of the Spanish Republic, and a rather similar reaction, more than three decades later, to the end of our involvement in Vietnam: I wanted as much psychological and intellectual distance as I could get from those events. In the case of Spain in 1939, this insistence on detachment was directly contrary to my response to other events of that period. When I left *New Masses*, I became immensely curious about how I had been suckered and had suckered myself about the true nature of the movement I had briefly served and abruptly abandoned. As a young Communist, I had been unfailingly enthusiastic about working for change in this society and about the radical journalism I had been practicing; yet at the same time, as I have noted, I was bored by Marxist-Leninist polemics and what was absurdly called Party "literature." Stalin's history of the Communist Party of the USSR was required reading in those days; I don't believe I ever finished it. Nor could I take seriously the theoretical journal *The Communist*, which was atrociously written and as patently dishonest as any sales brochure. As for the quarrels of the Stalinists with the Trotskyites and the Lovestoneites (the rival party, of which Bertram Wolfe and Jay Lovestone were leaders), I couldn't see what they had to do with organizing automobile workers in Detroit or sharecroppers in Mississippi. Once I left *New Masses*, though, I began to devour the very material I had previously scathed as soporific and irrelevant. It was obvious to me now that it was anything but irrelevant: a Party member's obligation was not to the auto workers or to the sharecroppers but to Soviet foreign policy and the *obiter dicta* of *The Daily Worker* and *The Communist.* I also found it amusing— grimly so, absurdly so—and as I plunged into my research, I became something of an expert on the factional wars. I wrote a piece for *The New Republic* which I called "Factions on the Far Left"; in it, I tried to explain not only the major theological disputants such as the Trotskyites but such odd splinters as the Fieldites, a tiny deviationist group led by a Mr. and Mrs. Field, whose home had recently been picketed by their own followers, crying, "Mr. and Mrs. Field are no longer Fieldites."

But the war in Spain was different. On the streets of New York a few bones may have been broken, but no lives had been lost. I had overcome my pacifist instincts and felt quite passionately about the Loyalists' defense of their government. I had volunteered for the Abraham Lincoln Brigade and had been rejected as physically unfit. (Later it became altogether clear to me that actually I had been rejected as *politically* unfit.) Suddenly, in that dreadful autumn of 1939, I understood that the side I had supported, for which friends of mine had fought and died, was hardly less brutal and repressive than the Fascists, that both sides were being manipulated by totalitarian governments. Had Guernica been destroyed by German Junkers and Heinkels or laid waste by Loyalist incendiaries and machine gunners? Had Franco's treatment of Loyalist sympathizers been worse than the Communists' treatment of Socialists and anarchists? . . .

VII

For the next two years, I scratched out a living as a free lance. Malcolm Cowley, on *The New Republic,* had occasional assignments for me, as did Eugene Lyons, who was editing *American Mercury* and was well disposed toward anyone who had broken with the Communist Party. Someone, I forget who, put me in touch with a group of young Socialists who were getting out a weekly newsletter named *Uncensored*, a kind of antiinterventionist fact sheet. I did some work, unpaid, for it and for *The Call*, for which I wrote a number of articles on the 1940 presidential campaign. One of the financial backers of *Uncensored*, though not himself a Socialist, was Quincy Howe, then an editor at Simon & Schuster. He was working on a book about contemporary journalism—to be titled, somewhat misleadingly, "How to Read a Newspaper"—and he hired me as a researcher. I was still something of a dilettante in radical politics. I had been disturbed, but not greatly, by the Moscow trials and by the other evidences of repression and tyranny in Soviet life. But I had told myself that what went on in Russia was not really my business, that I would not allow myself to be deflected from working for socialism here by evidence of injustice in another society—one in which, as I understood it, injustice had been rampant for centuries. What bothered me about the Soviet-Nazi pact was not so much the fact that Stalin had come to terms with Hitler as the fact that I, an American Communist, was expected to applaud and defend this unholy arrangement as a means of achieving peace in the world and socialism in the United States. There was, I guess, an element of chauvinism in this—chauvinism and, of course, ignorance. To me, the defendants in Moscow were spectral figures, men with strange names—Kirov, Bukharin, Zinoviev, Kalinin, Kamenev—and uncertain pasts. For all I knew, they no more deserved my sympathy than Al Capone in Chicago or Harry Daugherty in Warren Harding's Washington. I probably thought of Trotsky as a Russian Aaron Burr or Benedict Arnold. It was Alfred Kazin who put flesh and blood on these disembodied figures for me.[2] He knew what they had done, what they had written, what they stood for. He had been brought up, as I had, in Brooklyn, but in a part of it—Brownsville—in which names like Kamenev and Zinoviev evoked images as vivid and as

[2] Alfred Kazin, at twenty-four, was already established as a leading literary critic; he arranged for me to do some reviewing for the Sunday book section of the New York *Herald Tribune*. He and his first wife, Asya, lived only a couple of blocks from me in Brooklyn Heights. I saw a good deal of them in that period (and much of Alfred in later years), and they were an important part of my life.

recognizable as the names Jimmy Walker and Al Smith (or those of movie stars and ballplayers) evoked in the Brooklyn I knew—more so, in fact, for Alfred's Uncle So-and-So had known this one, or been befriended by that one, or been abused by yet another one, or had grown up in the same village as still another. The Kazins had friends with similar knowledge; they could all talk for an evening about events in the Soviet Union as confidently as if discussing a play they had just seen or a novel they had read. Listening to them, I was not only greatly instructed but shamed into a kind of intellectual responsibility that I had up to then lacked.

Another new friend was Robert Bendiner, the managing editor of *The Nation*. Bob had been on *New Masses* in a capacity like mine, but he had quit early in 1937, some months before I joined the staff. He had none of Alfred's intensity—his grandparents had come from Hungary, by way of Indiana and Ohio, to the coal-mining country of western Pennsylvania, where he spent his early years—but he was well served by an independence of mind and spirit that made it impossible for him to put up for long with any conformity. He had a wit that deflated pretension and was often prankish. (On a *New Masses* article defending the Moscow trials, he had slugged the heading "Dostoyevsky Rides Again," which seemed unfunny to whoever was the A. B. Magil of the time.) Bendiner commissioned me to write some articles for *The Nation*, one of which led to a memorable trip to the South.

The Klan had not been much heard of for several years, but early in 1940 there was a killing in Anderson, South Carolina, that seemed to foretell a resurgence. Someone had sent *The Nation* some notes and newspaper clippings; Bob turned them over to me to assemble as an article, and I did so—it was my first piece for the magazine. *The Nation* did not feel it could finance a trip to Anderson to cover the trial, but I was eager to go, and I put together a kind of miniconsortium for the purpose, with small sums from the *Jewish Daily Forward*, the Federated Press (a news service for trade union papers), and the Worker's Defense League, a Socialist-spon-

sored civil-rights and civil-liberties organization. A day or so before
the trial was to start, I went by train—it turned out that the only
train was the mail train, so I rode on the sacks—to Anderson, a
rather sleepy little county seat, and checked in at the John C. Calhoun, the only hotel in town. The next morning, while seeking press
accreditation at the Anderson County courthouse, I met Thomas L.
Stokes, of the Scripps-Howard newspapers—the only other journalist (except for two or three South Carolinians) covering the story.
Tom was a Georgian, a man of high integrity who had recently won
a Pulitzer Prize and the displeasure of some of his New Deal friends
for exposing political hanky-panky with public-works funds. He, too,
was registered at the John C. Calhoun, and so were a dozen or more
national and state leaders of the Ku Klux Klan. Tom suggested that
we join them all for lunch in the hotel dining room, and though the
idea sounded about as enchanting as occupying a ringside seat at a
lynching bee, I could see it was the sort of opportunity a good
reporter ought to seize. We sat down with the Klansmen not only
for lunch that day but for just about every other meal during the
week or so of the trial. They were more like a group of farmers,
clerks, and millhands than the pack of murderous night riders I
expected to encounter. In fact, none of my preconceived stereotypes
held up. The Imperial Wizard, the national head of the Klan, who
was on hand, was neither imperial nor even imperious in bearing.
He was James Arnold Colescott, a pudgy, round-faced veterinarian
from Terre Haute, Indiana, who took some pride in being the first
man from north of the Mason-Dixon line ever to hold the office.
The Klan henchmen who were on trial had taken part in no lynching, and neither race nor religion had figured in the murder. The
victim was a young white garage mechanic (I am not sure, but I
think I described him as a black militant in my *Nation* article), and
what had led to his death was a request from his wife that the Klan
persuade him to give up his drunken, lecherous, and spendthrift
ways. The local Klansmen, outraged at the man's neglect of his
family, picked him up in a truck, took him out to Fox Swamp

outside of town, and stomped him; as enforcers they were overzealous, and he died as a result of their ministrations. One of the stompers was a physician who pronounced him dead on the spot. They picked up the body and deposited it on his front porch with a note of regret. Donnalee Dale, the first female district attorney in Bilbo County, riding by in the morning, discovered the body—a fact that had a lot to do with the case's coming to trial. The defendants were promptly arrested in a pool parlor to which they had repaired.

It was for this homicide that the defendants were on trial, and the brass of the Klan had come to Anderson to stand by them as honorable men and upholders of public morality, whose only mistake lay in underestimating their own strength. But they were found guilty as charged by an all-white jury and sentenced to six months on the chain gang. Colescott, noting my interest in the Klan, invited me to cover a similar trial in an Atlanta suburb (expenses paid). A white insurance salesman was the victim. Same verdict, same sentence. I went home to write a rather different story from the one I had come to write.

I worked briefly on *The Nation* thereafter as an assistant editor— James A. Wechsler, a junior editor, had left his job to become a reporter on *P.M.*, and I replaced him—and at the end of 1942, when *The Nation* let me go, I became the editor of *Common Sense*, a liberal monthly whose founders and coeditors, Alfred Bingham and Selden Rodman, had gone into military service. (I was exempt from the draft for physical reasons never disclosed to me, but I assume that I was disqualified for being blind in one eye.) After a bit less than a year, I departed, partly because of differences with the management, partly because the job required administrative work, in which I had little interest and for which I had little aptitude.

By late 1943, when I was twenty-eight, I was once again unemployed. I had spent the past six years as an editor and sometime writer. I had left *New Masses* because of political disagreements. I had been fired from *The Nation*. On *Common Sense* there had been a conflict of personalities. After leaving *Common Sense*, I decided that I wanted to spend all my time writing. I was confident I could make a living at it, and I hoped that in time I might write for *The New Yorker*—a hope I shared with many writers of my generation. *The New Yorker* seemed to many of us the best magazine in America, perhaps the best in the English language. I knew no one there and was anything but confident of being able to meet the magazine's standards. I admired it more than any magazine I had ever read, for its style and accuracy, for its journalistic eclecticism, for its humor. Though *The Nation* and *Common Sense* had been a relief after *New Masses*, they were essentially political trade journals, and the writing was, by and large, indifferent, or worse. As I have written elsewhere: "Their view, to borrow from Emerson, was that there is no history, only mass movements and the faiths they live by. They were interested less in the people whose names turned up in their pages than in the gospels those people propounded." I was still interested in politics, but in more than just politics, and I was interested more in writing than in any particular subject.

3

Journalist, Observer, and Critic

I

In mid-May 1944, I was asked by William Shawn, then managing editor of *The New Yorker*, to join the staff. I was twenty-nine, seven years out of college, married, a father, and supporting my family by writing for various magazines and newspapers. I preferred to have a steady contractual arrangement of some sort, and I had applied to *The New Yorker* some months earlier (my birthday is May 5, and I remember that I applied before I was twenty-nine and was hired after), and been rejected. I had shown Shawn an article I had done for *Harper's* on a New York politician, Representative Vito Marcantonio, who was a Communist in the Republican Party. "We don't publish exposés," he said. (He certainly couldn't say that today.) But in the next *Harper's* I had an article on Thomas E. Dewey, then governor of New York and soon to be the Republican candidate for President. It became, within a few weeks, something of a sensation. It had a catchy title—"The Man in the Blue Serge Suit"—and it turned out to fill the needs of some of Dewey's Republican critics and, when he got the nomination, those of the Democrats. (It was distributed to all delegates and alternates at the Republican convention and later reprinted in the hundreds of thousands by the Democrats.) After my Marcantonio experience with Shawn, I thought it would be idle to ask him to read the Dewey piece, but within a few days after its publication, and well before it became the center of a controversy, he telephoned me and asked me to come to his office. He had liked the article very much, thought it qualified me to join the staff as a writer of Profiles, and offered me a drawing account of seventy-five dollars a week, which was twenty more than I had made at *Common Sense* and seemed a princely sum—provided, of course, that I could earn it. (A drawing account is analogous to an advance against royalties; what is paid out in money is owed back in words.)

In the first year or so, I saw rather little of Shawn or of others on the magazine. My office was four floors below the main editorial offices, and I might as well have been in another city. I was in a suite of two or three rooms, which I shared with three or four other writers—the cast changed many times—and I had no sense of being part of an institution. This had both rewards and frustrations. The main compensation was the camaraderie in the suite. The writers I remember best are Joel Sayre, George Leighton, and Rufus Jarman. The latter two had joined the magazine just about when I did; Sayre had worked on it in the 1930s. He was more or less of Harold Ross's generation and of those who had been with the magazine almost from the beginning—James Thurber, E. B. White, Alva Johnston, John McNulty, Joseph Mitchell, A. J. Liebling, and S. J. Perelman. A great barrel of a man, with an Old King Cole head and given to rollicking laughter, Sayre was, among many other things, an amateur classical scholar. He had been a professional football player, a bodyguard to a White Russian admiral, a city and sports reporter for the old New York *Herald Tribune,* and a Hollywood script writer. He was the author of what is still one of the best novels about New York, *Rackety Rax,* and having him nearby was, for someone like me, like having at hand a friendly guide, a Dutch uncle, and a well-stocked reference library.

Leighton was a recruit from *Harper's;* in fact, he had worked closely with me on my early pieces there. A gifted editor and a splendid journalist, he was a man at once gentle and eternally angry. He was eccentric in the extreme. Once, on *Harper's,* he sought a change of pace by taking a few weeks off to join a road gang on Staten Island; while in our fifteenth-floor *New Yorker* suite, he bought a bolt of cloth and a tailor's pattern and, with no previous experience, made himself a suit. He had one odd source of income. As a schoolboy at Phillips Exeter, he had written, as a class assignment, a one-act play based on Abraham Lincoln's correspondence with the Mrs. Bixby who had lost five sons in the Civil War. It was produced at the school and picked up by the Samuel French company, which supplies play texts to amateur performers all over the world, and for decades scarcely a day went by when he did not find in the morning mail several royalty checks in small denominations—five, ten, fifteen dollars—from school and other amateur companies on every continent. In the early 1930s, finding himself unemployed, he thought of an ingenious plan for making money: reasoning that few door-to-door salesmen got around to visiting the islands off the East Coast of the United States, he got himself a boat and a Fuller Brush franchise and—apparently with considerable success—sold brushes and other Fuller knickknacks to residents of offshore islands from Maine to Florida. He and the magazine were not well suited to each other. When I first knew him, he was an idealistic liberal. But something soured him—I suspect it was the discovery that by no means all liberals had the kind of integrity he expected of them—and he turned into an out-and-out reactionary. He would come into the office with a copy of the New York *Daily News,* then in its most benighted period, and say that it was the only honest paper in the city. Nothing he wrote for *The New Yorker* in the year or so he was on the staff ever appeared; some of it was brilliant in its way, but too full of bile to be publishable. When he left, he joined the staff of the Senate Republican Policy Committee, then dominated by extreme conservatives. I saw him now and then in Washington, but the intellectual gulf between us was too broad for leaping. He died in 1974, and by then I had not seen or heard from him for many years.

Jarman was a misfit of another sort. A hulking, hard-drinking Tennessee hillbilly, he had been a reporter on the Atlanta *Constitution* and the St. Louis *Post-Dispatch* before coming East. According to Brendan Gill's *Here at The New Yorker,* in which Jarman is renamed Horgan, he was probably hired because Ross was so awed by the reputation of the *Post-Dispatch* that he thought anyone who worked for it could just as well work for him. I read some of Jarman's early magazine pieces—mainly in *The Saturday Evening Post*—which struck me as superior journalism, and I can vouch for his skills as a raconteur in the great Southern tradition, but even so, he and *The New Yorker* were not made for each other. One problem was his gullibility. He had a two-part Profile on Norman Rockwell published and then wrote one on a man he understood to be an eminent surgeon. But when the checkers began working on the story they discovered that the man was an imposter, without any medical credentials whatever; this might have made an even better story, but Jarman and the editors evidently didn't want to get into that. After a year or so, Jarman left and became a star reporter for *The Saturday Evening Post* and the author of an authorized biography of Conrad Hilton, the hotel magnate. He later found his true métier as a teller of tall Southern tales on Arthur Godfrey's radio program.

Others moved in and out of our suite, but they were transients—seasonal employees or displaced persons, often victims of the craze for structural alterations that seizes *The New Yorker* management from time to time. I remember that after a friend was moved to a nineteenth-floor office, he left it for a few hours one day only to find on his return that a staircase to the twentieth floor had been partially installed and that his desk was at the bottom of it. I have had at least a half-dozen offices since my first one, and have on occasion shared them with other writers, but my memories of that suite are among the most vivid of my thirty-five years on the magazine. Still, we were a unit unto ourselves, and not *The New Yorker.* My contacts with Shawn in those early months were mostly by telephone or memoranda. And most of what passed between us had to do with whom or what I was to write about. I had some ideas for Profiles, and so did he. But either mine didn't interest him or had been reserved by other writers, or his seemed inappropriate to me. Nothing had been said of this when he took me on. I assumed—wrongly, as I later learned—that Shawn wanted me to function mainly as a political writer, which was all right with me provided I could, in time, prove myself in other fields. Ross didn't want any national figures written about in his magazine. For an outsider to qualify for a Profile subject, he had to have some connection with New York—to have lived or worked there at some point, or to have some business or professional tie to the city. It was a rule that was sometimes broken, like all *New Yorker* rules, but not, in Ross's time, very often. "I don't mind having a local magazine," he was said to have said, "or even an international magazine, but I'll be damned if I want a *national* magazine." When A. J. Liebling said that he would like to write about the West, Ross said, "I've been there, Liebling, and there's nothing in it for us." It was several weeks after I took up residence before I found any subject that seemed right to both Shawn and me, but it seemed an eternity to me. We finally settled on a pleasant but not very exciting man, Newbold Morris, president of the City Council of New York. Morris, a liberal Republican and a protégé of Mayor Fiorello La Guardia's, was an inveterate reformer, a man of indisputable integrity, and a political innocent. He was also a member of the New York aristocracy—a descendant of Gouverneur Morris's, a signer of the Declaration of Independence—as well as a figure-skating champion, a patron of the arts, and an astute observer of city life and government. As it turned out, having a subject was not much better than being without one. When I set out to write about Morris, I was overcome by my first really serious attack of writer's cramp; it was caused by my conviction that *New Yorker* prose had to glitter in every sentence, that nothing less than perfection would do. It took me two or three weeks to compose an opening paragraph worthy of the magazine. Each succeeding paragraph came only with extreme difficulty. Finally, in the autumn, I sent my copy to Shawn, who found it acceptable and wrote me a note advising that he found the articles "very adroit," a phrase I found most bracing after those months of sweat and uncertainty.

II

Shawn was my editor on the Newbold Morris articles and on most of my other early ones. As I now set out to write about him, I can see that he is going to prove a most difficult subject. Ross was at most a two-dimensional character. Shawn has more than three dimensions. Ross—or at least the Ross I knew—was all of a piece, and what he was showed clearly in his appearance, his dress, his voice, his idiom. Almost everything about him was on the exterior, visible and audible. Nothing of the sort is true of Shawn. It was often said of Ross that in both appearance and manner he seemed most improbable as the editor of a sophisticated urban magazine; there was truth in that, but at least he was well cast as a newspaperman, which, essentially, is what he was. Nothing about Shawn's appearance—except, perhaps, his look of gravity and an occasional chuckle that bespeaks his grasp of anything under discussion—says much about his character or his interests. He comes no closer than Ross did to fitting what seems to be the common image of what the editor of *The New Yorker* should look like. He is of somewhat less than average height for an American male of his generation. He is round-faced, often rather flushed, and solemn. The solemnity, perhaps, comes as much from his dress and manner as from his actual appearance. His dress is conventional; the hues are invariably dark. His manner, though far from stiff, is formal, almost courtly. Seeing him on the street or in a restaurant, one would despair of finding any clues as to his occupation; he could as well be a doctor, a professor, an undertaker, a banker, a scientist. Nor would hearing him be of much help. His voice is hushed, almost as though he were talking to a pewmate in church. He has no regional accent, no special rhythm. His style, both in writing and conversation, is excellent and often eloquent, but though it is surely distinguished, it is not distinctive, except perhaps in its quiet intelligence and in its moderation. Once when I was at a rather large luncheon with him, I heard an attractive, ebullient young woman tell him of something that her sister had written that was, she felt, exactly right for *The New Yorker*. "Oh, Mr. Shawn, you'd love it. It's simply fabulous. It's fantastic!" she said. "It sounds as if it might be pretty good," Shawn said. The search for precision, for avoiding extravagance and overstatement is characteristic of him, but it is not—perhaps for this reason—distinguishable from that of anyone else who shares the same virtues.

There is much that is distinctive, though, in the relationships that Shawn establishes with others. What strikes most people on first acquaintance is his insistent politeness, his adherence to a social protocol. I have once or twice managed to follow him through a doorway, but only by some ruse, such as pretending I have left something behind. It took twenty-three years—I counted them with fascination—for us to go on a first-name, or diminutive, basis. Up to then it was always "Mr. Rovere" and "Mr. Shawn." I don't know how this struck him, but after the first four or five years, by which time I knew him as well as I knew most of my friends, it struck me as absurd. But things had gone far beyond the point at which any change might seem easy and natural, and I, a junior in both age and rank, had no intention of initiating a new mode of address. Finally, in 1967, writing me a note about an article he seemed particularly to like, he began with "Dear Mr. Rovere," went on to comment on my work, and concluded with "This formality has been going on for too long, so I will begin to end it. Sincerely, Bill." Even so, he would often forget, and so would I, that a change had been made, and there were in consequence some awkward, amusing moments. It is a strange fact that those who know him well almost always refer to him publicly or among themselves as "Shawn." In this book, there are some people other than family whose first names or diminutives I can use with ease, but not Shawn's.

Shawn's style in handling people is one I have encountered nowhere else. I was never close enough to Ross to know how he functioned as the head of an organization. I have the impression that he delegated authority—if not widely, at least frequently—and by the time of my arrival, certainly, Shawn was something more than Ross's principal deputy. As far as I know, he did not consult Ross or anyone else about taking me on, and I do know that no one else interviewed me. The magazine then, as now, had three editorial departments— fact, fiction, and art. Shawn was, and is, sovereign in fact. I do not know how independent the fiction and art departments were of him. Katharine White—Mrs. E. B. White—and Gustave Lobrano were the principal fiction editors, and the tension between them, I learned from Lobrano, was high. James Geraghty was the art (cartoons, covers) editor; they were all answerable to Ross and to some degree, I suspect, to Shawn.

After Ross's death, there was an interlude in which, according to an announcement on the bulletin board, the magazine was to be run by a triumvirate—Shawn, White/Lobrano, and Geraghty. According to Brendan Gill, Lobrano harbored hopes of being Ross's successor, but I do not believe that anyone else had much doubt as to what would happen. What would happen was Shawn. Whether there was any serious infighting I do not know, but there was never any question in my mind, or in the minds of most people I knew that Shawn would prevail, as he did. (He was named editor about three months later.) At this stage, I knew Lobrano much better than I knew Shawn, and I am rather inclined to think that his breadth of interests and his editorial capabilities were equal to Shawn's, but it was clearly Shawn who had had Ross's confidence and that of the preponderance of the writers. The magazine is first of all a *journal,* and Shawn was the editor who was first of all a journalist.

There are several keys to Shawn's success in the post-Ross period. The first is that he is a superb editor, both in the narrow sense of being a tidier and tightener of manuscripts and in the large sense of having the intelligence and imagination to give the magazine a broad range in the field of ideas and in criticism while maintaining it as a compendium of fiction, poetry, reportage, and satire in both prose and art. It is hard to imagine what *The New Yorker* would have been like if Ross had lived on through the 1950s and 1960s.

DECEMBER 7, 1951—Harold Ross died last night.* I was at Mother's when I heard about it. I had just phoned Eleanor to tell her what train I'd be taking, and was talking with Mother when the phone rang and Eleanor said she'd just heard—or seen—on television that Ross had died in a Boston hospital. . . . Now I will say something I feel foolish saying. I was stunned. I see now why the word is a good one for the occasion. I was not shocked. I was not saddened—as of that moment. Yes, I was stunned. Sadness came in the morning, in the office. Shock never came.

I had gone down to the office yesterday, Thursday morning, to finish up my piece on Key West. Didn't know Ross was back in the hospital. While I was talking to Shawn during the final editing of the piece, a little matter came up on which I thought Ross might have a good idea. I asked Shawn if Ross would read the piece. "No, he won't." That about ten-thirty. Ross was to be operated on at one. At one I went to lunch at the Blue Ribbon with Brendan Gill. Nothing more until evening. I had dinner with Will Chasen and Shelley Appleton. Walked around a bit, then back to the office at about nine-thirty, to pick up my stuff before going home. As I went in the building, Shawn was coming out of the elevator. He stopped me and said he thought we'd need another session on the piece because of some difficulties that had arisen. Ross was already dead. But Shawn hadn't been told. Or had he? Ross's old friend Hawley Truax, I learned from Sandy Vanderbilt this morning, had called Shawn from Boston, where he was staying while Ross was hospitalized, and had suggested that Shawn go home immediately and await a call. Truax, apparently, was afraid that

* EDITOR'S NOTE: This entry and the entries that follow are from Rovere's journal.

Shawn would faint if he told him the news in the office. So when I saw Shawn in the lobby, he was on his way home. This morning he told Sandy that earlier he had had a premonition. Could he have failed to guess Truax's news? I can hardly believe it. Bob Bendiner had called this morning to suggest lunch, so I suggested he join Harvey Breit and me. I was glad to have a lunch date. The atmosphere in the office was unbearable. Uneasy. No one knew what to do with himself. I can't describe it now. But it was a good thing to get away from. I was also glad to have a piece in this issue. E. B. White is doing an obituary for it. No one envied him the job.

And of course I am glad to have worked for Ross for seven years. I do not for a moment doubt that he was the greatest editor of our time, perhaps the most creative editor who has ever worked in this country. I was not close to him, but I knew him as well, I suppose, as any of my generation of writers did. Mostly, I would meet him just by accident around the office. Now and then when I was in the place he would stop by for a talk. I remember that the first time I met him I was on the point of quitting the magazine. I owed it a lot of money. I had just finished the Edward J. Flynn Profile, after many horrible writing sessions, and I didn't like it at all. I told Shawn I thought I'd be happier and more productive if I went somewhere else. He said we'd have lunch one day and talk it over. The day came, we went to the Algonquin, and there in the lobby, lurking in a shadow, was Ross. He joined us, obviously by prearrangement. We did not talk about my going or staying during the whole meal. (Meal was hardly the word: Shawn had a soft-boiled egg, as I recall it, and Ross a bowl of corn flakes.) But when it was over, it was understood—at least by me—that I was staying. As an extension of the treatment, I spent the afternoon with Ross, who took the Flynn piece over from Shawn. I am ever so glad it worked out that way. I kept on owing the magazine money until either late last year or early this year, I forget which. At any rate, it took almost six years.

In his heavy-handed book on Ross [*Ross and "The New Yorker"* (Garden City: Doubleday, 1951)], Dale Kramer says that Ross had me do the Letter from Washington because I was the only one able to write about Washington as if it were a foreign city. That is nonsense. Principally it was because Ross felt that I could write a political piece that dealt with issues without giving the reader a feeling that I was committed one way or the other. He wanted someone who wouldn't be selling a bill of goods. He thought I was objective. He also thought that I could extract a little fun from politics. However, when I went to work on [Senator Joseph] McCarthy last year, he was very much pleased and said so.

I must go through my disorderly papers and see if I kept any of my notes from Ross about pieces. Some of them were very nice, and I should like to have them. . . .†

DECEMBER 10 (SUNDAY)—It occurred to me that Ross's contribution is in some ways on the order of Ezra Pound's. If I understand Pound's contribution properly, it was nothing more

† EDITOR'S NOTE: Rovere did keep Ross's notes about his Profile of Frank Hogan, "The Prosecution Factory"; the following are excerpts from them:

1. It's not "of course" here so far as I am concerned, and the "but" in this sentence is nonseq. Wouldn't a simple statement be better? No supposition reader remembers clearly. People don't remember such dates. Also, should get in here the length of the D.A.'s term. Vital to story. Several references to terms, but story doesn't tell what a term is. Did Dewey serve one four-year term, or what? What is length of term?

6. Don't know quite what "single doorway" means here. Get no picture from it.

45. Can an arrest be a person?

65. This is brutally long para.

68. By God, I've never seen a telephone in a courtroom in my life.

82. What's illicit about liquor these days? Thoroughly respectable, isn't it?

or less than a reinvigoration and purification of the individual word. It was a contribution not so much to poetry as to language. Much can be said about Ross's contribution to journalism, to general criticism, but I think the noblest contribution *The New Yorker* has made—and the one that springs primarily from Ross—is to human speech, to words in our time, to communication between man and man. Ross functioned in a day when the printed word had lost much of its dignity and worth. There were, for one thing, so many printed words. Writers turning out words by the thousand every day, editors editing words by the tens of thousands every day, readers reading in great globs—all lost their sense of the meaning and value of the single word. Even someone I love and respect, Arthur [Schlesinger], suffers from the loss of the sense of the single word. (Not much, but noticeably, and it should not be so.) Now, Ross had the word-sense. And he had the energy to put out a weekly magazine built not of articles and stories, not even of sections and paragraphs, but of single, holy words. He either attracted the writers who had that sense or he imbued with it those who didn't have it at the start. I think he won much of the battle— as much as anyone ever does. He got it over to writers, he got it over to many readers, he showed that the thing was altogether wonderful.

III

The Letter from Washington was Shawn's idea—not Ross's and not mine. In 1948 I had persuaded Shawn to let me cover the presidential candidates, Dewey and Truman, and when I left the campaign trains I assumed that I would go back to writing on nonpolitical subjects. After my Profile on Howe & Hummel,‡ Ross had me typecast as a specialist on crime. He wanted me to do a

‡ EDITOR'S NOTE: Howe & Hummel was an unwholesome law firm that did business in New York from 1870 to 1905.

history of Murder, Inc., the name the press had given to some homicidal industrial racketeers working out of Brooklyn and preying on the garment district in Manhattan and on truckers throughout the city; his friend, Mayor William O'Dwyer had, as district attorney of Kings County, successfully prosecuted several of the alleged leaders,[1] and Ross thought that the mayor would give information that no one else had. (I soon found that O'Dwyer was an almost matchless source of misinformation.)[2] Ross also wanted me to salvage James Thurber's biography of Houdini. And I was editing, for Roger Straus, an anthology of the literature of New York City. Though all these projects eventually foundered, they were the sort of thing I wanted to do, and not the least of my regrets about taking the Washington job was that it pretty much put an end to this kind of work. I have now not written a *New Yorker* Profile for more than thirty years, and, except for some book reviews, have written no more than a dozen or so pieces that could be described as nonpolitical.

It never occurred to me, in 1948 or earlier, that *The New Yorker* would even want a Washington correspondent. I did not know then

[1] I say "alleged" because I began to doubt that there was any such thing as Murder, Inc. The newspapers had led the public to believe that it was an organization of guns for hire, that anybody who wanted someone murdered need only pay a fee—which varied according to the resources of the customer, the importance of the victim, and the difficulty of the job—and have the work done expeditiously. As far as I could learn, the only known victims of the mob were its own unruly members or outsiders who seemed a threat to the syndicate.

[2] I never understood the friendship between Ross and O'Dwyer, who—at least when sober—was a boring man. He had a roguish look and a charming Irish accent, but most of what he said was dull and platitudinous when it was not evasive. Yet, unaccountably, O'Dwyer seemed to be the guest of honor at the magazine's twenty-fifth-anniversary party, at the Ritz, which I remember as being one of the gayest affairs of its sort that I ever attended. I suspect that it was O'Dwyer who sought out Ross, and that Ross was flattered. Whatever the truth, the friendship yielded one good Ross story, perhaps apocryphal. Ross one day got a parking ticket in the city. Having learned that politicians often put in the fix for their friends, he called the mayor and asked if his office could take care of the matter. Of course, O'Dwyer said. A week or so later, curious about how such things work, Ross called O'Dwyer and asked what he had done. "Nothing to it," the mayor said. "I just paid the fine." If the story is true, Ross, I am sure, was disappointed.

that several Washington regulars—among them Marquis Childs and
Dick Strout—had submitted pieces they thought might be pilots for
a Washington column, and that Ross had turned them down—not
because he found the writing unsuitable but because he found
Washington uninteresting. When he agreed to Shawn's suggestion
that I be given a try, he did so, he later told me, because he felt that
Washington was becoming an "international city," like Paris and
London. I was not sure what he meant by this, or whether *he* knew
what he meant; Washington was no more "international" in 1948
than it had been five or six years earlier. (In fact, it seemed a good
deal less so, with the war over, the Roosevelts gone, and Churchill
no longer turning up as a White House guest.) Up to then, Ross
seemed to be saying, it had been no more worthy of his magazine's
attention than Philadelphia, where, as he saw it, nothing of interest
had happened since the signing of the Declaration of Independence. (He didn't want to clutter up the pages with news from any
American city except New York, but he particularly didn't want to
hear anything about Philadelphia. Brendan Gill's theory is that this
odd animus can be explained by the fact that *The Saturday Evening
Post,* which was Ross's idea of what a good magazine should be, was
published there. Gill once wrote an article about a black banker in
Philadelphia, and it was not printed until Ross was on a fishing trip
in Colorado.) And Ross felt that if we did add Washington to the
other capitals, we shouldn't write about it more than once a month
(the Paris and London columns appeared every two weeks), and not
at all in the summer. "Not much goes on there then," he said.
"Everyone I know gets out when the weather turns hot—unless
there's a war or something." He knew perhaps a half-dozen people
in Washington—James Forrestal (the first Secretary of Defense) and
a few other New York lawyers and bankers, most of whom he had
met through John O'Hara, who cultivated people of their sort.

Ross was, in fact, skeptical about the whole enterprise. "So far, so
good," he would say after each of the early Letters. "I hope there's
enough there to keep you going." I was relieved to hear him talking

this way, for I was anything but eager to spend all, or even much, of my time in Washington. We were then living on Quaker Lane, in Hyde Park, and it was working out very nicely for Eleanor and me and the children, all three of whom were then under five; I might well have declined the assignment if I had been asked to pack up and move to Washington. (But I would probably have agreed, for having a department of one's own meant security of a kind, and in our seven years of marriage, we had not known much of it.) We had moved to the country on the assumption that I could do all my writing and much of my research at home. I had quarried *Howe & Hummel,* which paid for the place on Quaker Lane, in a library two hundred miles from New York, and had written it in a farmhouse in West Brookfield, Massachusetts.[3] The Profiles of John Gunther and Henry Sell were written on Quaker Lane. I had been a few weeks on the road with Truman and Dewey, but nothing I then had in mind would have required more than an occasional one-day trip to the

---

[3] Someone—I can't remember who—told me about the library of the American Antiquarian Society in Worcester, about twenty miles east of West Brookfield. I went there one day and met the director, an elderly and urbane gentleman named Clarence Saunders Brigham, who lighted up when I told him I was writing an article about a disreputable New York law firm that had gone out of business some forty years ago. He was a New Yorker, and he had known about the partners as a young man, especially about Hummel's work on breach-of-promise and alienation-of-affection suits. He knew so much about them, in fact, that I suspected that he might once have been a victim of the firm. But to me the great discovery was that library. It contained the largest collection of American newspapers in the country—and easily the best preserved. The Antiquarian Society was an institution primarily supported and patronized by people concerned with genealogy. If one wished to establish one's qualifications for membership in the Sons or Daughters of the American Revolution, the place to make the effort was at Worcester, in the Antiquarian Society. But such aspirations were a bore to Brigham and his colleagues, and they were eager to assist in a project like mine. Suddenly I had a large and well-trained staff at my disposal—the genealogy business slackened off a bit in the summer—and before I knew it, the article I had planned became two, then three, then four. I put aside the writing for the time being and drove each day to Worcester to follow new leads, of which there were many. Implausible as it seemed, a library used largely by social climbers had a complete file of *Woodhull and Claflin's Weekly,* a publication edited by the only woman to run for the presidency and an early member of Karl Marx's First International. The sisters—Victoria Woodhull and Tennessee Claflin—had been Howe & Hummel clients, and the only other file of their revolutionary paper was in Moscow.

city. (I was researching much of Murder, Inc., in the newspaper files in the library at Vassar.) The thought of moving again—to Washington or anywhere else, but particularly to Washington—would have been appalling. I had been to Washington perhaps eight or ten times for *The Nation* and *Harper's*, but I knew the place only as a power center; it interested me the way Hollywood would interest someone writing about movies, or the way Rochester, Minnesota, might interest a physician or a hypochondriac. I knew almost no one there—only some of the reporters I had met while following the candidates. Moreover, although I was getting to like the idea of being away from New York, I would not have wanted to be that far away. From Hyde Park it was easy to go to the city—less than two hours by car or train—and return in the evening. Washington was almost three times as far, and in 1948 there were no shuttle flights. When I went there, I would, as a rule, take an evening train from Poughkeepsie, get on a sleeper in Penn Station, wake up at dawn in Union Station.

In the beginning, Ross and I—and perhaps Shawn, who has not to this day, as far as I know, ever seen Washington—thought I might write about the city the way Janet Flanner and Mollie Panter-Downes wrote about Paris and London—write about it, that is, as if it were a foreign metropolis. I was quickly disabused. From Paris and London they could bring news to American readers. They could write not only about urban life in another country but, since they were really national correspondents, about anything happening in France and England. Politics was only part of what they were reporting. They could write about artists and writers and musicians, about architecture, about films and theater, about sports, about crime, about dress, about restaurants, about anything that interested them and might interest readers of the magazine here. There were few ways in which I could model my work on theirs. Except that Washington is a one-industry town, and in many ways a Southern one (then, at any rate; now it is much more part of the Northeast), there was little about life there to distinguish it from any of a dozen or

more other American cities. Moreover, it worked on the same calen-
dar as the rest of the country. What became fashionable there si-
multaneously became fashionable in New York, Chicago, Los Angeles, and (perhaps a few days later) Poultney, Vermont. Washington,
in short, was not a place where new ideas were generated or new
trends of thought set in motion; in this respect, there was more to
be said for Philadelphia. In Paris and London, our correspondents
were part of a small band of Americans—fifty or so—reporting on
developments that struck them or their editors as worth looking
into. The Washington press corps was huge, with several reporters
for every politician who might conceivably do or say something
worth reporting. I found this most depressing. For at least a few
months, I thought of myself as being in direct competition with
Time and *Newsweek,* and to some extent with the *Times,* the *Herald
Tribune,* the *Post,* and a number of syndicated columnists. The
weeklies had large bureaus of full-time correspondents; they had
their own people in the White House almost on a round-the-clock
basis. Several reporters were assigned to the House and Senate and
to the more active committees. There were about two dozen people
who did nothing but cover the State Department. I felt that it was
important for me not to come close to duplicating anything the
weeklies were doing. I went to Harry Truman's press conferences
whenever I could, but what was the sense of writing about them
when the *Times* would print the entire transcript, as well as several
columns of analysis, the next morning? Though there had been as
much competition, man for man, on the campaign trains, the problem then was simpler. That was politics in motion—a peculiar and
almost closed society highballing over plains, prairies, and mountains. It was, as I wrote, like life in a carnival or a medicine show.
(For a time, we seemed to be playing the same towns as Brink's
World of Mirth, a circus that toured the Midwest; the audience was
different not just every few days but several times a day.) Washington was static, the scenes and the backdrops always the same. The
best thing I could do, I reasoned, was to poke around for stories that

no one else seemed to be doing, to seek out approaches that no one else seemed to be taking, or to write in anticipation of events to come. In the first Letter from Washington the magazine ever published, in its issue of December 25, 1948, I wrote about the plans that had been made, months earlier, for the inauguration of the President in January. There were some nice ironies in this. The Congress had voted an unprecedented sum of money for the ceremony and for the revels that were to follow. More money than ever before had been spent for the pile of lumber on which Harry Truman was to be sworn in on Capitol Hill and for the reviewing stand on Pennsylvania Avenue. But the Congress that had planned these lavish displays was Republican—the very one that Truman had campaigned against—and the inauguration they were to celebrate was to be that of the first Republican in twenty years; had it been clear that the President would be a Democrat, Congress might have let him be sworn in on a pair of soapboxes and watch the parade from a White House window. I rang every change I could on this and other ironies. Expecting Dewey to be their new boss, bureaucrats who had served under Roosevelt and Truman were doing whatever they could to accommodate themselves to the prospective new order. I learned of one agency head who had been cleaning out his files of everything except evidence that he had been on excellent terms with Republicans. "Truman's reelection," I wrote, "may be a unique instance of the maintenance of the status quo's being the most upsetting thing that could have happened."

I covered—more extensively, I think, than anyone else—the treason trial of Mildred Gillars, a shrill and leathery blonde who, as Axis Sally, ran a disc-jockey and talk show on Berlin radio during the war with the aim of undermining the morale of English-speaking troops. The trial featured some odd witnesses for the prosecution—ex-Nazis seeking to ingratiate themselves with their conquerors and explain away their past as the result of misunderstandings or mistaken identities. One was a man named Werner von Plack, who, to escape conscription into the German Army, wormed his way into a high position in the Foreign Ministry by leading his superiors to believe that he had very good connections in an important American city, Hollywood, where he had been a wine merchant for a few years—a very obscure one according to defense witnesses. I spent a day following some vacationing high-school students on a guided tour of the headquarters of the FBI, gawking at the bullet holes in the clothing of dead criminals; at the shooting range on which the agents practice bringing such people low; at the displays of handcuffs and other restraining devices. I investigated what the Muslim community was doing (not very much, but I made a story of it). I got hold of a study of racial segregation in Washington that no one else seemed much interested in—separate cemeteries for dogs and other pets owned by whites and nonwhites—and summarized its findings, among them the fact that the leading champion of separate and unequal treatment was Ulysses S. Grant III, head of the District Commission.[4] I got a certain amount of satisfaction out of some of those early pieces, and as I read the best of them now, they seem gayer, livelier, less solemn than what I was writing several years later. It was marginal stuff and often thin, but I worked hard at making something of it, and Ross encouraged me to go on. Still, I began to feel that I was somehow cheating myself and the magazine. Washington wasn't Paris or London, but it was surely more than some adolescents being shown through the FBI's Grand Guignol, more than the trial of a minor war criminal, more than the paradox of Republicans financing some high living for the Democrats. And in what sense was I competing with anyone by steering clear of the main events and looking in on the sideshows? This couldn't have

[4] Ross was less than enchanted with this last piece, and said as much in a note to Shawn. I have no copy of the note, but I remember it almost word for word. Most of it was devoted to explaining that racial problems were far more complicated than I seemed to understand, and that this he knew from his experiences as a reporter in San Francisco, New Orleans, and Panama. And so on. He concluded this way: "I don't see why this magazine has to draw every Abraham Lincoln in town. I guess we've got to print this, but I hereby file a protest." That last sentence showed me that the editor I worked for was no true bigot. For similarly offending Freda Kirchwey and Alvarez del Vayo, of *The Nation*, I had become unemployed.

been what Shawn had in mind when he made me a Washington correspondent—or what I had in mind when I agreed to give it a try. The big story in Washington in 1949 was foreign policy— NATO was in the making, Berlin was blockaded—and here I was writing about cops and robbers.

I took my problem to Shawn, and he solved it in a characteristi- cally simple and, to me, liberating way. I should not, he said, think of myself as being in competition with *Time* or *Newsweek* or the dailies; they were in the news business, and we were not. *The New Yorker* had no obligation to "cover" anything; we did have an obliga- tion to be thoughtful, informative, provocative on occasion, and, whenever possible, entertaining. My job in Washington was not to "report" on the White House or anything else—except in the way that a reviewer might "report" on a book. I was to be a kind of critic or reviewer of what was going on there. My job was not to chronicle the action itself but to find what meaning I could in it, and to find out what the best-informed and most reflective people *thought* about it.

As I write now, this point of view has a rather odd and ironic ring to it, for *The New Yorker,* under the pressure of events and under Shawn's editorship, has become increasingly a journal of advocacy. It has stopped short of endorsing candidates, but not very far short. No attentive reader could ever have supposed that the magazine stood on neutral ground when Nixon and Kennedy were running for President. Or that it took no position on civil rights or Vietnam. I have myself written as very much a partisan—though never, or rarely, in the Letter from Washington. And Notes and Comment is often flagrantly political—often in a way that Ross would not have tolerated—and Shawn has developed a new heading, Reflections, under which some of us have hectored the movers and shakers and told them how we think they should go about their business. The two articles that in 1968 made up my *Waist Deep in the Big Muddy* were originally published under that rubric, though I can hardly think of one less appropriate; a more suitable one might have been

Screams, for the pieces were less a series of reflections than an outburst of anger and torment, a prolonged cry of pain over Vietnam. But of that, more later.

I was pleased with the vision of myself that Shawn had given me. The office of critic was one to which I had aspired ever since my last year in college. If I had had the gifts of an Edmund Wilson or an inheritance on which to live, I might have devoted myself to it. Ever since West Brookfield, I had wanted to become a specialist in eighteenth-century English literature; I was still soaking myself in Johnson and Boswell, in Pope and Walpole and Burke.[5] This new approach to my writing from Washington would be something less than a fulfillment of my ambition—Washington was a less edifying place than the London salons and taverns in which part of me had settled, but it was a step forward. In 1955, attempting to analyze my thinking, I wrote: "I believe that it is at least theoretically possible to bring to public affairs the sympathy, hope, objectivity, and rigorous discrimination that a conscientious critic brings to literature, painting, music, architecture, or any other form." Today I would not put it quite that way, for I have grave doubts about the relevance of aesthetics of the kind I had in mind. I sense in those words a confusion of categories. When the critic confronts a book or a play or a piece of music, he is dealing with something that stands alone, that is finished and complete in itself. If it deserves a future it will have one, but whether it survives for a few years, decades, or even centu-

[5] The house in West Brookfield was a delightful one—an old, comfortable New England farmhouse, built around a central chimney with three fireplaces, one or another of which we used on chilly evenings. Also, it had a fine library, assembled, I gathered, by a scholar with a particular interest in English writing of the eighteenth century and in certain twentieth-century British novelists, among them H. G. Wells, John Galsworthy, and Arnold Bennett. Somehow, I had missed the eighteenth century in my scattershot reading, and in those July and August evenings I developed such a passion for Dr. Johnson, Boswell, Horace Walpole, and their contemporaries that I decided that if I were ever free of the need to spend all my time earning a living, I would devote myself to becoming an authority on the period. I have never been free of that need, but the passion has not entirely subsided, and I still read Dr. Johnson with great pleasure. He is more alive in my imagination than any other British writer, which may speak poorly for my imagination but not, I think, for my ability to recognize a powerful, civilized, and unfailingly entertaining mind.

ries, it will—though it may be seen in different lights and weighed by different measures—be unchanged, beyond revision, beyond the possibility of being compromised by whatever may follow it. Politics belongs to a different order of things, and the critical method, though it can certainly yield insights, can be misleading. I think I saw this most clearly in the years that followed John Kennedy's death. When Kennedy first sought the White House, I was unimpressed. His years in the House and Senate were, except for two or three prophetic speeches on foreign policy, undistinguished. He had written a book, *Profiles in Courage,* which seemed to me no better than second-rate. On the other hand, I greatly admired him for his campaign in 1960—a splendid display of verve and of cool, sharp intelligence. He brought the same qualities to the White House, and when he died I found myself writing about his "style," his "perception," his "passion for excellence." These were critical value judgments of mine, and I suppose they are as valid now as they seemed to me then. But a few years later I began asking myself what Kennedy's legacy really was. What was there to him besides style and grace? And what did these have to do with Vietnam? I think it possible that if he had lived he would not have pressed on there as Johnson did, but there is also reason to suppose that he would have done exactly that. He had, after all, surrounded himself with hawks, and there was the indisputable fact that he had upped Eisenhower's modest ante by 400 percent. How does one weigh wit and elegance of phrase against such folly? Or the absence of style in an Eisenhower or a Carter against their caution?

What pleased me at the time was that Shawn had given me a modus operandi of the kind that editors generally discourage and that more enterprising journalists disparage. If I was to do my own thinking and report on the best and clearest thinking being done, it meant that I could use my colleagues as "sources." It is generally held to be a bad thing—almost a violation of professional ethics— for a correspondent to do what is known in the trade as "thumbsucking," or picking the brains of other correspondents. An article that comes out of the members' bar of the National Press Club is generally held to be less worthy of publication than one that is produced by a reporter with muscular legs tracking down miscreants and occasional messiahs in government departments and agencies. Yet here I was with a license—almost an order—to suck my own thumb and pick the best brains I could find. And on any given day in the Press Club bar, more good minds could be found than on the floor of the United States Senate during a close and important vote.

IV

In the thirty years in which I wrote the Washington column, the intellectual caliber of the press corps has, I think, greatly improved. In the earliest days, I thought it clearly inferior to what I had encountered in New York, where the city hall reporters were closer students of municipal problems than the members of the city council. In 1948, and for several years thereafter, life in the White House press room was about like life in the press room at police headquarters on Spring Street—poker and pinochle games in continuous progress, desk drawers serving as liquor cabinets, *Daily Racing Forms* being gravely studied, bored and generally disheveled men sitting around waiting for someone to tell them that something was about to happen. In subsequent years—beginning no later than the first days of the Kennedy administration—the place took on something like the atmosphere of a seminar in one of the better graduate schools. There were then a good many first-rate minds in Washington, the most respected being Walter Lippmann, whom I was soon to meet and find myself writing about.* He was, of course, the

* EDITOR'S NOTE: In 1950, Rovere was commissioned by *Flair* to write an article on Lippmann. The article appeared in the terminal issue of that magazine. Rovere was deeply distressed by the editing and wrote an open letter on the subject addressed to his colleagues:

November 17, 1950

   I wish to disown responsibility for an article on Walter Lippmann soon to be published under my signature in *Flair*. Although it is a fact that I wrote what quintessential political critic, and he was not to be seen in the Press Club. (Like Proust, he wrote in a cork-lined study in his home, the former deanery of the National Cathedral, on Woodley Road.) But there were other reporters who tended to be somewhat frustrated because they were under orders *not* to do exactly what Shawn had urged me to do—to exercise their critical faculties and form and express judgments of their own. The wisest of the lot, in my opinion, was Dick Strout, of the *Christian Science Monitor,* and he was one of the most experienced. He had been in Washington since Warren Harding's day (and is, at over eighty, still there, writing in *The New Republic'*s T.R.B. column, with all the verve and energy of a man in his twenties). And there was Tom Stokes, of Scripps-Howard, the gentle, poetic, tough-minded Georgian I had met when I covered the Ku Klux Klan trial in South Carolina eight years earlier. And Alfred Friendly, of the Washington *Post;* Marquis Childs, of the St. Louis *Post-Dispatch;* Paul Ward, of the Baltimore *Sun;* Scotty Reston, of the *Times;* Bob Donovan, of the *Herald Tribune;* and the waspish Joe Alsop, the man it took so long a time to get to like. The British, whose journalists then seemed better educated and more literate than ours, had some of their finest correspondents in Washington. Alistair Cooke, like me a transient from New York, was often there for the Manchester *Guardian. The Economist* and *The Observer* had a succession of brilliant men (there were then few women in any of the bureaus) in Washington. On the Truman train in the summer of 1948 I had spent a lot of time with Leonard Miall, a correspondent for the British Broadcasting Corporation and later one of its high executives, and Rene McColl, of the

will appear as mine in this peculiar publication, I feel quite justified in disclaiming responsibility, on the ground that no writer is fairly represented by a piece of work from which, roughly speaking, every third word is missing. I do not wish to suggest that my original manuscript was either a work of art or a piece of flawless logic; I do, however, feel that I must ask such friends and associates of mine as may chance on this article in barber shops or beauty parlors that they refrain from judging me on the basis of it. Left to myself, I can produce as wild a nonsequitur as the next man, and I don't see why my final score should include any that I didn't turn out on my own account.

Richard H. Rovere

Beaverbrook empire, one of the funniest men I have ever known and a fine writer.[6]

I soon developed a regular and quite agreeable routine for getting out my Washington pieces. Once every three or four weeks, I would leave Hyde Park—generally on a Sunday evening—and arrive, by sleeper, in Washington Monday morning. (This mode of travel, so pleasant and comfortable for me then, is today all but obsolete, and most disagreeable when it does exist.) I would check in at the Willard Hotel, a splendid old pile that fronted on Pennsylvania Avenue and magisterially stretched the long, sloping block of Fourteenth Street between the avenue and F Street. The Willard closed down in 1968, after the riots following the murder of Martin Luther King, Jr. (not so much, I think, because of the riots as because it was suffering the fate of many inner-city hotels—competition from motels on the outskirts and from the classier, glassier chain hotels in other parts of town), but it still stands with the kind of massive grace of the Plaza in New York, which is the work of the same architect. It was directly across Fourteenth Street from the National Press Building, which housed the Washington offices of most of the large news agencies and, on the top two floors, the National Press Club. Given my assignment, I need hardly have ventured beyond these two buildings. The club had, in addition to the usual facilities, a small press room with battered desks and chairs and ancient typewriters, and I often shared it with a few other transients and some regulars who had no offices of their own. There was a hungry-looking

[6] McColl's interest in politics had less to do with ideas than with the possibilities of journalistic mischief making. He once made life miserable for a Hyde Park neighbor of ours, the Reverend Gordon Kidd, pastor of St. James Episcopal Church, the Roosevelt family parish. The daughter of Hetty Green, the Witch of Wall Street, had died and willed a very large fortune to his church. Asked by a New York newspaperman how he planned to spend the money, Kidd said, "I don't know what to do with it—I really don't," meaning, of course, that he had as yet come to no decision. Rene seized on this and wrote a story—bannered throughout the United Kingdom—on how one church in a small American town was so rotten rich that it couldn't think of a way to get rid of millions. Dr. Kidd was besieged with hundreds of letters from impoverished British rectors telling him that they could think of many good uses for the money and please send some of it over right away.

correspondent for some vegetarian journal in California who had his meals at his desk—quantities of celery, raw carrots, and onions, and some comestibles foreign to my experience—and one from a sectarian publication who seemed to get his information, or it may have been his inspiration, from a dog-eared Bible, in which he looked up something every few minutes. I spent many evenings writing in that room, which commanded a matchless view of the Washington Monument, the Lincoln Memorial, and the well-tended grass and gardens reaching down to the Potomac. As a rule, I would have breakfast in the club with friends, who were fortifying themselves with coffee—and sometimes more spiritous liquids—before going to their offices on lower floors. If I had no specific plans, as was often the case, I would consult the Washington *Post,* which each morning listed the day's goings-on in the city. I often checked congressional committees that were holding open hearings, and if I found one, as I frequently did, I would go up to Capitol Hill and spend the morning, and sometimes the better part of a day, there. If I was bored by one hearing, I would leave and walk around in search of another. I seldom found one that I wanted to write about, but I think I learned a good deal. Nothing that Washington has to offer comes closer to theater than congressional hearings. Floor debates tend to be set pieces—displays of precooked and inferior rhetoric, simulated conflicts. But in the hearings there is often a real clash of interests and philosophies, and those that have not been set up to draw large crowds of spectators often offer a chance to study the style and character—unbuttoned, as it were—of the participants. And at times the practice yielded unexpected dividends. I think I was one of the first writers in Washington to discover what in time became known as McCarthyism. One pleasant day in May of 1949, I found myself at a noisy hearing of charges of alleged American mistreatment of a number of German SS men—members of an outfit known as the Blowtorch Battalion—who had some years earlier been accused of massacring Belgian civilians and American troops at a crossroads village named Malmédy. The noise came mostly from an obscure young senator from Wisconsin, Joseph McCarthy, who was disrupting the proceedings and accusing the investigators of whitewashing some Americans who, he said, had conducted their own atrocities. The investigation was a sham, a fraud, and an outrage, he shouted, and he stormed out of the hearing room, saying that he was going to take the case to the public. Curious as to what he was making such a fuss about, I walked out behind him and asked what kind of case he thought he had to take to the people. He invited me to his office and I spent a dizzying hour or two watching him shuffle papers and rattle off names and numbers that told me nothing except that I was in the presence of a con artist of considerable talent. A few months later, that talent was everywhere on display, and remained so for a run of four years.

Being a one-man, part-time bureau, I had to leave much of Washington unexplored. Agricultural policy, for example, was very important in those days—the farm bloc kept Truman in Washington and Dewey in Albany—but I had not mastered its intricacies, and I did not think that my urban and suburban readers wanted to hear much from me about price supports for corn and wheat, soy beans and dairy products. I felt that I understood a bit about economic theory, but I was, and still am, weak on financial matters, and though the windows of the Willard gave on the Treasury and the Department of Commerce, I cannot recall visiting either place. Until the Cold War turned hot and I began writing about Korea—in the magazine and, with Arthur Schlesinger, Jr., in a book, *The General and the President,* about Douglas MacArthur and President Truman—I did not report on the military controversies of the time. (In some ways, I would now like to retract much of what I did write then.) Fond as I was of lawyers and judges, and fascinated as I was by the questions that preoccupied them, I did not—after looking in on the prosecution of Axis Sally—pay much attention to the judicial branch. I was summoned to an occasional tea by Felix Frankfurter, but our talk—I should say, *his* talk, for the great jurist's guests were his audience—was mostly gossip, sometimes trivial, sometimes rather nasty. Nor, except for its committees, did I do much about the House of Representatives, for it is too large and disorderly, and is, because of its rules, seldom the scene of interesting debate. (Neither, most of the time, is the Senate, but it is at least a place where ideas can be dealt with seriously and at length, and perhaps once a year it comes close to deserving its claim of being the world's greatest deliberative body. Or perhaps I should say that it does so once every two or three years, for I cannot think of more than ten interesting debates in three decades, and I cannot, at the moment, recall any in the last several years.) My Washington, especially in those first years of the Letter, was largely politics, economics (in the broadest sense), and foreign policy—increasingly foreign policy. It was the White House, the Senate, the State Department, and the embassies. And the National Press Club. With my mission, I had little need to know anyone simply for the sake of knowing him or to cultivate anyone simply because of power or prestige. I could best spend my time seeking out those whose minds and characters seemed worth examining, and these were often people who held no office at all—staff officials, advisers, and the like. In the Truman years, I saw much of two lawyers, former New Dealers then in private practice. One was Benjamin Cohen, half of the celebrated team of Corcoran & Cohen, which drafted much of the landmark legislation in Roosevelt's first term. His was, I think, one of the most luminous and clarifying intelligences then in Washington, and, despite his partisan commitments, he was a man who could rise to Matthew Arnold's command to "see the object as in itself it really is." It was exciting to me to observe his mind at work as he sat in his bachelor apartment near Dupont Circle and, in his reedy, quavering voice—his vocal cords, unlike his mind, were those of an old man—unraveled the tangled strands of high policy. The other lawyer, a very different sort, was Paul Porter—a huge, gregarious, flamboyant Kentuckian, then a partner in the prospering firm of Arnold, Fortas & Porter, which seemed to represent everything from organized baseball to indigent plaintiffs with grievances against the government. He had been one of Roosevelt's political strategists toward the end of the war and an adviser to Truman after it. If Cohen was the most lucid analyst of ideas, Porter, who defended many of McCarthy's early victims, was the shrewdest observer of people. He was also a prodigious drinker and eater, and a few years ago died a trencherman's death while trying to ingest too large a piece of food.

In 1948 the only senator I knew was Robert Taft, who seemed to me the most intelligent rightist in Washington. But by then he had become so embittered that one could hardly talk with him. He had reached a point at which he was less interested in leading the opposition to Truman than in making life miserable for the Dewey men (soon to be Eisenhower men), and before long this sober and seemingly dispassionate man was so embattled, so consumed by rage that he accepted McCarthy as an ally. A senator with as good a mind as Taft's was Thomas Hennings, of Missouri, who was a fine constitutional lawyer and hastened McCarthy along the road to self-destruction. Philip Potter, of the Baltimore *Sun,* once conducted a poll of the Washington correspondents he most respected (not a large group but a select one—ten or twelve) and asked which senator they most respected. The vote for Hennings was unanimous, or close to it. He was, when I knew him, clearly free of ambition. He may once have wanted to run for President or sit on the Supreme Court or gain a more influential place in the Democratic hierarchy, but in the late forties and early fifties he was content to do little more than put his mind to the task of exposing McCarthy's financial shenanigans and organizing the opposition to what was known as the Bricker amendment, a scheme for hobbling the President in the conduct of foreign policy. (Under Truman and Eisenhower, the White House appraisal of the national interest seemed more reliable than the Senate's; under Johnson and Nixon, the opposite view seemed true.) Hennings's modest ambitions were forced upon him by his alcoholism. He was given to binges that took him away from his office for days, sometimes weeks, at a time. When he was sober, though, he was very sober indeed—a man of precision of language and great circumspection. He was pleased to confide in me—in part, I think—because I was writing for *The New Yorker*. He was one of the few people around who read the magazine regularly—John Kennedy, whom I then did not know, may have been another. Hennings felt a special attachment to it because he had been at Cornell with E. B. White and Lobrano, and through them had met Ross, Thurber, and others. Even as the magazine became more and more national, more and more political, there was little interest in it in Washington. To be noticed in a sentence or two in the *Times* could be very gratifying to a politician from Wyoming; to be mentioned in passing by Arthur Krock was worth two or three columns in a wire-service story. But to be written about at length, favorably or otherwise, in *The New Yorker* was far less rewarding than an inch or two in *Time* or *Newsweek*. It was not until Kennedy was in office that I ever heard from the White House about anything I had written, and Carter was the only subsequent tenant who had an aide call me up to set me straight about anything. (The caller was the press secretary, Jody Powell, and he wanted to let me know that no ghostwriter had contributed to a particular speech; the call must have been on Powell's own initiative, for I doubt if Carter knew or cared what I had written.) On the whole, I was not displeased by this show of unconcern. I was writing *about* Washington, not *for* Washington, and was getting a good response from readers elsewhere, and also from my fellow journalists, most of whom did read the magazine. There was, however, one disadvantage to that indifference. Because *The New Yorker* was not a news magazine and because it did not have a Washington office, accreditation to the White House, to the State Department, and to the press galleries on the Hill could be obtained only with difficulty. Every time I went to a Truman press conference, I had to go through the same procedures as any out-of-towner whose claim might be that he was a second cousin of the President's brother-in-law, and my visitor's pass specified that I was not eligible to ask any questions. It was not until 1961 that I managed to get, from Pierre Salinger, a regular White House pass. When Nixon came in, it was rescinded. Small inconveniences. In any case, the kind of questions I might have had for Presidents would not have been answered in a press conference.

DECEMBER 25, 1948—This year has set me on a path I'll never leave.† Now I'm so plainly typed as a political writer that I'll make this my major work. I like this better than writing about memory experts, or even old-time lawyers, but it isn't quite my idea of the best fun in the world. I'd sooner write about literature, and I'd still sooner write about life. I may do a little of each, but politics is my specialty, and I won't try to evade it. It is my business now, and that is that. Without knowing why, I became a Communist in 1936. Communism was politics, though to me it was poetry. As a Communist, I wrote about Communist politics. Writing, I learned—a little. Learning, I gave up Communism. To see what went wrong, I learned—a little more. Gradually I got to know a few things. Nobody will believe me when I say that I'm really not especially interested in politics, but it's true. My interest in politics is probably equivalent to Lippmann's interest in literary criticism. My interest in criticism is probably equivalent to his in politics. But both of us are political writers.

† EDITOR'S NOTE: This is an entry from Rovere's journal.

4

Presidents and Politicians

I

I saw Franklin Roosevelt only twice, and then at a distance. In 1936, when I was a senior at Bard and campaigning for Earl Browder, I saw Roosevelt as he ended his campaign in traditional fashion, speaking to a Dutchess County crowd from the balcony of the Nelson House, in Poughkeepsie; the other time was in 1944, when George Leighton and I went out to Brooklyn to see a broken man ride hatless through a freezing autumn rain. As a child of the 1930s, I will die with my Roosevelt memories—not particularly fond but extraordinarily vivid—intact.

I traveled across the country with Roosevelt's successor in 1948 and found him engaging—more so, I think, than I would have found Roosevelt, and far more so, of course, than Thomas Dewey. I think I attended Harry Truman's press conferences more regularly than those of any of his successors. (When Eisenhower came in, the conferences were being televised, and I could observe media events —get their message—on the medium.) In 1948, the year I began the Letter from Washington, I left *The New Yorker* for a few months to do a series for *Harper's* on that year's leading presidential candidates—the beleaguered Truman, the Republican Senators Robert Taft and Arthur Vandenberg, and Dwight Eisenhower, whose party affiliation, if any, was unknown, though both Democrats and Republicans were busy courting him. When I went off for the stint at *Harper's*, I proposed to Shawn that after my return, in the summer, I might ride the presidential campaign trains and report on life aboard. The magazine had never done anything of the sort before, and, although I had written quite a bit about national politics, neither had I. Shawn—and, I suppose, Ross—thought it a promising idea, and early one September morning I boarded the Truman train at Union Station, in Washington, and stayed with it as it zigzagged across the continent to Los Angeles, where I picked up the Dewey train. This turned out to be the last cross-country railroad tour of presidential candidates. It seemed to me then a supreme adventure; I enjoyed it as much as any reporting experience I had ever had—and almost as much as my trip by Jeep, Land Rover, and bush plane about East Africa eighteen years later. The railroads then were still proud and competitive; they showed off the best of their equipment and put aboard the campaign trains the best of their service personnel. From a politician's point of view, I think, little was lost when campaigners took to television and traveled mostly on planes, but from a writer's point of view much was lost. On the Truman train there were about fifty reporters; on the Dewey train perhaps eighty (but not a single dictionary). (In later years, the hundreds of reporters who were flown about the country saw no more of the campaign than could be glimpsed from the highways between the airports and the downtown hotels.) Between stops, on the long hauls over the plains, the prairies, and the mountains, we had ample time to converse with the politicians and ample time to write. I had a bedroom to myself (car 1, compartment 1), and kept the upper berth down, for sleeping and an occasional nap; with a desk for my typewriter, the compartment served as a composite sitting room and office. Hotels are more comfortable and offer better facilities for bathing and the like, but this seemed to me a civilized, and certainly a leisurely, way of getting on with the business at hand.

I started out, naturally, with more sympathy for Truman than for Dewey—in fact, with much sympathy for Truman and almost none for Dewey—and though I tried to be nonpolitical in my dispatches, it was clear that I enjoyed life aboard the President's train more than life on his rival's. The Truman campaign had no help from Madison Avenue. It was an old-fashioned and rather sloppy operation, with schedules often fouled up and plans often mislaid. Truman's set speeches were written by amateurs—mostly his fellow politicians—and did nothing to elevate the level of discourse. But, unlike Dewey's, they were commitments. Dewey, confident of victory, spoke in platitudes, the more offensive because they were framed in *Reader's Digest* prose. (His principal writer, Stanley High, was an editor of that magazine and a master of its what's-right-with-America style.) Dewey was a polished elocutionist and a trained baritone. Truman, when he spoke with a script, had difficulty following it; he called his opponents "Republican mothballs" when the text said "Republican mossbacks." There was a conviviality on the Truman train that was missing on Dewey's. There was a twenty-four-hour poker game going on in the staff car. I was told that the President would sit in now and then, and that the liquor would stop when Bess boarded the train. We even had a theme song, with a refrain provided by the President. Earlier in the year, he had gone to California to receive an honorary degree from the University of California—a trip billed as "non-political" but with several stopovers and seemingly political speeches along the way. Asked to explain the "non-political" journey, he had said, "It's what I told you —I'm going out to Berkeley to get me a degree." The dean of the Washington press corps, Tom Stokes, set this to the tune of "Oh! Susanna," and we sang, "Oh! Susanna, don't you cry for me, I'm going out to Berkeley to get me a degree./The stars are out, the moon is full, the weather it is fine/And we're gunning for Tom

Dewey on the old Milwaukee Line." There were new versions and new verses as we crossed the Mississippi, snaked through the Royal Gorge, and steamed through the fertile California valleys.

My most vivid memory of the Truman campaign is of the stops made, often in darkness, in the railroad yards of small cities and towns. We seldom stayed more than ten or twelve minutes. Anywhere between twenty-five and several hundred people would gather behind the President's car (the armored Ferdinand Magellan, from which Roosevelt had often campaigned), and the President—a trim, perky figure materializing on the back platform through a parted blue-velvet curtain—would make a short speech, working in some allusions to local industries, problems, and personalities. His listeners were respectful but not notably receptive until the end of the act. "I'm the President," Truman would say, "and I'd like you to meet the President's boss." The curtain would part again, and Bess Truman, clutching a big bouquet, would emerge. She would smile and wave, and Truman would say, "And now I'd like you to meet the boss's boss." Again the blue curtain and the bouquet—and Margaret Truman. More smiles and more waves, and some whistles and puffs from the locomotive, and the Three Traveling Trumans would be off for the next town and the next cameo appearance. In my mind's eye, that blue-velvet curtain is the backdrop against which I see them. On the Dewey train, there was nothing of the sort—whistle stops, of course, and speeches featuring Democratic incompetence, softness on communism, and the like, but everything routine and businesslike. His managers had thoughtfully wired the sleepers and diners as well as the press car; we could hear the proceedings without scrambling off and on the train. Dewey's train, like those in Mussolini's Italy, ran on schedule. (Once when it got a second or two ahead and jolted the candidate on the back platform, he lost his cool and said, "That engineer must be an idiot," thereby losing a few more labor votes.) But its efficiency was boring. I got off the Dewey Special in Missoula, Montana, at 5 A.M. one morning and boarded the Olympian Hiawatha Milwaukee line, on my way home.

II

How distant a figure Truman now seems! Except for that jaunty, scrappy figure speaking from the Ferdinand Magellan in Sandusky, Ohio, in 1948, he is blurred in memory. It is hard to bring him into focus. The Truman years in Washington, while by no means a blank, are for me a series of much fuzziness and many shadows. Naturally, one had to admire anyone who could follow Roosevelt's hard act and do it with so much assurance and dignity—especially since dignity was not Truman's long suit. (Of Eisenhower in the White House he said, "That feller don't know as much about politics as a pig knows about Sunday.") And there was the way he stood his ground when McCarthy started snarling and clawing at him. His sponsorship of the Marshall Plan—and of General Marshall himself—was surely statesmanlike. Those were years of moral grandeur and years of moral squalor. Indeed, there was, as Eisenhower said, and as Adlai Stevenson later agreed, a "mess in Washington"—a very messy mess, not on a scale as grand or as dangerous as the one Nixon was to make, but a real mess nevertheless. The thievery was petty—a fur coat here, a freezer there, influence peddled for 5 percent of the take. But the people involved were a sorry lot and had no business being near the White House. It used to be said of Mayor Ed Crump, the larcenous boss of Memphis, that he was more than worth every dollar he stole—that he ran the city more efficiently than an honest but less gifted administrator might have done. (I don't know if Crump was that good or not, but such a case could be made for several other politicians.) The crooks in the Truman administration were no bargain. They rendered no service of value to Truman or to anyone else. And Truman covered up for them; of this I was, for once, a witness. When things were getting very sticky in the election year of 1952, Truman decided that the time had come to act, or make a show of acting. After casting about for someone—a tame Republican would be best—to conduct an "independent investigation" (independent of Congress, that is), and after being several times rebuffed, he called in my high-minded and not very bright friend Newbold Morris (subject of my first *New Yorker* Profile, eight years earlier), whose reformist urges were finding no outlet in New York, and who was spending his days punctuating wills and contracts in the family law firm. What Newbold lacked in the way of insight and imagination he almost made up for—as the Truman people were to learn—in rectitude and determination. He was as innocent of wrongdoing as of political sophistication. Truman had Newbold appointed as a special assistant to the attorney general, J. Howard McGrath—a hack from the Rhode Island organization who had served briefly in the Senate and as chairman of the Democratic National Committee—but the appointment was met with derision, as it was the opposite of putting a fox in the chicken coop. After his first meeting with the President, Newbold was asked by reporters where he planned to start. He would need a day or so to decide, he said—whereupon McGrath, who *was* the fox, moved in front of the cameras and, with a flourish of his fat cigar, announced that he would be happy to have him begin at the Department of Justice. Newbold was pleased; that would be as good a place as any. The fox gave his special assistant the largest, most richly appointed office in Justice (the size of a basketball court), a smashing blonde secretary who could neither type nor take dictation, a key to a private elevator, and an army of young lawyers eager to help him. The huge office suddenly became a warehouse of Justice Department documents, delivered to Newbold by the eager lawyers—mountains of reports, most of them tied with blue ribbon, on the triumphs of the FBI, on interesting cases tried in the past, on cases then pending, on the history of the department, on its relation with other departments, on just about everything but what he was supposed to be concerned with. He had submitted names of several people he wanted on his staff—lawyers he had known or worked with in New York, others recommended as experienced investigators—only to learn they would be put on the payroll as soon as the FBI granted clearances, a process likely to take longer than the few months his task was scheduled to consume. Meanwhile, he was invited almost every day to boozy, six-course lunches at the 1925 F Street Club. He was bathed with flattery and advised that his work should not be allowed to interfere with his private life. He need not be away from his New York office for more than two days a week for a month or so. Just go through some of those reports—read them on the train, take them to New York. Don't overwork. At one of these numbing lunches, he was told the long, sad story of T. Lamar Caudle, recently dropped as head of the Tax Division because, among other things, he had accepted a five-thousand-dollar commission on an airplane sale he had negotiated. Caudle, it was explained, was a decent and forthright man. He had not concealed his part in the transaction but had come directly to McGrath. Did Mr. Morris see anything wrong in such a deal? If a man wanted to sell airplanes, Newbold said, he should go into the airplane business rather than the Tax Division of the Department of Justice. That, he said, was exactly the sort of thing he proposed to look into.

Poor Newbold! Flimflammed again! Three New Yorkers who had known him at City Hall—Bob Donovan and Don Irwin, of the *Herald Tribune,* and I—had dinner with him one evening and told him he was a sucker, a patsy. We said that first he ought to renounce that awful title—Special Assistant to the Attorney General. Truman should appoint him head of a commission or put him on the White House staff—anything but an assistant to one of the most disreputable figures in town. At the very least, Newbold should demand space of his own outside of Justice, probably the most corrupt of departments. If this were denied, he should resign. Get rid of that secretary and away from all those lawyers. Ask for money to hire his own staff. Bring down some tough veterans of the La Guardia years. Even in those days not everyone working for the government needed an FBI clearance. What Newbold was doing had no connection with national security. He could hire consultants on a per diem basis. And he should keep after Truman and McGrath until he got subpoena power. (McGrath had requested this from Congress, but he had also requested the power to grant immunity to witnesses. This was more than Morris needed and more than Congress was likely to give. It was, we told Morris, McGrath's way of ensuring that he got no power at all.)

Within a few days, Newbold had an appointment with the President in Blair House. (The White House, lately declared to be a structural menace, was closed while workmen shored up its timbers and bearing walls.) Two days later, a statement was issued, in which the President said:

> I have had a good conference with Mr. Newbold Morris. . . . I am directing all departments and agencies of the government to cooperate fully. . . . Adequate funds will be provided. . . . I intend to see that Mr. Morris has access to all information he needs. . . . I am going to ask the Congress to give [him] subpoena powers. . . . Mr. Morris will have my full support. I hope he will also have the full support of Congress and the public.

Newbold did, finally, get moved—to the offices recently vacated by the Washington *Post*, down the street from the Willard Hotel and around the corner from the Press Building. And he was empowered to appoint his own staff. But the people he wanted were out-landers—New Yorkers. They still had to be examined carefully for ideological contamination by the FBI. Newbold had prepared a questionnaire requiring government employees to declare their sources of income, their assets and liabilities, their connections with private business—a questionnaire loosely modeled on a document used by the New York City Police Department, but a good deal shorter and simpler. The President had told Newbold that he thought the procedure a splendid idea—should have been done earlier. It would, of course, have been absurd to try to analyze the responses of two and a half million government employees in a few months, so Newbold planned to narrow the task by getting the names and addresses of employees in specific job categories. But nowhere was there such a list; in no one place was there data on the bureaucracy as a whole. A department-by-department search immediately encountered resistance. The Secretary of the Treasury, John Snyder, a Kansas City banker who came through the period with a clean record, thought it would be "demoralizing" for Treasury people to be asked such questions. It hadn't demoralized the New York police, Newbold said. He was still receiving his daily ration of irrelevant reports from Justice; couldn't they bring him, instead, some of the complaints of corruption he knew were piling up? The next morning, the deluge. The first complaint he read was from a farmer out in rutabaga country who protested that a bank was about to foreclose his mortgage. Newbold told me once that the only pertinent complaint he received came from a girl who rushed up to him one day in Union Station to say she had been employed by Justice for several months and had still to be given anything to do. It was a bizarre business.

Congress balked at providing subpoena power—some of the members had reason to fear that Newbold might use it against them. (Senator Karl Mundt, of South Dakota, a McCarthy ally, said, "It is difficult to see how Hitler himself could have cloaked his associates with more power to protect friends and punish enemies.") Still, Newbold might have managed without subpoenas—the newspapers were daily publishing evidence that could have been presented to grand juries, and Newbold was turning up information simply by asking for it. (When, for example, the lawyers from Justice were carting in all those irrelevant reports, Newbold asked the bearers if they were engaged in private practice; a number *were*, and saw nothing improper in it.) And Truman still had no complaints. On "Meet the Press," Newbold said some harsh things about the President's cronies—including Harry Vaughan, who was to Truman what, twenty-five years later, Bert Lance was to Jimmy Carter—and two days later, meeting with the President once more, he was told that he had full White House support. ("Keep after them," Truman said. "I'm not protecting anyone.")

I had a theory that Truman had made a deal with himself to keep close watch over the departments that dealt with foreign policy and military affairs—primarily State and Defense—and leave the rest pretty much to themselves. He chose men he could trust and respect —Dean Acheson, James Forrestal, George Marshall, Averell Harriman—for positions in which cronies simply would not do, and filled the other spots with timeservers. He knew that, unlike Roosevelt, he could not deal with thorny characters, like Harold Ickes, or with ambitious ones, like Henry Wallace, who were building constituencies of their own. He wanted to be a strong President, and he was, but he had to concentrate his strength on matters of high importance to him. I think he probably did want a clean administration and had brought Newbold in as something more than window dressing. After all, in the Senate, during the war, Truman had served as a kind of watchdog over public funds, a scourge of profiteers in defense and related industries; his wartime services, it had been estimated, saved the country many billions of dollars.

But if the President did not lie when he brought Newbold to Washington and pledged cooperation, he assuredly lied when, on April 3—a day after Newbold had been fired by McGrath—he held a press conference which included the following exchanges:[1]

Q: Why was Mr. Morris fired? Do you think his dismissal was justified?

A: The President said he couldn't answer the question.

Q: I wonder what is your opinion of the celebrated questionnaire of Mr. Morris.

A: The President said he had never seen one, so he couldn't answer a question like that.

Q: Mr. President, could I ask whether you have any reason to feel dissatisfied with Mr. Morris's work.

A: The President said he couldn't answer the question.

Q: . . . We understood that Mr. Morris was your man to conduct the investigation, and now he is fired, and you don't tell whether it is in your opinion a justified dismissal. It leaves Mr. Morris under a cloud.

[1] Truman did not authorize direct quotation without permission, but the record is verbatim except for the use of the third rather than the first person.

A: The President said Morris was hired by the Attorney General, brought down by the Attorney General, and the Attorney General fired him.

Q: Are we wrong in thinking he was your man?

A: The President said he wasn't his man. He said he never was.

What had happened was rather simple. Newbold had hand-delivered his questionnaires to McGrath's office, but they had not been distributed. When he asked what had happened to them, he was told they had been removed with the rest of the garbage. Newbold then proposed to McGrath that he begin his investigations by going through some files at Justice in search of much-rumored improprieties. McGrath said that this would be unfair; he would not stand for search and seizure. Morris would first have to produce specific charges; then the "relevant" files would be opened. This, of course, would leave time to sanitize the records. Newbold said that there was no point in going on if he were denied the access promised by the President to the information he would need. On April 3, McGrath met with Truman for fifteen minutes, and the next morning Newbold received a note from McGrath, stating curtly: "Your employment has been terminated." He went to see Truman, and the President asked him to resign, and he did. In a press conference that afternoon, Truman announced that McGrath himself was resigning.

Meanwhile, Joe McCarthy had discovered some connection between Newbold's law firm and a shipping company that did business with Communist China—the investigator under investigation. It seemed that United Tanker, with the sanction of the State Department, had delivered four shipments of oil to Communist China before the war in Korea, and that stock in United was held by the China International Foundation, a pro-Nationalist organization of which Newbold was the unpaid president. The foundation's profits were used wholly for such causes as providing college scholarships for students living under Chiang Kai-shek's rule in Formosa (now Taiwan). Newbold might have been complimented for finding a way to finance anti-Communists with Communist money, but instead he was screamed at by McCarthy for taking profits "soaked in American blood." Newbold had told his fellow Republicans that McCarthy was as bad as the Hungarian Communists then persecuting Cardinal Joseph Mindszenty—and this might have endeared him to the Democrats, but instead they had begun saying that he had been compromised, that his usefulness was at an end. It seemed possible that he had been fed to McCarthy and the subcommittee by some Democrat who wanted him out of Washington—perhaps the fox himself.

I had just returned to Washington from Chicago and Springfield, Illinois, where I had gone to gather material for a piece on Governor Adlai Stevenson. (It was becoming clear that Truman would support him for the 1952 nomination in the event he did not run himself.) The next morning, Newbold and I took the Morning Congressional to New York. We talked over the whole business, and I offered to draft a memorandum telling his side of the story. He declined the offer; this was to be his last involvement in government, and he would make no more public statements. He went back to punctuating all those wills and trusts and deeds. After 1948 I did not talk with Truman alone until 1957, when I spent a day with him in Kansas City; I was writing a piece about him and the opening of the Truman Library, in Independence. I remember his telling me how much time he spent reading American history, and I do not think that ten minutes went by without his imparting a fact that was not a fact or making some wildly inapposite allusion. I also recall his telling me that he had yet to be persuaded that the Russians had mastered atomic energy.

III

For almost a decade, the Republican rank and file and most of the Republican state leaders had wanted to nominate Robert Taft for the presidency. He was a symbol of tough, steady opposition, an unwavering partisan, a principled conservative, a man innocent of

Wendell Willkie's genuine and Thomas Dewey's bogus ecumenism. If General Marshall's stern disapproval had not forced Eisenhower to withdraw as a candidate, the 1948 nomination would have been the general's for the asking; as a Republican, he could have defeated any Democrat, or, as a Democrat, any Republican. As a consequence of his withdrawal, the 1948 Republican contest was between Taft and Dewey. Arthur Vandenberg, of Michigan, had been running since 1936, but in a lackadaisical and unconvincing way, and he was no match for men as determined as the senator from Ohio and the governor of New York. In the end, the Republicans settled—once again reluctantly—for Dewey, but I had had my say about him in 1944 (the *Harper's* article that led Shawn to take me on at *The New Yorker)* and had little further to add.

Of the politicians of the period, Taft and Vandenberg interested me the most, though for completely different reasons. Except for their Midwestern origins and their Republican loyalties, the two had nothing in common. Taft was a man of formidable intellect and unbending will. Vandenberg was a genial muddlehead, a garrulous mediocrity who owed his celebrity largely to the very lack of the resolve and purpose that Taft had in such abundance. Of Taft's father, the twenty-seventh President, Theodore Roosevelt said that he "meant well, but meant well feebly." Of Vandenberg, it might have been said that he never quite knew *what* he meant, and of Taft that there was no way in which a word like "feeble" could be used to describe his intentions or anything else about him. In 1948 Taft seemed certain to have a large place in this century's history whether or not he ever served in the White House. Vandenberg's star, it then seemed, would shine about as brightly as that of Alben Barkley, Truman's Vice-President—another jolly and essentially frivolous statesman. As it has turned out, traces of Taft's power and influence can be found almost nowhere, while there is only an element of hyperbole in Dean Acheson's 1962 statement that "Vandenberg stands for the emergence of the United States into world power and leadership as Clay typified the growth of the country

[and] Webster and Calhoun the great debate of the ante-bellum days." When I knew them both—Vandenberg died in 1951, Taft in 1953—it seemed unlikely that this would be the case a mere three decades later. Three decades hence, things may be different, though I have no present reason to believe they will be.

I say that I "knew" Vandenberg. I recall talking with him once or twice for a few minutes, but I don't remember what we talked about. One did not have to know him in order to judge him, any more than one has to know an actor one has many times seen on the stage; everything came out in the performance. Taft, of whom I saw a good deal in the last five years of his life, was no performer. He was a deeply, darkly introverted man, sober, even somber, in appearance, yet capable—increasingly in the last days—of an almost ungovernable passion. One day he could be sweetly reasonable and ready for sharp, unsparingly self-critical analysis, the next wildly irrational. In public and in private, his manner seemed ill-suited to his profession —cold, starchy, reserved, forbidding. It always struck me as odd that anyone so seemingly colorless, so ungregarious, should have a following numbering in the millions. He dressed like a loan officer in a small-town bank. He was gawky—all arms and legs. In his fifties, he was almost completely bald, but until his terminal illness he looked younger—like an "elderly schoolboy," I. F. Stone once wrote. Alistair Cooke said that he looked like a bespectacled grapefruit. His voice was dry and singsong, and his speech, except when he was angry, and sometimes even then, was flat, lawyerlike, schoolmasterish, often impolitic. In floor debate, it was never his style to say that, much as he respected the views of the able and distinguished gentleman from Old Catawba, he found it necessary to differ with his esteemed colleague. Not Taft. He would take the floor to say, "I have never heard such tommyrot" or "I think that's stupid." Yet, though he was hardly a clubbable fellow, and his rudeness must have given offense to some, he was respected enough to be chosen majority leader when the Republicans regained control of the Senate; it was said that there were at least a dozen senators who would follow any lead he gave, while not one would do the same for Vandenberg, a master of parliamentary etiquette and persiflage. Taft was a master of plain talk and compression. Just after the war, when some foods were in short supply, the administration brought in a Madison Avenue public-relations wizard, Charles Luckman, to mount a campaign for what he called "economy in the use of certain foods through personal restraint." He urged all Americans to join in a "broad national effort" to be "selective in consumption . . . and to conserve vital supplies." Asked how he thought the goal might be met, Taft said, "Eat less." When this leader of American conservatism—and he led the movement as no one since has ever done—addressed himself to questions of the day, he did so with no mention of the flag, the Founding Fathers, the American home, the family, or the honored dead. I never heard him speak of "Americanism" or invoke the sanction of God, or even of Washington or Lincoln. He never made the eagle scream, and he never identified himself with the silent majority. He was not much impressed by majorities, silent or otherwise.

Though I never thought of him as a reactionary, his instinct generally was to react—to oppose change whenever change was proposed. On some matters he reversed himself—federal aid to education, for example, and to housing—and did so, I thought, rather gracefully. (He would say, "Well, I've changed my mind," or "I guess I was wrong about that.") But he thought that liberalism of the kind represented by the New Dealers and by the clubhouse types around Harry Truman was, in the first instance, cynical and, in the second, fraudulent. He affected contempt for Easterners, though he was very much a product of an Eastern education (the Taft School, Yale College, and Harvard Law School) and came from a city—Cincinnati, hardly a frontier settlement—about as Eastern in atmosphere as Philadelphia. I often wondered why he bothered to see me, a product of New York who wrote about him first for *Harper's* and then for *The New Yorker* and the New York *Times*. He might well have been put off by the very title of my first article—

"Taft: Is This the Best We've Got?"—and by my conclusion that he was a good man, "but not good enough." If so, he never mentioned it. I never brought up the fact that a decade earlier I had been a Communist, but someone on his staff must have checked me out before our first meeting. I don't imagine he would have cared one way or the other. Except in what I think of as a prolonged manic period—which lasted roughly from mid-1950, when he stooped to encouraging and echoing McCarthy, until mid-1952, when, all passion spent, he accepted his last defeat at the hands of the "moderates"—he was a committed civil libertarian. He was outraged by Truman's plan to draft the striking miners, and as a member of the Yale Corporation he stoutly defended the right of a Stalinist to remain on the faculty as long as he discharged his professorial duties satisfactorily. (This at a time when liberals like Sidney Hook and Irving Kristol were saying that academic freedom had its limits, and that it should not be granted to those who would destroy it.) And Taft was not the sort who welcomed publicity, favorable or otherwise, for its own sake. I think he simply enjoyed trying out his views and his reasoning powers on someone who he knew had a different outlook.

In describing Taft as a "principled conservative," I mean only to suggest that he was a man of principle—that he took his beliefs seriously and, most of the time, sought to apply them responsibly. He did not, as far as I could see, adhere to any economic or political orthodoxy. Some of his views might have alarmed conservative thinkers like Milton Friedman. For example: "I don't even pretend to know what causes depressions. I haven't met anyone who does know, but I certainly wish I could find the answer. The business cycle is a very puzzling thing. I wish we could learn to understand it and to stabilize the system without wrecking it. No one is going to be persuaded by arguments about the long-range achievements of capitalism in raising standards of living if it is all at the expense of periodic plunges into mass misery." Once, when he was carrying on about "Socialist" tendencies in the Truman administration, I asked if he thought socialism would be the ruin of Britain and the Scandinavian democracies. "No, no," he said, "you're missing the point. I have never criticized the British for going Socialist. It may work for them and suit them very well. England is a small country with a fairly homogeneous population. They govern themselves better than we do. In countries like England and Sweden, things are more manageable than they are here. All I've ever said is that socialism would be a disaster here. This government can't even run an efficient mail service." He had no great faith in private enterprise. He felt about it much as Churchill felt about democracy: that there was not very much to be said for it except that—for us, at least—it works better than any other system could. Unlike Eisenhower and many other Republicans, he was not much impressed by the merchant princes and the captains of industry. When Eisenhower announced his cabinet appointments—"nine millionaires and a plumber," they were called by the press—Taft was appalled. Just as he believed that politicians should stay out of business, so he felt that businessmen should stay out of politics. "Eisenhower thinks that anyone who has made a lot of money must be a good economist," he said. "It's ridiculous. Just because someone can sell a lot of cars, it doesn't mean he can run a government department. There's no reason to think that a man who's done well in private life will do well in public life."

There was a kind of ideological insouciance in Taft's approach to specific issues. How could he advocate federal intervention in the housing industry when he thought government so incompetent and wasteful? "The free-enterprise system doesn't do well when it comes to housing," he said. "It can provide food and clothing efficiently, and power and transportation. But it simply doesn't provide the housing the country needs. I don't know why. You'd think the profit motive would work in the construction and management of housing, but it just doesn't. So there seems to be no alternative to having the government step in. It won't do it well, but there you are. And the government has to be in education, too. That's a simpler case. Education has always been outside the system, or mostly outside it. There's no money in education, and I guess there shouldn't be. It has to be a public function."

Taft was denied the Republican nomination four times—in 1940, 1944, 1948, and 1952—always on the ground that, beloved of Republicans though he was, he was a sure loser. And this, of course, was true. He was a splendid party leader and a power in Washington, but he could never have been elected to national office. Though he kept muttering (as Barry Goldwater and Ronald Reagan were later to do) that if the people didn't have to choose between Tweedledee and Tweedledum, more of them would vote and a conservative could win, I doubt if he really believed this. At least in his era, this was not a conservative country. In any case, he was an inept candidate. When he sought the nomination in 1940, at a time when the farm vote was important, especially for a Republican, he was widely quoted as saying, "I know the country has got to do something for the farmers . . . but I'm not sure yet what to do." His advice on the food problem—"Eat less"—was a model of candor and succinctness, but it was not well received, particularly since it came from a man who was leading the fight to remove price controls. And it was politically close to suicidal for him to say—as he said on October 5, 1946, after the Nuremberg trials of Nazi war criminals—"The hanging of the eleven men convicted will be a blot on the American record which we shall long regret." It haunted him for years. How could any American in 1946 lament the passing of men who the previous year had been running death camps and directing operations against American troops? Taft, of course, was not talking about the guilt of the defendants or the justness of the sentences. He was speaking as a lawyer, at a conference on "The Heritage of the English-Speaking People" at Kenyon College, in Ohio. He was questioning the legitimacy of criminal trials under ex-post-facto statutes. He saw them as "policy clothed in the forms of legal procedure," and this bothered him, as it bothered many able and circumspect jurists, among them Justice William O. Douglas;

Judge Learned Hand, of the Circuit Court of Appeals in New York; and his colleague Jerome Frank. But they were not candidates, and their misgivings were not big news.

The Taft I have been writing about is the one of whom Walter Lippmann said in 1940 that for the Republicans to nominate him would be a disaster for the nation and an ordeal for the candidate; Lippmann, who knew him longer and better than I did, also said, after Taft's death, "The inner core was the solidest part of Taft, and at the center he was so genuine and just, so rational and compassionate, that he commanded the confidence of men when he could never convince them." This, I think, is a bit off the mark. It would have been no disaster if Taft had been nominated in 1940, for there would have been no chance of his being elected. And while he was a "just" man, in the sense of being generally fair-minded, I do not think the word "compassionate" quite fits him. He had a good record on civil liberties but a poor one on civil rights. He opposed the Marshall Plan and foreign aid in general. Moreover, there was that two-year period—1950–52—in which very little that he did was defensible on any grounds. On March 22, 1950, a month after McCarthy began talking about Communists "making policy" in the State Department, Taft met with some reporters—I was one of them—to explain his position on this latest of Washington sensations. He said that while he had no particular faith in the accuracy of McCarthy's claims, he had urged McCarthy to go ahead anyway, and had advised him "to keep talking, and if one case doesn't work out, proceed with another." He later said that he had been misunderstood and misquoted, but a half-dozen reputable newspapermen used the above words in their stories, and a day later Philip Potter, of the Baltimore *Sun*, talked with Taft and came away with the same quotation. For sheer callousness, this matched anything McCarthy ever said. *Keep talking, and if one case doesn't work out, proceed with another.* Imagine what would be said of a prosecutor's office that acted on that basis, or a chief of police who told his officers to arrest everyone in sight until the law of averages worked in their favor and turned up a few thieves. "It is doubtful," I wrote, "if American history provides an instance of a man comparable in stature and prestige to Taft saying anything as subversive of democratic values and the values of any civilized human society as the words of encouragement offered McCarthy by Taft."

And there was more—much more. When, in the middle and late 1940s, other Republicans and more than a few Democrats began talking about Roosevelt's "sellout" at Yalta and the "betrayal" of Poland and other countries in Eastern Europe, Taft did not join them. Speaking of Yalta in 1948, he went no further than to observe that President Roosevelt made "certain agreements" that gave the Soviet Union "wide interests" in Manchuria and Poland. Even after the Stalinists took over in Czechoslovakia, he said he had "no knowledge of any Russian intention for military aggression." (This served his isolationist view; he wanted no more involvement in Europe or anywhere else.) But then McCarthy came along; Taft scented political pay dirt in foreign policy. It was as if the discovery suddenly drove him mad. He began talking about "this pro-Communist administration" and the "betrayal of America at Yalta." He spoke now of the "delivery of Manchuria to Communism," of "the State Department's plan for Communist victory," of the "continuous sympathy toward Communism . . . which inspired American policy." In speech after speech, he explained that "Dean Acheson was determined to let the Communists take Formosa." There was then no way one could speak of him as a decent, fair-minded man. In a 1952 *Harper's* article—"What's Happened to Taft?"—I tried to compare him to Shakespeare's Cassius. It was possible, I wrote, that Taft saw Truman and Eisenhower—both of whom he expected to oppose that year—as Cassius saw Caesar: "Ye gods! it doth amaze me a man of such feeble temper should so get the start of the majestic world and bear the palm alone." Knowing more about politicians now than I did then, I would not make such an analogy today. Taft, who had seemed so atypical, reverted to type. He was, moreover, desperate. He knew that his fourth try for the presidency had to be his last. If Eisenhower got one term, he would probably get two, and in 1960 Taft would be seventy-one—too old. And he may (though I doubt it) have known that he was soon to die.

By early July of 1952, when the Republican National Convention opened in Chicago, it was clear to just about everyone that Eisenhower would be nominated on the first ballot. (Since the advent of television, first-ballot nominations have become routine. The most devoted of viewers cannot stand much more tedium.) It was a convention that plainly would have loved to nominate Taft. But Dewey and the people who have been beaten about the ears ever since for rigging things at Republican conventions prevailed—and so it was Eisenhower. Despite the fact that it nominated this moderate man, it was rather an ugly convention. Both McCarthy and MacArthur addressed the gathering, and received much greater acclaim, as I recall, than Eisenhower. When it was over, Taft went to the family's retreat in Murray Bay, in Quebec. It was reported that he spent two months sulking; he must also have spent some time thinking and coming to terms with himself. At any rate, a new—or at least a different—Taft emerged from the north country. He took no part in the Republican campaign, but he called on Eisenhower at Columbia University and said he would work for those parts of the new administration's programs that he found himself able to support. (It was clear in September that Eisenhower would win handily; a transition office was already at work in the Hotel Commodore.) In the Senate after the election, with the Republicans now a slim majority, Taft took over the party leadership and placed his followers in key positions. For the few months that remained to him, he was as much in control as Lyndon Johnson was to be in his great years. "In his fifteenth year in the Senate," I wrote in March of 1953, "and in the year following his defeat in one of the great party struggles in American history, Robert A. Taft of Ohio has ascended new heights of power and prestige." At the time, one could only speculate as to what kind of use he would make of his power. Would he try to impose his will on Eisenhower, or would he accept, as a good party man, the new President's leadership? I think he wanted to make a success of the first Republican administration in twenty years. One of his first acts was to take on the McCarthyites and fight for the confirmation of Eisenhower's choice for ambassador to the Soviet Union, Charles Bohlen. It was a squalid business. Bohlen was a career Foreign Service officer, a favorite in Acheson's State Department, a Kremlinologist accused of being a favorite in the Kremlin also. Also, there were charges—wholly unfounded—of homosexuality. But Taft, who thought there were far more important things in life than who was to represent Eisenhower in Moscow, saw Bohlen through. Responsible now for putting together winning combinations, he became more conciliatory, less brusque in manner. At the same time, he was determined, I think, to put his own stamp on the Republican legislative program. He had little respect for Eisenhower's bankers and manufacturers, and hardly more for the President himself. Asked how he intended to deal with some troublesome money problem, Eisenhower had said that he thought he could use "the Federal Reserve and all that stuff." "God help us," Taft said. But he lived only through the shakedown phase of the new administration. He had seemed well enough when the year began, but cancer struck suddenly and spread wildly. In the last weeks, he could hardly make it down the Senate aisle. He died on July 31, 1953.

Four years later, a Senate committee led by John F. Kennedy was given the mission of selecting from among all the senators who had ever served in the upper chamber five whose portraits would grace the Senate reception room. Three inevitable, obligatory names led the list—Clay, Calhoun, and Webster. Then came Robert M. La Follette, the great Wisconsin liberal of the 1920s, and Taft, the great conservative of the next two decades. It was a season for honoring Taft for the integrity that had characterized him during all but those two shameful years when McCarthy and McCarthyism flourished and Taft endorsed them. Earlier, soon after his death, Congress had appropriated funds for a Taft memorial on the Capitol grounds—a rather dreadful carillon tower mentioned in the guidebooks only because of its unique setting and the fact that no other member of Congress has been so honored for his service on the Hill. But does Taft belong among the five greatest? This seems arguable to me. John Kennedy's approval, explained in *Profiles in Courage*, rests on the courage Taft displayed in questioning the Nuremberg trials. That did take courage, though not more than standing against McCarthy when Taft stood with him—or, years later, opposing the war in Vietnam when Lyndon Johnson was riding high, or inviting Richard Nixon's wrath when the penalties were severe. I would think that at least as good a case could be made for William Borah, of Idaho, or George Norris, of Nebraska. Taft's special qualities needed neither a stone monument in Northwest Washington nor a framed likeness in a reception room.

However that may be, he is more deserving of any honor than Arthur Vandenberg, the amiable windbag from Grand Rapids. Yet Dean Acheson would have Vandenberg as the second greatest of the Great Five. "A good case can be made that Vandenberg's achievements exceeded those of any of the five, except Henry Clay," he said. What achievements? Actually there were none—nothing comparable, for example, to Taft's drafting and sponsoring the Taft-Hartley Act, a law once despised by liberals and trade unionists but now, for the most part, accepted as a necessary brake on the power of big labor, which has at times been as inimical to the public interest as big business. Still, Acheson had a point—a melancholy but nevertheless valid point. "Without Vandenberg in the Senate from 1943 to 1951," he wrote in *Sketches from Life of Men I Have Known*, "the history of the postwar period might have been very different." What he meant by this was that if Vandenberg, the ranking Republican on the Senate Foreign Relations Committee and a man with a long history of isolationism, had not undergone a swift and widely publicized conversion in 1945, the United States might not have joined the United Nations, and there might have been no Marshall Plan, no North Atlantic Treaty, and no American military presence in Europe in the early, dangerous postwar years.

Without Vandenberg in the Senate, Roosevelt and Truman might have suffered the fate of Woodrow Wilson. And—if one accepts Acheson's geopolitical logic—without Vandenberg Western Europe might have been governed by Communists and occupied by Soviet troops.

It is, of course, possible to argue that without Vandenberg in the Senate things would not have been very different. It is hard to believe that one man could have kept us out of the United Nations (Henry Cabot Lodge the elder was abetted by a "band of wilful men" in keeping us out of the League of Nations), blocked the Marshall Plan, and kept the Communists out of Western Europe. What is unarguable is that Vandenberg was immensely useful to Roosevelt in his last days and to Truman in his early years in the White House, and that he made foreign policy a bipartisan affair in the crucial last half of the 1940s. And all this came from a single speech, delivered in the Senate on January 10, 1945, in which he, once the most unregenerate of isolationists, announced his conversion to internationalism. It was a dreadful, gassy bit of oratory, in which the key sentence was "I do not believe that any nation hereafter can immunize itself by its own exclusive action." Those words alone—a commitment to collective security—were quite enough. But Vandenberg, whose prose was as mushy as Taft's was gritty, fancied himself a man of letters—he had been an editorial writer on the Grand Rapids *Herald* and had written a few short stories for *Collier's*—and he had, according to his diaries, rewritten the speech ten times, each time making it a larger anthology of tautologies. (The phrase "honest candor" turns up about a dozen times, now and then with reinforcement, as in "honest candor devoid of prejudice or ire" and "honest candor on the plane of high ideals.") Had anyone else delivered the speech, it would have received no attention or been treated as a candidate for *The New Yorker*'s Wind on Capitol Hill Department—but because it was Vandenberg's, the "electric effect," as its author put it, "was instantaneous." Indeed it was. "It cannot be said of many speakers that they affect the course

of events," Walter Lippmann wrote a few days later, and years before Acheson found room for Vandenberg in the pantheon. "But
this may well be said of Senator Vandenberg's speech if the President . . . will recognize promptly and firmly its importance." Roosevelt was very prompt. He took fifty reprints to Yalta and handed
them out as IOUs from the Republican Party. Roosevelt made Vandenberg a member of the American delegation at the founding session of the United Nations in San Francisco, and thereafter it
seemed that no international conference could be described as official unless Vandenberg was on hand. Indeed, when James Byrnes
was Truman's Secretary of State he told the President that he would
not attend any such meeting unless Vandenberg was at his side.

In the Vandenberg story can be found a rather stirring lesson in
the political uses of rectified error. "His prior history of isolationism," Acheson wrote, "was an asset which he never allowed to die."
He couldn't afford to: his new career, which made him a world
traveler and a world celebrity, and which he found much more
congenial to his gregarious and sybaritic tastes than his old one, was
firmly based on the fact that he had been wrong before he was right.
Taft experienced conversion more than once (generally, except in
the McCarthy years, from an unreasonable position to a reasonable
one), but he lacked Vandenberg's sense of timing, drama, and publicity. Each change of mind was, as he saw it, a concession of past
error. For him there were no dazzling illuminations. In Taft's last
years, Vandenberg was working—or so he said—on a life of St. Paul.

Vandenberg has a small but secure place in history. Early in 1979,
when Republicans in the Senate were becoming uneasy over President Carter's foreign policy and felt that the time might have come
to abandon bipartisanship, Howard Baker, their principal spokesman, said that "Vandenberg was right in his time, but I think we're
right in our time." His colleagues, many of whom were small children in Vandenberg's day, knew more or less what he meant. The
name Robert Taft seems to have no resonance at all. I do not recall
its even being mentioned at the 1976 Republican National Conven-

tion, which, as one liberal Republican put it, was essentially a contest between one right-wing faction and another. Taft's kind of conservatism—and Vandenberg's, too, for that matter—no longer exists. It is impossible to imagine Taft saying, as Barry Goldwater said, that "where fraternities are not allowed, Communism flourishes," or, as Ronald Reagan put it, "If you've seen one redwood, you've seen them all." (Taft's hobby—his only one—was planting trees.) Taft was a conservative of the British Manchester school. The conservatives who flourished a quarter century later were far more dogmatic, though it is difficult to say where their dogma, apart from anticommunism and Cold War ideology, came from. Taft's principal backers were the industrialists of the Midwest. Now the geographical base of American conservatism is in the South and the Southwest. Today, cities like Chicago, Detroit, and Cleveland are pretty much in the same boat as those on the East Coast, and as they decay and lose ground to what not long ago were frontier settlements, the old tensions are no longer to be felt. Were Taft in the Senate today, he would probably be calling for aid to the cities and might regard the Sunbelt with the kind of hostility he once reserved for the East. This might have been quite irrational, but he was no stranger to the irrational.

IV

It was through the late Herman Kahn, the director of the Roosevelt Library, in Hyde Park, that in the summer of 1948 I met Arthur M. Schlesinger, Jr., who was then in the early stages of research for *The Age of Roosevelt.* I had known Herman for only two or three months. He had moved up from Washington, where he had been on the staff of the National Archives, and he and his family were living in a house not far from ours. He was forty—a plump, bouncy, pink-cheeked, bright-eyed, and unfailingly cheerful man with a mind that was at once tough and playful, and with an apparently inexhaustible store of ideas and insights. A historian by training—at Minnesota

and Harvard—he was a fine scholar but in no way a pedant. Whenever, in those days and for many years afterward, I wanted to test an
idea or a line of analysis, he was the first person to whom I turned,
and a good deal of what I wrote—particularly in the first years in
which I covered Washington for *The New Yorker*—was as much a
product of his thinking as of mine. He was a guide and counselor to
a generation of Roosevelt scholars; though he wrote almost nothing,
he knew the field better than most of them. He returned to Washington in 1961, and in 1968, when he retired to teach history at
Yale, he was coordinating and supervising the work of all the presidential libraries in the National Archives system. He died in New
Haven in 1975.

Herman and Arthur and I lunched together once or twice a week
in a grubby diner in Hyde Park, and Arthur, who was living in a
rented room in Poughkeepsie, spent a good many evenings with
Eleanor and me on Quaker Lane. For the next three summers he
was our houseguest much of the time, and in 1951 we collaborated
on a book, *The General and the President*. When I first knew Arthur, he was thirty and already one of the best-known members of
the Harvard faculty. He had won a Pulitzer Prize at twenty-eight for
a work, *The Age of Jackson*, that he had actually completed two
years earlier. In his late twenties, he was established as a leading
spokesman—along with Reinhold Niebuhr, Eleanor Roosevelt, Herbert Lehman, and Hubert Humphrey—of the liberal wing of the
Democratic Party. (His views on the politics of the period were set
forth in *The Vital Center*, a collection of articles and essays he put
together in the summer of 1949.) Partly, I think, because of his
precosity and partly because he tended toward overkill in controversy, he was widely held to be a rude and arrogant young man,
intolerant of those who disagreed with him and contemptuous of
those who knew less than he did. Arthur in print and in debate
could indeed seem arrogant, though I think he was generally fair-
minded, and I know he was open to criticism, for I subjected him to
quite a bit of it. His manners were formal and courtly in a way that

seemed rather dated. Eleanor, a close student of the mores of the houseguest, found him exemplary: considerate, avuncular with the children, ready to lend a hand with the dishes or any other household task, and a good deal neater than her lifetime houseguest. He suffered fools—of whom a good many would pass through the Rovere household in the course of a summer—not gladly, perhaps, but with patience and good humor.

Unlike many who have achieved success early and seemingly with little effort, Arthur was generous, often to a fault, in his praise and encouragement of the efforts of others. When I read his appraisals of other writers, I put a fairly heavy discount on what he said, and I would double it if he was writing or talking about anyone I knew to be a friend of his. His sense of loyalty could cloud his thought. When our Truman/MacArthur book was published, we appeared twice on a radio talk show that often pitted right-wing critics against liberals. On both occasions, we were stoutly defended by a fellow journalist, a decent and amiable man who enjoyed beating back our assailants. A year or two later, this writer published a book that seemed to me and to others a shoddy and misleading piece of work. One day, I saw a newspaper advertisement that displayed in bold type an endorsement by Arthur—"MUST READING FOR EVERY AMERICAN," or something of the sort. When I next saw him, I said, "Arthur, that was a terrible book. What do you mean, 'Must Reading for Every American'?" "Well," he said, "he defended us twice. Don't you remember?" I said that I did indeed remember, but that that didn't make his book a good one. "Maybe you're right," Arthur said. "I guess I shouldn't trust my judgment of people I like. I never seem able to see the flaws in their work." Not that he was all kindness and charity. He was also assertive, proud, and severe in judgment. If his manners in social occasions were elaborate and elegant, his manner in combat could be fierce and withering, abetted by his gift for irony and his controversialist's edged tongue. But he was never ferocious in behalf of any shackling orthodoxy or mean and self-serving policy. His jousting defended a humane skepticism, human rights, and human freedom, and—in a phrase I think he taught John F. Kennedy to value—human diversity.

In any case, his intellectual and physical energies were, as they still are, extraordinary. He would work in the library a full day; join us for a swim, drinks, and dinner; spend the early evening turning out a couple of book reviews or a magazine article, then rejoin us for a nightcap and conversation. If he had an evening engagement in New York, he thought nothing of driving the ninety miles to visit friends or see a show, and then driving back for a few hours' sleep before going to the library in the morning. Our house at the time was noisy and often chaotic, with three children under eight, often accompanied by friends and animals. None of this fazed Arthur. He slept and wrote in a bedroom off the kitchen. When he was organizing his thoughts for what he was about to write, he shut the door (which of course did not keep out the noise), but when he was actually at work on the typewriter, with a cigar clamped firmly between his teeth, he would throw open the door and let the children swarm all over the place, as if it were a schoolyard during recess. For me, thinking and writing have always been part of a single process; as I have noted, I am often unsure of what I want to say—of what, in fact, I think—until I formulate it in sentences and paragraphs. For Arthur, the physical act of writing seemed little more than transcribing by machine what had already been worked out in his mind to the last detail. Given a period of relative quiet to get his thoughts in order, he could have written in a boiler room or a zoo, and the house on Quaker Lane was often a combination of the two.

After four years of almost no political writing, I was getting back into it at the time I met Arthur. I was writing my *Harper's* series about the 1948 presidential candidates on my leave from *The New Yorker*. Arthur, too, was writing about current politics, but he was frankly partisan, while I did my best to cultivate a journalistic objectivity and neutrality. I think we agreed more than we disagreed, but I could never have been the kind of activist he was. My experience on *New Masses* had left me with a residue of guilt—a rather light one, as I look back on it, in comparison with those whose involvement had been deeper and lasted longer. Arthur was a founder and an officer—at one time national cochairman—of Americans for Democratic Action; though I thought it a worthy organization, I never became a member, partly because I felt that as a political journalist it would have been improper for me to belong to any organization that sought to influence elections and legislation. But even without any such restraint, I was disinclined to become a special pleader of any sort. In later years, I would do quite a bit of special pleading, but I wasn't ready for it then. I enjoyed watching politicians, and I enjoyed the company of some, but, unlike Arthur, I had little taste for the sweat and swirl of political life. I liked having a ringside seat when I could get one, but I did not want to be in the ring or in anyone's corner.

When Arthur went to the White House in 1961 as special assistant to the President, he assumed a post for which he had been in training longer than Kennedy had been in training for the presidency. I remember once—it must have been ten years earlier, in 1951—when Arthur stopped off with us in Hyde Park on his way from Cambridge to Washington. He was exhilarated by the prospect of being in Washington, where he had appointments with Harry Truman and other luminaries. Cambridge was all very well, he said, but the real world was in Washington. That was where things were done, not just talked about. Eleanor and I said that if we had to make a choice between being in Washington and being in Cambridge, we would probably choose Cambridge. No, Arthur said, we didn't know what we were talking about: the academic life is stultifying, the political life invigorating. He stopped off again on his way back, full of tales of high adventure. As it happened, I was about to set off for Washington myself, where I had been invited to have tea with Felix Frankfurter, a close friend of Arthur's, in his Supreme Court chambers. When I arrived, Frankfurter began regaling me with a rapturous account of a weekend he had just spent in Cambridge. The weather there had been lovely, the atmosphere peaceful, the conversation elevated and stimulating. Such a contrast, he went on, to Washington, where he had to spend so much time talking with people who had nothing to say. He made some unflattering generalizations about his fellow justices, and some even more unflattering ones about their wives. In Cambridge, though, the company had been altogether delightful. I said I found this rather amusing, and told him of my recent conversation with our mutual friend, who found in Cambridge all the faults that Justice Frankfurter found in Washington, and vice versa. "Why, you know why that is, don't you?" he said. I replied that I thought I did, but I wondered what his explanation was. "It's simple," he said. "I'm very fond of Arthur, but he is not like us. You and I have no interest in power, but Arthur loves it. He likes to be near it, he likes the feel of it, the smell of it. Only someone like that could prefer Washington to Cambridge." I said I thought he might be right; I did not, of course, say that I found it quite delicious that Frankfurter, of all people— the man considered by many to be one of the great movers and shakers of the century—should be speaking of power as something he abhorred.

Arthur had zest for more than power. He is one of the most sociable people I have ever known. As long as I have known him, he has been a compulsive partygoer and party-giver. In the Kennedy years, his partying would have undone even a man who had little in the way of work to tax his energies. And his zest was all the greater when there were attractive women around or in the offing. Eleanor has always been amused by her memory of a scene with Arthur in a dining car on the old New York Central. She and Arthur were in aisle seats, facing each other across the table, when a girl with quite sensational legs walked slowly through the car. Table talk stopped as Arthur positioned himself to command the full sweep of the aisle. He was rather heavy in those days, and as he leaned away from the table, Eleanor braced herself to break his fall and keep the table settings from going down with him. The girl passed through the door at the end of the car before the crash could come, but it was a near miss. In 1952, he and I were in the same hotel in Hollywood, he as a speechwriter for Adlai Stevenson, I as a reporter for *The New Yorker*. Some movie barons were giving a fund-raising party for Stevenson, and not only the candidate but his staff had been invited. A full complement of starlets was to be on hand, and Arthur could hardly contain himself. Before he took off, he was in my room asking me if I saw a hair out of place and whether his choice of tie and shirt was all right. I gave him my approval—I hardly know a bad choice from a good one—and said that I hoped the starlets were as gorgeous and as pleasure-bent as had been promised. He was radiant when he left and altogether dejected when, a few hours later, he returned to the hotel. What was the trouble? No starlets? "There were plenty," he said, "but I never talked to one of them. As soon as I got there, some producers got me in a corner and began asking me questions. 'Professor, can you explain the federal system to us?' 'What do you think of the loyalty-security program?' 'Professor, do you think the Electoral College ought to be abolished?' 'What will happen on Wall Street if Stevenson wins?' Here I am lecturing a bunch of movie oafs on the goddamned federal system and the Electoral College when I can see Ava Gardner barely ten feet away. All evening long, I never got near anyone except a bunch of producers."

In 1951, shortly after Truman relieved MacArthur of his several commands in the Far East, Arthur and I collaborated on an article for *Harper's* about the affair. Then we decided to make a book of it. It was my first—and only—venture in collaboration, and I thoroughly enjoyed it, though I am not sure I could have done it with anyone else. Arthur did some of the work in Cambridge, and I did some in Hyde Park and in a cottage we rented for a few weeks on the Rhode Island shore. But much of it we did together in the living room on Quaker Lane, with children and dogs underfoot. I wrote an opening chapter on the tumult in the country when MacArthur returned home from Korea and then came to Washington to address Congress and set the Potomac afire; Arthur did a long biographical section on the general's career through the Japanese occupation; I did a running history of the war in Korea; and together we composed a closing section on the hearings in Congress and on what we thought would be the consequences for American foreign policy. I do not think a reader could easily tell who wrote what or find much evidence that two hands were involved. We did not, as I recall, make any sort of effort to accommodate the style of one to that of the other. We both wrote fairly standard English—what Cyril Connolly called "the common style"—and we organized the material in a quite strict chronological order. Neither of us was an expert on either Asian or military affairs, but nobody picked up any serious mistakes, and in any case the controversy was essentially an American one, with political and constitutional implications that might have been the same if MacArthur, instead of being an American overlord in East Asia, had been an insubordinate commander of a post in Georgia or Arizona. The book, as it turned out, was a mild critical success but a commercial dud. By the time it appeared, late in 1951, the passion the affair had aroused earlier in the year was pretty well spent, and not many people wanted to go through it all again in a book.

In 1978 I was a member—an observant if not a particularly helpful one—of a task force (I wish the term could be reserved for military and engineering projects) dealing with reform of the presidential-election process. The task set us (Arthur also was a member) by the Twentieth-Century Fund—a foundation with impeccable Establishment credentials—was to find a way of making certain that the candidate most Americans voted for and the President installed every four years were one and the same person. Because of the structure and workings of the Electoral College—that creaky and anachronistic apparatus conceived in "fatigue and impatience," John Adams wrote, at the Constitutional Convention in 1789—it has happened at least twice that the man with a majority of popular votes was denied the presidency, and there have been several close calls. The obvious solution is to do away with the Electoral College and hold direct elections. But this would lead to, among other things, a proliferation of candidates, and would weaken, if not destroy, the two-party system, which all the members of the task force, like most Americans, regarded as a force for stability and order.

The question is a vexed one, and we vexed it further through several day-long meetings in a stylishly appointed conference room in the foundation's headquarters on New York's Upper East Side. Until close to the end, it looked like a Mexican standoff. But we finally did produce a proposal that was adopted by our members with a single dissent, and that a partial one. M. J. Rossant, the head of the fund, said in his report: "By going over their differences again and again, the . . . members ultimately produced a proposal that artfully solved the problem." I am not sure that it solved the problem "artfully" or otherwise, but it was ingenious, and it drew favorable responses in the press and elsewhere. It was not, however, the product of our deliberations, of our "going over [our] differences again and again." It came—just about as we were to agree on failure —from Arthur, who had missed most of the earlier meetings and arrived late at this one. He sat down, put his cigar aside, and said that he thought matters might be resolved simply by keeping the Electoral College—indefensible as an institution but firmly anchored in history and tradition—and, in addition, giving each state and the District of Columbia an additional two votes, to be cast for the winner of the national popular majority. Thus the candidate with the most votes would have a bonus of 102, enough, in all imaginable circumstances, to ensure his entry to the Oval Office. I am hardly an expert in these matters, but many members were, and I gather that no one had ever thought of this startlingly simple compromise. It was gimmicky, and it begged several questions of principle, but there is a lot of useful gimmickry in American democracy—the balanced ticket, for example—and there are questions of principle that will be forever begged. The task force quickly adopted the proposal as its own. I asked Arthur later if the idea had come to him as he sat there listening to the frustrated experts or whether he had thought of it before. He wasn't sure.

I don't suppose it likely that Arthur's plan will be written into the Constitution in his lifetime or mine, but I'd like the record to show that it was his plan, not that of a committee made up largely of political scientists—a breed for which he has often revealed his contempt. (I think he regards most of the "social sciences" as suspect, even outlaw, disciplines, which properly belong under one rubric—"history.") And there are many additional things for which others have got credit but that in fact sprang from Arthur's fertile mind. When, in his later books, I find him quoting Adlai Stevenson or John and Robert Kennedy or George McGovern, I wonder to what extent he is really quoting himself. Many of their best lines were originally his.

V

Sometime in the winter or spring of 1952, at Arthur's urging, I went to Springfield, Illinois—by rail, via Chicago—to spend the better part of a day talking with Adlai Stevenson. Arthur wanted to see him get the nomination, and bugged me until I did a piece. I liked Stevenson instantly—and enormously. My memory now holds only two or three things about that first meeting. At lunch, I recall, he brought up the subject of A. J. Liebling's pieces on Chicago, which were then appearing in *The New Yorker*, or had lately appeared. They were causing an uproar in Chicago, and no Illinois politician should have shown any approval of them. But the governor said that he found them delightful and generally true, and he didn't seem to care what use I made of this intelligence. If we talked much about national politics, I don't recall it. We did talk a lot about Illinois politics, especially about corruption. (That day, or a day or so before, he had had to demand the resignation of a staff or cabinet member who had been caught stealing.) We must have talked of many other things, too, but I no longer recall what they were. Stevenson's position on the nomination then was that he didn't want it, but I think this meant only that he didn't care to be either Truman's heir or Eisenhower's adversary. He wanted, surely, to be a national figure; he wanted to be written about. I left Springfield with an armful of handouts.

I covered the 1952 Democratic convention in Chicago, but I didn't see Stevenson alone—nor did I, as far as I can remember, when I covered his campaign on the Coast. However, I was in touch with the Springfield headquarters through Arthur, and perhaps John Bartlow Martin, and I wrote a passage that Stevenson used in his Labor Day speech in Detroit, and I passed along to him any other ideas that came to mind.

A year after his defeat, in the fall of 1953, I spent another day with him—this time at his place in Libertyville, Illinois. He had returned from a round-the-world trip, and Lester Markel, editor of the Sunday New York *Times Magazine*, asked me to go out and do an interview. I recall the day as delightful and relaxed; one of Stevenson's boys was with us for a few minutes, but otherwise we were completely alone. It must have been cook's day out, for he got together a lunch of sorts from the refrigerator. Later, we spent a lot of time walking about the grounds. He was pleasant but depressed. Though everyone was saying that the campaign and the trip and his writings had established him as a world figure, he said he couldn't see that this was true—all he'd heard about on his trip was Eisenhower and Joe McCarthy, and more about the second than about the first. I don't think I saw him again until the 1956 convention and campaign. We talked a bit during the campaign, and he was dispirited, saying that he wished he could change places with me— writing about the damned thing rather than being it.

In the Kennedy and Johnson years, I saw him perhaps a halfdozen times—mostly at Arthur's, once at the White House correspondents' dinner, when Gore Vidal implored me to introduce him to Stevenson, and I reluctantly and awkwardly did, fearing that Stevenson would resent it because of Vidal's play *The Best Man*. Stevenson did not seem too pleased, but he put up with it and talked for quite a while with Gore. I saw him once at the United Nations, when I was doing a piece on U Thant for *The Saturday Evening Post*, and we talked a couple of hours. I'd had a hard time seeing Thant—he wasn't giving out individual interviews—but Stevenson intervened in my behalf; he was at the time quite high on Thant, though discouraged about the United Nations, which he thought the Russians were determined to wreck. At our last meeting, at Arthur's, I was relieved to find him pleasant and detached and funny. After Kennedy's death, I had been told, he had been quite difficult; high ambition had been reborn, and he had done everything he could to persuade Lyndon Johnson to pick him for the vice-presidency in 1964. Some of his means had been unattractive. On the day he died—July 14, 1965—I was talking with Eleanor at lunch, and an "if" occurred to me: suppose there had been a deadlock at the Democratic convention in 1960, and Stevenson had been the beneficiary. Who for Vice-President? John F. Kennedy, most likely. Had this happened, that July 14 might have been the occasion of John Kennedy's being sworn in as President.

Though I knew Stevenson only slightly, I felt very close to him, in part because I admired him and in part because of what I kept hearing about him through others—Arthur, of course, and John Bartlow Martin, Bill Shannon, Bill Blair. And at the time I first met him, he was, except for Wendell Willkie, the only presidential candidate I had really known at all. I had talked with Truman and Dewey and Eisenhower and Taft, but Stevenson, I felt, was my sort, and I very much wanted him to win, though later I was glad that he had lost. I can't imagine what the future will make of him. From my point of view, he performed admirably at the United Nations, but it cannot be said that he performed greatly (who ever has, in a role like that?), and whatever he accomplished was at the cost of his independence, once his most valuable asset. I think he was at his best in the Eisenhower years. He was not a formidable critic of the administration, but he held up a certain standard of responsibility and gaiety for the dissidents. It was always heartening to know that he was there and that he was able to command some twenty-odd million votes. I agree with Arthur that he contributed more than any other living person to the Democratic Party that came to power with Kennedy in 1960. In fact, it seems to me that Stevenson made Kennedy possible. Their differences in age and manner and temperament concealed a remarkable similarity. Both had a self-depreciatory style. Both enjoyed the company of intellectuals—and very often the same intellectuals. More important, both saw the need for firm alliances with the intellectual community, and both believed that the assistance of intellectuals was necessary in running campaigns and governments. In his two campaigns, Stevenson brought together at every level the people who manned the Democratic Party in 1960. They got their experience in 1952 and 1956, and in 1960, when there was at last a chance for victory, they were there and well seasoned. It was far easier for Kennedy to surround himself with eggheads, because Stevenson had done it before him. Stevenson had fought antiintellectualism with fair success—especially in the party, but also in the country at large. Among the Stevenson people who worked for Kennedy were Arthur, Ken Galbraith, Newton Minow, Willard Wirtz, Fred Dutton, Justin Feldman, George Ball, John Bartlow Martin, and God knows how many others—even, in a way, Ted Sorensen, who was a bequest from Senator Paul Douglas, of Illinois. And many of the better congressmen. John Brademas told me that his whole career was founded on the enthusiasm fired in him by Stevenson. I know that the "quality of life" business which became such a cliché in Lyndon Johnson's Great Society was first Stevenson's—out of a memo by Arthur.

Yet it has always seemed to me in retrospect that a Stevenson victory in 1952 would have been a disaster for the country. Not long before his death, I talked one evening with him about his years in national politics, and I asked him if he felt, as I did, that it had been good for the country that Eisenhower rather than he had become President in 1953. Though I am sure I did not need to, I stated the case as I saw it: only a Republican, and perhaps only a Republican who was also a military man, could have accepted the settlement that Eisenhower accepted in Korea. The Joint Chiefs of Staff, with solid backing in Congress and encouragement from the State Department, would have gone to the brink of war with China, and perhaps beyond the brink, in backing Chiang Kai-shek; a President lacking Eisenhower's high repute as a strategist would have found it difficult to restrain the Pentagon. McCarthy was on a rampage, and he would not have been brought low in 1954 if there had been a Democrat in the White House; only a Republican President could have done the job. The Democrats had held power for two decades, and many of them had been corrupted by it; the Republicans needed an exercise of responsibility as a brake on their accelerating irresponsibility. At least on a point-by-point basis, Stevenson agreed. If he could have won at all, it would have been only by a hair. The country would not have accepted his military judgments over those of the Joint Chiefs. He would have been as bloodied as Truman was by McCarthy, Nixon, Taft, and William Knowland (who had cried "Munich" when Eisenhower disengaged in Korea). As Truman's heir, he would have been an implausible cleanser of the stables. Stevenson found the argument by his friend Walter Lippmann persuasive—that the case for Eisenhower in 1952 was not unlike the case for George Washington as the first President. There were finer minds than Washington's, and men of broader vision, but he was the one who had the respect of all factions, who was perceived as a healer. And such a perception was then, as in 1952, the most important thing. The people looked upon Eisenhower as a man above partisanship, who might unite the country as he had earlier united the commands in Europe. I had great fondness and admiration for Stevenson, and I voted for him both times against Eisenhower, but I was more relieved than regretful when he did not win. I felt glad for Stevenson's sake. I think that Eisenhower did the country a considerable service in his early years as President. His stolidity was an asset; it was not the right time for an activist President.

VI

I suppose that if there was one figure in public life for whom I had an instinctive dislike and distrust—apart from transparent demagogues and frauds like Joe McCarthy and Richard Nixon—it was John Foster Dulles. In this I was hardly alone. My friend Peter Lisagor, of the Chicago *Daily News*, used to say that if Dulles had a choice between telling the truth and lying, and if he had nothing to gain or lose either way, he would choose to lie. I would not put it quite like that, for I doubt if Dulles ever found himself in a situation in which he did not calculate profit or loss, but his capacity for duplicity was as great as his ambition and as repellent as his piety. Even his Presbyterianism seemed to me to have no fire—I had, after all, grown up with some rather fiery Presbyterians. Dulles, in contrast, seemed to have the kind of piety one often finds at businessmen's luncheons. He was a hardheaded lawyer who could be terribly ruthless. And he was almost gutless in the McCarthy period. He thought of himself, no doubt, as a Cold Warrior, convinced that the times demanded this of him and that the important thing was to advance Eisenhower's policies, whether or not somebody got hurt in the process. He had a sound appreciation of the nature and the realities of power; his ideological crusade, I thought, was simply good politics. His ambition, formed as a very young man, was to become Secretary of State—a position held by his grandfather, John Watson Foster, under Benjamin Harrison—and he worked as hard to achieve it as he worked to amass a fortune and to become, as was often reported, the highest-paid lawyer in the country. So strong was this ambition that Wendell Willkie, when I was seeing something of him in the months before his death in 1944, blamed Dulles rather than his adversary, Dewey, as the cause of his downfall in Republican politics. Dewey, in Willkie's mind, was not the tough and rather gifted politician others thought him to be, but a hollow man, a puppet manipulated by Dulles. Dulles was determined to be Secretary of State, yet he could not gain that office unless a President named him to it, so, in Willkie's view, Dulles invented Dewey and put the young governor in his debt, financially and intellectually. He arranged things so that Dewey, if elected, could appoint no one else. Thus, it was not the insubstantial Dewey but the conniving Dulles who eliminated Willkie in 1944. This was, of course, a paranoid view, but Willkie was not normally given to such delusions, and it suggests something of Dulles's ability to outrage his contemporaries —and those, like me, who were not his contemporaries.[2]

My first encounter with Dulles was at the Republican National Convention in Chicago in 1952. It was in the basement pressroom of the Conrad Hilton Hotel, where copies of the party platform were being distributed. Dulles was the author of the foreign-policy section, and he was there awaiting congratulations. When I read his condemnation of the Democratic administration for standing by in 1939 while the Baltic republics were being annexed by the Soviet Union, I approached him and asked what he thought the Democrats—or any Americans—could have done about this. The annexation had taken place two years before we were at war, when he himself was giving money to the America First Committee and denouncing the interventionists. Dulles looked at me—he looked, I wrote, like "a Founding Father with bloodhound eyes and jowls and the bearing of a weary banker"—as if I were at once stupid and impertinent. "They were in office when it happened, weren't they?" he said. Stupefied, I replied that Herbert Hoover was in office when the Japanese invaded China—should Hoover have been held to account for that? He said nothing more, and neither did I.

It was then quite certain that Dulles would be Eisenhower's Secretary of State. The general's debt to Dewey was a large one: it was the governor's troops who had taken on and repelled the Taft forces at the convention. Dewey, the kingmaker, had called Dulles "the

[2] I suppose it also suggested a tendency on Willkie's part to see politics as a conflict between lawyers with corporate clients. As head of Sullivan & Cromwell, Dulles would clearly wield more power than the district attorney of New York County, or even the governor of New York State.

world's greatest statesman,"[3] and if Dulles was something less than that, he was also one of the few Republicans who could claim any sort of expertise and experience in foreign policy. He had been part of the American delegation at the founding of the United Nations in San Francisco, and he had served the Truman administration in a number of advisory capacities. He had helped draft and negotiate the treaty with Japan. He had served briefly—and by Dewey's appointment—in the Senate. He was qualified as no other Republican was, and to have chosen anyone else Eisenhower would have had to go outside the party and settle for a career diplomat, or a military man like George Marshall.

By 1953, when Eisenhower took office, the Cold War was (at least by my reckoning) well into its third phase. The first, which had begun in 1946, had ended by 1950, when there was no longer much fear that the governments of Western Europe, particularly those in France and Italy, would be taken over by the Communists. After that, the fear was of invasion—of the Red Army's moving out of the satellite countries and across the undefended plain that stretched to the Atlantic. The invasion of South Korea was read as evidence that the Communist nations were ready to risk aggression to add to their real-estate holdings—or, as it was assumed at the time, to Moscow's. In retrospect, it seems unlikely that Stalin or any other Russian leader ever had any such intention in Europe, but fear of invasion brought NATO into being and overcame all resistance to rearming the Germans. By 1953, that fear had largely subsided. Stalin was dead, and power—political and military—was once more in balance; it was thought that the West, like the East, could negotiate from what Dean Acheson had called a "position of strength." Acheson's successor as Secretary of State, John Foster Dulles, did not share this view and did his best to block all efforts at diplomatic accommoda-

---

[3] This was when Dewey himself was an active candidate for the presidential nomination. It led me to ask why Dewey did not step aside in Dulles's favor. "Surely," I wrote, "the 'world's greatest statesman' deserves the world's greatest job, and surely the world's greatest job should be graced by the 'world's greatest statesman' when he is of the right nationality and has the proper requirements of birth, age, and party."

tion, but Churchill thought it time to talk with Stalin's heirs, and so did Dulles's patron, Eisenhower, and the two were laying plans for a "parley at the summit of the nations," in Churchill's words. To prepare for this, the Prime Minister proposed a tripartite meeting—Britain, France, and the United States—in Bermuda in early December of 1953.

The Bermuda conference was the first of its kind that I covered, and so little came of it that I wrote, just a few hours after the official closing, that "one has the feeling that it never took place at all." Though I was in Europe on other business at the time of its announcement, it seemed a good idea for me to go to Bermuda. The New York newspapers were on strike—their correspondents were filing from St. George, but the presses in New York stood idle—and Shawn thought I might provide a service of sorts by going; at the last minute, our enterprising business representative in Europe, George Woodward, got me aboard a press plane from London by bumping a *Time* correspondent. As it turned out, I performed no service at all, except by reporting a few speculations and some of the sideshows—but then neither, really, did any of the three or four hundred other journalists who had flown in from several continents. If anything worth reporting did happen, which seems doubtful, the effort to conceal it was so successful that no leaks were possible. The American press was billeted at the Castle Harbour, the luxury hotel that Henry Sell (subject of one of my *New Yorker* Profiles) had once rescued by filling it with free-loading Broadway and Hollywood celebrities. The conferees—Churchill, Eisenhower, and Joseph Laniel (easily the least memorable of all postwar French Premiers)—held several sessions in the Mid-Ocean Club, on what was surely the most heavily fortified golf course in history. Churchill, the host, was no believer in open covenants openly arrived at. The Mid-Ocean Club was ringed by barbed wire, and outside this fence were British troops with all manner of military vehicles at their disposal. Offshore, there was a small armada of British warships ready to repel any seaborne intruders. All this in addition to the security staffs brought in by the Big Three. There was no security at the Castle Harbour; none was needed, for there was nothing we could do there except eat, drink, and sleep—and now and then ride rented bicycles to the shopping centers in search of duty-free bargains. Briefing officers held briefings to tell us that all was going well and to explain that they were under strict orders to go no further. They could divulge nothing about the goings-on at the clubhouse.

Some of the sideshows, though, were amusing. The French had agreed to the meeting somewhat reluctantly, and it was perhaps on this account that their forgettable leader, M. Laniel, arrived in St. George in garments that might have been appropriate for a gathering in Spitsbergen. He was a victim, his spokesmen said, of a heavy *rhume*—a head cold that required much bed rest and layers of thick woolens. The ailment was reported around the world (except in the New York newspapers), and nothing could have affronted the Bermudans more than to have it broadcast abroad that one of their distinguished guests suffered an affliction that was all but outlawed in the colony. They had thought of the conference as yielding millions in free publicity for the resort, and now the world was looking at pictures of a visitor arriving on their summery isle dressed in what appeared to be three overcoats, mufflers galore, and a fur-lined hat. A bit of the damage was undone when, on the last day, it was announced that British wonder drugs, administered by Churchill's physician, Lord Moran, had relieved some of the Prime Minister's symptoms, but it was still a fact that the medical bulletins on the indisposed Gaul were bigger news than almost anything else that was happening, or not happening, in Bermuda.

The best show, naturally, was the one staged by Churchill. His body was already feeble, but it housed an anything but feeble spirit, and he was an extraordinary impresario. As host, he was the first to arrive and the last to depart. When he went to the airport to greet and bid farewell to his guests, all the cameras and all reporters' eyes were on him. He had summoned from Jamaica to Bermuda a detachment of the Royal Welch Fusiliers, a colorful outfit that, on parade, is a kind of walking museum of British military history. Sometimes known as the Pioneers, the men marched not with swords and muskets but with axes and picks. The fusiliers' dress featured, among other colorful things, a broad, flowing ribbon down the spine to keep the grease on the regulation pigtail from soiling the uniform, and their mascot was a goat with gilded horns. Churchill zeroed in on the goat as the cameras zeroed in on him. Just as a visiting dignitary would emerge, smiling and waving, from the plane door, Churchill would pat the mascot and say, "Stout fella, eh, stout fella," and then proceed to the second order of business, which was to greet the arriving Eisenhower, Laniel, Dulles, Georges Bidault. This ritual took place six times in all, the last when Eisenhower and his party left. As sometimes happens in large crowds, an inexplicable hush descended, and just as Sir Winston was fondling the goat, the redoubtable and ubiquitous Merriman Smith, of United Press International, was heard loud and clear across the field, saying, "Jesus Christ, the old man must be queer on goats." The old man took no notice, as with one hand he stroked the beast's beard and with the other waved good-bye to the presidential party.

In revisionist histories of the period, Churchill is almost a war criminal, along with Truman, Acheson, Dulles, and many others. In my history of the 1950s, he holds a large and honored place for having, to paraphrase him, led the West toward jaw-jaw negotiations and away from war-war confrontations. The Bermuda conference he called was a dud, but at least the participants, in their last and only communiqué, acknowledged that East-West relationships were in a new phase, and that "the danger of aggression now seems less imminent." I am inclined to think that Eisenhower had an intuitive awareness of this, and that he was always prepared to keep Dulles on a short leash. But in 1953 he was a new President—indeed, a man new to politics—and often an inattentive President. I suspect that, if nothing else happened at Bermuda, Churchill strengthened Eisenhower's resolve to be master in his own house—to let Dulles talk recklessly but to pursue no reckless course in American foreign policy.

VII

The good that Eisenhower did—largely by doing so little—was accomplished, I felt, in his first term. In that term, he got us out of Korea and McCarthy was got rid of—not necessarily by the administration's actions, but it couldn't have happened, I believe, under a Democratic administration. The country simmered down, and was less divided and embittered than it had been—certainly less so than it is today. There was no Bay of Pigs (although it was prepared then), there was no Vietnam (although Eisenhower, or at least Dulles, may have sown the seeds of Vietnam). Eisenhower served eight years and didn't get the country into a war. This criterion, to my mind, is the most important of all. There was one other accomplishment of the first term which was significant and for which I think he deserved a lot of credit: the understanding he reached with Stalin's successors that nuclear war was out of the question as an instrument of policy for both countries. He was able to rally to his own person a large majority. He was a symbol of unity. By the time of his second administration, in 1956, he had done for the country about all the good that he was capable of doing; new divisions were beginning to appear, and new problems, and he wasn't ready for any of them. Very little can be said, I believe, in defense of the second term. In 1955, at Geneva, he had started the process we now call détente, but in the ensuing years (unless Eisenhower's invitation to Khrushchev to tour the country in 1959 is counted), little was done to advance it, and the period approached its end with the fiasco of the Paris summit meeting that never took place: the Russians had just shot down the U-2 reconnaissance plane and imprisoned its pilot, Gary Francis Powers. And finally, in those ominous days of 1960, there was the horrible spectacle of the President of the United States, on what was to have been a triumphant Asian trip, floating around in the Western Pacific looking for a country that would let him in, while the Japanese tried to decide whether or not they could control the student mobs so he could visit Tokyo. In the end, they concluded that the President would not be safe in their streets.

I found the years from 1957 to 1961 sterile and depressing, at least in Washington. Eisenhower had survived his illnesses, but he was fatigued and irritable, and a pathetic figure during that last year in the White House. The economy was stagnating, but to Eisenhower this was natural law—it had thus been explained to him by the bankers, the automobile men, and the soft-drink barons he thought of as master economists because they had taken so much out of the economy—and when Congress sent him legislation designed as stimulants he responded with a dreary succession of vetoes. And many of his key appointments had proved disappointing; Truman's had run to mediocrities, but at least they were political mediocrities—they were political people in the sense that Eisenhower's were not. Eisenhower ran to men like Charles Wilson, his Secretary of Defense, for whom very little could be said, and to automobile dealers like Douglas McKay and Arthur Summerfield. At least Dulles was a professional and probably Eisenhower's most distinguished appointment. The civil-rights movement was gathering strength and developing some brilliant leaders, but the President, if not hostile to it, was strictly neutral and never uttered a word of moral support. To the end of his tenure—indeed, to the end of his days—he declined to express approval of the 1954 Supreme Court opinion (Brown *vs.* Board of Education) on racial segregation in the schools, and one of the great regrets of his political career, he said, was his appointment to the Court of Earl Warren, the author of that decision. This from the man who had championed Richard Nixon and made Sherman Adams his chief of staff.

During Eisenhower's first term, I had known a few people in the White House—Maxwell Rabb, a New York and Boston lawyer who was a kind of resident liberal; Emmet John Hughes, a Time, Inc., alumnus and a speechwriter for Eisenhower; and James Hagerty, the press secretary, with whom I had little contact except when making travel arrangements. Rabb left early in the second term; Hughes was absent more than he was present. Later I knew Malcolm Moos, the speechwriter who was the author of Eisenhower's warning about the "military-industrial complex"—I doubt if the warning would have occurred to Eisenhower if it had not occurred to Moos. But the people I knew were not really in the know themselves; had I known others in the executive branch, it would have profited me little, for not much was going on there anyway. Consequently, when I was not seeing my journalistic colleagues I spent most of my time in Washington on the Hill. The man whose company I most enjoyed and found most valuable, Senator Hennings, was still, despite the alcoholism that would soon kill him, an astute and witty observer. I sometimes saw Hubert Humphrey and Lyndon Johnson, and I saw a good deal—what reporter didn't in those days?—of George Reedy, then an employee and an unqualified admirer of Senator Lyndon Johnson's and later, after a disillusioning time as press secretary to President Lyndon Johnson, a harsh critic and the author of two of the most perceptive books on the presidency ever written. In those depressing days, I found myself devoting more and more of my time to matters far from Washington and current politics. I wrote a piece for *Esquire* on Ezra Pound, which turned out to be helpful—as the editors and I had intended it should be—in getting him released from St. Elizabeth's Hospital. For a George Orwell anthology, *The Orwell Reader*, I wrote an appreciation of the writer whose journalism had much influenced mine. I was on the editorial board of *American Scholar* and wrote for it often. And I put in a good part of 1958 and 1959 working on *Senator Joe McCarthy*, the first book of mine that was neither a collection nor a collaboration.

The Eisenhower years ended for me with the Khrushchev trip of 1959, one of the few events I covered but never wrote about, for just as the tour was ending I came down with an affliction that turned out to be viral pneumonia, and by the time I was well enough to write, there was little to report that had not already been reported by the four-hundred-odd reporters who dogged the Russian party from the East Coast to the West Coast and back again. I do not know what led Eisenhower to bring the Soviet leader here. Perhaps it was a kind of revenge on Dulles; it could never have happened while Dulles lived. Or it may have been a kind of advance reciprocation, to ensure that Eisenhower could go to the Soviet Union and be greeted by the masses as he had been in India—a reception for some reason more gratifying to him than any accolade he had experienced here. At any rate, Khrushchev came, saw, did not conquer, and was not conquered. He did score something of a public relations success, however, and he probably learned something. He flew from Moscow to Andrews Air Force Base, near Washington, in a pretentious Russian jumbo jet and then went by train to New York. From the Maryland-Delaware border until the tunnel under the Hudson, the landscape is megalopolis all the way—factories, mostly antiquated, with smokestacks belching pollutants, and, except in parts of Philadelphia, residential districts that the authorities have neglected to condemn. Along most of the route, both sides of the track are the wrong side of the track. Where there are no factories or houses there are malodorous swamps unfit for manufacture or habitation. It was a scene that would have appalled Marx and driven Dickens to eloquent outrage. Not so Khrushchev. According to Henry Cabot Lodge, our chief United Nations delegate, whom Eisenhower had chosen as the Premier's cicerone, Khrushchev admired it greatly. "This was industrialism," Lodge said. "I think he envisioned the good society as Newark multiplied by a factor of several thousand—an uninterrupted stretch of Wilmington, Chester, Camden, and Elizabeth from Leningrad to Vladivostok." And so it was with New York. Khrushchev demanded to see Harlem, presumably so that he could report to his countrymen on its unspeakable degradation. He had been prepared to descend into an inferno; what he saw was, as he told Lodge, a community better housed than many a Moscow neighborhood. After a courtesy visit to Eleanor Roosevelt in Hyde

Park, he, and we, were off for Los Angeles, where Mayor Sam Yorty greeted him with ideological cheap shots aimed less at the visitor than at the right wing of his own constituency. A promised visit to, of all places, Disneyland was called off because neither the local police nor the State Department's security force could guarantee safety. Then a visit to the Paramount movie studios, to see the filming of a sequence of *Can Can,* starring Shirley MacLaine and a leggy chorus. Khrushchev found it lewd (or at least Mrs. Khrushchev did) and an occasion for some strident comments on American— never mind that the story and the setting were French—decadence. He threatened to fly home, via Vladivostok. If he had any intention of doing so, he may have been dissuaded by an unusually warm welcome in—again, of all places—Santa Barbara, a center of conservatism that, probably through some finagling on Lodge's part, produced hands for the Bolshevik leader to shake and babies for him to kiss, in sharp contrast to the angry confrontation with anti-Communist labor leaders the next day in San Francisco.

From the time of Khrushchev's arrival in Washington, the press had been clamoring for him to hold a news conference. He did not want one, and Lodge put no pressure on him. However, someone suggested that he might walk through the train on the Los Angeles– San Francisco leg to let the reporters—who up to then had hardly been nearer to him than the crowds—get a close-up look. I was at the time in the company of Mary McGrory, of the Washington *Star,* and Murray Kempton, of the New York *Post.* Mary had invested in a Russian-English dictionary, and the three of us improvised a little speech. The English text went about like this: "Mr. Chairman, the American press is glad to have this opportunity to see you. All of us are eager to have you give us some of your impressions of the places and people you have been seeing, and we ask you to agree to hold a news conference before the trip is over." Mary put it down on paper, and rehearsed it until Khrushchev, attended by interpreters and security guards, reached our car. After shaking hands, she began her little piece. She had got no further than the first sentence when Khrushchev stopped her with a raised hand and said, through his interpreter, "We know the American press is glad to see us. Who does not know of John Reed?" and moved brusquely on. It was in many ways an astonishing response; we three did indeed know of John Reed—two of us having been active in radical politics in our youth—but we were surely in a small minority. Reed, the romantic American journalist who had written a concise and moving history of the Russian Revolution, *Ten Days That Shook the World*, and had been buried in the Kremlin forty years earlier, may have been a folk hero in the Soviet Union (though even this may be doubted), but he certainly isn't one here. Even among journalists, he has never been the kind of cult hero that, say, Richard Harding Davis once was. Could Khrushchev really have believed that there was a bit of John Reed in each of us? Perhaps he did; perhaps he thought that his unfavorable press notices were the work of our employers, who turned glowing reports of his triumphs in America into anti-Soviet polemics. If so, I, for one, misread him, for I do not think he was a hard-shell Marxist Leninist. I think he had a fair understanding of an open society; it seems to me that such an understanding is essential to anyone who wishes to cling to power in a closed society. He had made some shrewd observations on American life and had picked up some ideas he thought should be applied in the Soviet Union. When he saw what the automobile had done to our large cities and when he learned of the car-rental business, he said that if the Russians ever reached our degree of affluence it would be wise for the state to go into rental operations, to discourage needless congestion and personal ownership (as distinct from private ownership, ideologically a banned term).

I was back in Los Angeles the following year for the 1960 Democratic convention. Most of the New York delegation was on my plane; Gore Vidal, who was a candidate for the House, a couple of other Dutchess County delegates, and I had shared a cab to the airport. Flying made Vidal rather morbid, and before we had left the ground he began to speculate on how we would fare in the newspaper stories of our crash. "I know my obituary would get more space than yours," he said. "I think it might even make the front page." A few seconds before the plane started taxiing to the runway, a nun boarded and headed for our row and the empty seat next to Vidal. "I don't want to sit beside her," he said. "Would you mind changing seats?" We shifted seats, leaving me in the middle and the nun by the window, but the respite was brief; there was some mechanical difficulty and we made an unscheduled stop at Salt Lake City. Another intimation of mortality. Some new passengers, bounced from an incapacitated plane, boarded ours, and among them was another nun, who, perhaps under instructions from on high, took the aisle seat across from Gore. This time, there was nothing to be done, and Vidal fidgeted until we touched down in Los Angeles.

By early 1960, it had seemed clear that John Kennedy would get the Democratic nomination and probably the presidency. The people who had worked for Stevenson in 1952 and 1956—Schlesinger, Galbraith, and a number of others—were depressed by the thought of a third Stevenson try, particularly if, as seemed more likely than not, Richard Nixon was to be his opponent. Kennedy was tougher and less vulnerable. I was not, at the time, much attracted to Kennedy; indeed, the event that moved me most at the convention was the demonstration that followed Eugene McCarthy's eloquent plea for Stevenson's nomination. But I realized that Nixon might have cut Stevenson to pieces, and I was relieved when Kennedy was the convention's choice.

VIII

In 1962 the historian Daniel Boorstin published *The Image, or What Happened to the American Dream*, a work that impressed me in many ways, particularly in the distinction it made between events and what Boorstin called "pseudo-events." In this world, he wrote, there are occurrences of two kinds. Events develop either out of unexpected occurrences, like earthquakes or famines or great discoveries, or as a consequence of some human necessity, such as procreation or the satisfaction of hunger or some other ineluctable demand. Pseudo-events happen because someone arranges for them to happen. A conversation that arises when friends meet on the street is an event; a newspaper interview or a press conference is a pseudo-event. With events, time is, as a rule, beyond control; we fall sick or die not at a moment of our choosing but when some force beyond us intervenes; with pseudo-events, time is negotiable—they are, Boorstin wrote, "planned, planted, or incited." In politics—at least in American politics—elections are events, arranged not by people but mandated by the Constitution, and most of what happens between them are pseudo-events.

Kennedy's 1961 trip to Paris and Vienna was, for the most part, an event. There was mounting tension over Berlin and Southeast Asia; Kennedy and de Gaulle, then Kennedy and Khrushchev, had to come to some kind of understanding. (An understanding might have been reached by representatives of the heads of state, but summitry had become a habit, almost an institutionalized one.) War by miscalculation was a danger recognized by leaders on both sides of the Iron Curtain, and a good case could be made for a face-to-face meeting of the leaders of the superpowers, at which they might declare their purposes, tell one another what they would and would not tolerate, and settle on the spot what differences they could. But what seemed like a diplomatic mission of great urgency had a strange, almost farcical beginning. The first stop out of Washington on the way to the meeting with de Gaulle in Paris was Boston, where five thousand Massachusetts Democrats had come to dinner, at a hundred dollars a plate, to pay off their 1960 campaign debts and to celebrate the President's forty-fourth birthday. The scene was the Commonwealth Armory, its cavernous interior draped with soiled and rumpled bunting and God knows how many thousand yards of frowsy green drop cloths—the latter, presumably, to honor the first Irish-American President. One wondered what de Gaulle would have made of it. Here was a young man of great personal wealth and cultivated taste who had just been installed in the most powerful office on earth spending a long evening eating atrocious food and enduring hours of even more atrocious oratory, all to raise money for the party that had just *won* a national election. There were eighteen speakers in all, only one of whom—Robert Frost— Kennedy could have thought worth listening to. (The old poet spoke briefly and said to Kennedy that he hoped when the American met with the Russian there would be more of the Irishman than of the Harvard man in him.) Would Khrushchev have understood how it could be possible that when the White House asked if the President might deliver his remarks early so he could get a good night's rest before departing for the historic meetings, the Democrats turned him down? After some last-minute negotiations, two or three speakers were, in fact, persuaded to withdraw, and Kennedy was moved up a couple of notches, from fifteenth or sixteenth place to thirteenth. He received, of course, a great ovation, but hardly greater than that accorded Howard Fitzpatrick, the sheriff of Middlesex County, who was under indictment on criminal charges in connection with the escape of two prisoners from the county jail. And what would de Gaulle have made of the fact that the sheriff, an entrepreneur as well as a law-enforcement officer, was also the caterer who had provided that dismal banquet?

The thirteenth speaker—the President—ended his remarks with some words inscribed at the base of a statue of William Lloyd Garrison in Boston's Public Garden: "I am in earnest. I will not equivocate. I will not excuse. I will not retreat a single inch, and I will be heard." These words of a militant abolitionist seemed singularly inappropriate, if not, like so much of Kennedy's rhetoric in those days, reckless. To be sure, he was going to Paris and Vienna to be heard and to demonstrate his earnestness, but he knew very well that he would have to yield several inches here and a yard or two there, and that his mission, to be successful, might require occasional equivocation. He had, indeed, been carefully briefed to equivocate. He was to try to talk de Gaulle into accepting the concept of an integrated multinational nuclear force, but he was not to use those terms—not to breathe such words as "multinational" or "integration" in the great man's presence. The Americans wanted the French to take their NATO and their United Nations responsibilities more seriously—for some time, the French had not picked up their part of the tab for the United Nations—but de Gaulle was accustomed to bridle at a mention of either organization, especially the latter, which led him to carry on about *"les nations désunies."* And there was to be no big talk about the need to defend West Berlin. The thought of spilling blood for any German territory was anathema to the French, and, in de Gaulle's view, quite unnecessary; he was wholly convinced that the Russians would not dare to challenge the occupying forces. One of the purposes of the stay in Paris was, of course, for Kennedy to ingratiate himself not only with the French President but also with the French people. With the former he seemed to do rather well. De Gaulle had known three American Presidents—Roosevelt, Truman, and Eisenhower—and for all of them he felt little but contempt. Roosevelt had been arrogant and unappreciative; Truman and Eisenhower were ignoramuses. Kennedy, on the other hand, was literate, sophisticated, and respectful, and it did not hurt that he had brought along a wife and a press secretary who had French ancestors and spoke de Gaulle's language with some fluency. The French people, though, saw and heard little of the American President. De Gaulle may have liked Kennedy, but he saw no reason to let this foreigner—or any foreigner—conduct a personal public-relations campaign in France.

In contrast to Kennedy's 1961 trip, his 1963 trip to Germany, Ireland, England, and Italy was a pseudo-event. No crisis impended. There was nothing to be decided by anyone. There was no reason for the trip to take place except that Kennedy and some of the politicians he was to see and be seen with wanted it to, and if the press and broadcasting people had decided it was not worth bothering with it would not have taken place. It was staged so that we could write about it and talk about it and record it on film and tape. Before we started, I wrote that it would be a "super-pseudo-event" —or, rather, a series of them. ("Pseudo-events," Boorstin had written, "spawn other pseudo-events in geometrical progression.") It was, in any case, a remarkable journey. What Kennedy was trying to do, I thought and wrote, was to establish himself as a European politician—an American seeking support abroad in the way he would seek it at home, and with much the same methods he had used in his campaign for the presidency. De Gaulle was his Nixon, Konrad Adenauer was his Mayor Richard Daley of Chicago. He was determined to go to Berlin in June, because de Gaulle had planned a trip there in July (on the Fourth of July, no less), and Kennedy wanted the West German vote—the vote registered by people on their feet in the streets. He may have hoped for the same in England, but by the time he got there the Macmillan Government was under siege because of the multiple sexual escapades and political indiscretions known collectively as the Profumo Affair, and the meetings of the President and the Prime Minister were held not in London but in Birch Grove, Sussex, arranged to deflect publicity rather than to attract it. The visit to Italy was to have been another exercise in crowdsmanship, but it could not be counted a success. Rome was distracted. The Christian Democrat government of Amintore Fanfani had recently fallen. Pope John XXIII had died a month earlier and been succeeded by Cardinal Montini, whose coronation as Pope Paul VI took place just before Kennedy's arrival. There was nothing pseudo about these events. The President did see the new Pope—a family friend—who endorsed civil rights in the United States and disarmament in the world. But the Italians were not greatly concerned with such matters as the multilateral nuclear force, test-ban treaties, or even the fate of Berlin. The crowds in Rome were thin and the heat was oppressive; at the Vatican, a husky young member of the Swiss Guard fainted from heat prostration as Kennedy went by.

On the other hand, the visits to Germany and Ireland were, as pseudo-events, enormously successful. I have never seen such crowds as those that turned out in Cologne, Bonn, Frankfurt, Wiesbaden, and Berlin. When Kennedy came to New York toward the end of the 1960 campaign, there had been enormous crowds—a good many more than a million people showed up altogether—and in some places they had got so out of hand that the motorcade was trapped inside them. Even so, not one in seven New Yorkers had turned out in those autumn days, whereas in West Berlin that summer about 60 percent of the total population rallied around. About a million and a half people were in the streets or, if not actually on the pavement, on the roofs and balconies—anywhere they could find a place—and the first-aid stations had to handle numerous cases of near suffocation. "The President's motorcade," I wrote on July 26, "has just completed a forty-mile swing around the city, which means that it passed forty miles of Berliners standing never less than four or five deep on both sides of the street." It struck me—six months before Dallas—as an extraordinarily risky undertaking. The crowds were orderly and the police and security people efficient in keeping the way clear, but there could have been ten thousand assassins in those crowds, with no defense against them. And Kennedy reveled in the crush, which struck me as uncharacteristic. He did not, as a rule, relish being in the middle of mobs. He needed them, but they made him uneasy, as he told me one evening shortly before Election Day in 1960, when his hand and arm were almost bloody from handshaking in and around Philadelphia. "Thank God, I won't be going through this on Tuesday, win or lose," he said. And at home, the President had counseled the civil-rights controversy to get "off the streets and into the courts." But in Europe now, he was seeking to get foreign policy out of the courts of primary jurisdiction—the parliaments, the chancelleries, the United Nations—and put it on the streets. He was a carpetbagger, a foreign agitator crying, *"Ich bin ein Berliner!"*

And he got caught up in the mob spirit himself, losing his celebrated cool. "There are some who say in Europe and elsewhere, 'We can work with the Communists,' " he said in the Rathausplatz. "Let them come to Berlin." But it was part of his policy to work with Communists; he had said so in a speech at American University, in Washington, a few weeks earlier, and he was shortly to send Averell Harriman to Moscow in search of a deal. His bellicose words were pleasing to the Berliners but chilling to most of the allies, and our ambassadors all over Europe were compelled to explain that the President didn't quite mean what he had said.

Although the Irish tour in 1963 was a pseudo-event almost devoid of political intent or content, it enabled the President to enter a few corrections on the record. In his speech before a joint session of the Dáil, he sent a message to Khrushchev, saying that in his view there are "no permanent enemies," adding, "Hostility today is a fact, but it is not a ruling law." For the rest, despite a good deal of sham— and in part because of it—the trip was a high-spirited lark that provided good copy and good film. It was, in a way, a mock miniversion of the sort of journey that many Americans have undertaken in search of their roots. Kennedy was not serious, and certainly not sentimental, as others were, though the phrase "sentimental journey" seemed to occur somewhere in every newspaper account. His mind was relaxed and playful, as when, in Cork, he introduced a traveling companion, Monsignor Jeremiah O'Mahoney, as the "pastor of a poor, humble flock in Palm Beach, Florida." He went along cheerfully with the sham. The Boston Kennedys knew little of their Irish forebears, and had made no great effort to find out more. There was reason to believe that Kennedy's paternal great-grandfather, Patrick, had come from County Wexford, possibly from a village named Dunganstown, but there was no reason at all to believe that Patrick's homestead was the Dunganstown cottage that became a souvenir shop when Kennedy became President. It was even less likely that in 1846 Patrick Kennedy had gone to the town of New Ross, at the mouth of the River Barrow, to board a ship for Noodle's Island, in Boston Harbor. (In James MacGregor Burns's 1960 biography, *John Kennedy: A Political Profile*, it is said that "doubtless he boarded a Cunarder at Cork or Liverpool and crossed the Atlantic in the crowded steerage.") But the stories about Dunganstown and New Ross had a plausible sound, and everyone went along with them. Kennedy made an appearance at the putative homestead—where the pigsty had been converted into a mount for television gear and the farmyard had been paved with concrete so that the presidential party would not be standing around ankle-deep in the mud—had tea with some neighbors, walked around a bit, and left without entering the souvenir shop. And at the supposed port of embarkation, New Ross, he and the rest of us met a man who was every bit as impressive as anyone we had encountered on the trip and a good deal more entertaining than the movers and shakers Kennedy had been coping with. He was Andrew Minihan, a highly cultivated local manufacturer, whose integrity was as bristly as his beard and rough tweeds. The chairman of the New Ross Town Board, he had been assigned to represent the community at the festivities. He agreed to do so, he told us, because he liked what he knew of the President—and he seemed to know a lot—but he was also a man who knew a pseudo-event when he saw one, and he found much of his task vexing. "Every man must justify his existence somehow," he told a group of us in the bar of the New Ross Hotel, "but I've better ways of justifying my own than standing around with your American G-men and arguing whether the northeast corner of the dais should be *there* or *there.*" To him, Secret Service agents were G-men, and one of his "theres" was a spot on the barroom floor, which he pointed to with a toe; the other was about four inches away. "And I'll not live," he went on, "to see a sight more ridiculous than your G-men combing out dung piles to see if we've planted bombs and merciful God only knows what else in them." The ultimate affront had come, he said, when the Americans inquired when he planned to remove a dung heap of impressive size and bouquet that stood on the dockside not far from where the President was to speak. "Remove it?" he told them. "I've no plan to remove it! As a matter of fact, we thought to add to it. It would be good for the character of your President to have to cross a veritable alp of dung on his way to the New Ross speakers' stand." Matters reached such a pass that our ambassador, Matthew McCloskey, was forced to intervene, with the help of some brass from the Foreign Office in Dublin. Whereupon Minihan remarked that of course he had planned all along to dispatch the odoriferous heap, but didn't want to be ordered about by some presumptuous and officious G-men. He explained himself to the President, who was charmed by him and by the knowledge that the two of them were engaged in a shameless but harmless fraud.

"In the summer of 1963," Arthur Schlesinger wrote in *A Thousand Days*, "John F. Kennedy could have carried every country in Western Europe." This was hyperbole, but it was, I think, Kennedy's aim—or one of them—to build an international constituency. Even if de Gaulle had given him more of a chance, I doubt if he could have made much of an appeal in France, where he was too far to the left for the conservatives and too far to the right for the radicals. But he stirred the Germans, partly because he stirred them up, and he was immensely popular with the British. Had he lived and gone on with these tours, he might have become the world figure Franklin Roosevelt was. Roosevelt did it without putting in any personal appearances—he traveled only in wartime, and with great secrecy—but Kennedy, too, was becoming known to people who had never seen him or heard him and would not have understood him if they had.

There is a stoic side of Kennedy's temperament, which may have been born of his intimacy with pain and of his several brushes with death, that leads him to turn aside almost any discussion of his attitude toward himself.* He is an endlessly speculative man and, his friends believe, an uncommonly inward one. But as a general rule he regards his own experience of

* Editor's Note: Shortly after Kennedy's inauguration, Rovere started working on a Profile of the President for *The New Yorker*, but he abandoned it several months before the assassination. This passage is excerpted from that unfinished piece.

himself as being as unprofitable a subject for speculation and discussion as the weather; and when he is asked to reflect upon the present state of his own mind and consciousness he is likely to respond in coldly analytic terms or oblique wisecracks or in short flights of irony.

As far as is known, he has only once dealt with a head-on question about his own inner reactions toward his present position. This was on a jewel of a day toward the end of the summer of 1961. He was sitting on a broad and handsome lawn in Newport, Rhode Island, talking about whatever came to mind with three old and good friends, none of them members of his administration. It happened to be at a time when the newspapers were running some detailed accounts of the problems that his adversary of the preceding year, Richard M. Nixon, had been having with former Governor Goodwin Knight and other eminent figures in California politics. It happened, too, to be at a time when Kennedy had had more than the usual presidential novice's share of troubles. The Bay of Pigs, though behind him, was unforgotten; he had been to Paris, where de Gaulle had been cool, and to Vienna, where Khrushchev had been chilling; there was tension over Laos, Berlin, and the Congo; it was clear that the superpowers would shortly resume nuclear testing; there had been several congressional rebuffs. But this moment in Newport was one of powerful contrast. A spectacular sunset was in the making. The marine traffic on Narragansett Bay was busy, orderly, and fascinating to watch. While the President, as physically relaxed as it is ever possible for him to be, puffed on his excellent pre-Castro Havana cigar and let his questing mind play over varying matters of interest, a handsome, sturdy battlewagon of the United States Navy steamed past the lawn on which the President sat. Colors were dipped in homage and respect to the Commander in Chief, all hands were on deck in shining uniforms, the ship maneuvered faultlessly against the backdrop of the fine sunset. One of the President's friends was deeply moved. A small lump rose in his throat; though hardly a more sentimental man than Kennedy, he nevertheless became aware of a patriotic glow about the temples. It seemed a proper occasion for the large question the friend had up to now hesitated to put. He turned to Kennedy and boldly put it: "What do you *feel* at a moment like this? What is it *like* to be President?" The President grinned, looked at his cigar, flicked its ash, and said, "I don't know, but I'll tell you this—it sure beats being pushed around by Goody Knight in California."

Irony is the language the President speaks a large part of the time. It infrequently finds its way into his public statements, for its capacity for being misunderstood makes it one of the poorest mediums of public communication. Yet it can be very useful as a technique of polite though not dishonest evasion, and it is for this purpose, one imagines, that the President uses it when asked to turn his inward sensibilities outward. "He does not use words that carry a high charge of feeling," an associate has said. "There are ways in which he is very much like the last President from Massachusetts—Coolidge. When he describes something as 'interesting,' you are safe in assuming that he has gone about as far as he can go in expressing enthusiasm."

No President since Lincoln has begun a term with problems as grave and as numerous and as bleak in terms of available solutions as those Kennedy has faced in his first two years. Certainly none of his recent predecessors confronted anything like what he has had to confront. Franklin Roosevelt took office in a period of suffering and vast dislocation, but he had, or thought he had, the remedies at hand, and the naysayers in Congress could have caucused in an alcove. Truman had to decide, almost right away, whether or not to use the first atomic bomb, but Truman in those days regarded himself principally as the executor of Roosevelt's political estate, and when those men in whom Roosevelt had placed the most confidence recommended that he go ahead, the decision was not too difficult. By contrast, Kennedy's lot has been unenviable in the extreme. He assumed office with nothing that could be called a mandate. In almost every crisis, the road he has taken has been as perilous as the road he has not taken, and he has had to follow it in the knowledge that it would lead him to a place where he did not care to go. In his first month in office, he had to come close to the brink of war in Laos. In his third month, it was the agony of the Bay of Pigs. Neither history nor Eisenhower could be faulted for this one. The CIA and the Pentagon had set it up, but Kennedy could have knocked it down— or, armed with the Monroe Doctrine, he could have gone in with a few obsolete jets and a few platoons of Marines, and that would have been the end of Castro—though, of course, that would also have been the beginning of much else, perhaps even more anguishing. In May of 1962, he authorized the resumption of nuclear testing in the atmosphere—a course of action he hated. "I was anti-test in my guts," he said, and indeed he was. He did not proceed until he had devoted sufficient study to the question to become, according to his science adviser, Dr. Jerome Wiesner, "the leading American authority on the problem." He concluded that testing was necessary—that is to say, that there was somewhat more jeopardy in not testing than in testing. What seems "necessary" and therefore "right" can, however, often give terrible offense to the guts. His commitment in principle to disarmament is of the sort that in another man might be described as a passion, yet in fact he has accelerated the arms race. He deemed it inadvisable to smash the Berlin Wall, and he decided that Castro should not be blasted from the Caribbean; the shameful wall still stands, and Castro still struts and taunts and tyrannizes. Kennedy would be the last man to complain much about his luck, however. He was brought up on W. E. Henley's "Invictus," and he really believes that sort of thing. Yet the feeling is widespread in Washington that in his first two years he was given an exceedingly bum rap by history.

The President is an uncommonly restless man. When, in public, he saws the air with his right forearm or admonishes his left hand with his right forefinger, the gestures are not forensic or elocutionary. He is the very opposite of a self-dramatizer. He is simply responding to a law of his being that requires that some part of his body always be in motion. In ordinary conversation, seated, he is always doing something other than sitting and talking. Kennedy "never merely sits in a chair," Fletcher Knebel has written. "He bivouacs in it." When a boston rocker was put in his office, it was reported that his physician, Dr. Janet Travell, had prescribed it as back therapy. Plainly, though, it satisfied other needs. In it, he maneuvers about and he rocks. The fingers of his left hand are always in motion; he drums on tabletops and chair arms, he taps his teeth, he massages his ankles, he tidies up papers that don't need tidying up. When circumstances permit, he paces. In more or less formal conferences, he stays more or less put, though never at rest, in his chair, but in smaller gatherings he moves from his chair to the far end of his desk, and back to the chair, and about the room. There is a touch of the claustrophobe in him, and he often works with the door to the office of Mrs. Evelyn Lincoln, his secretary, wide open—thus being visible and audible to the large numbers of people who troop in and out of her office. In seasonable weather, he does a good deal of his small-conference pacing on the White House lawn, opening the french windows in his office and summoning his visitor to join him on a nervous stroll, which may include a stopover in the children's play area. Physical relaxation and ordinary quietude come very hard to him. He likes movies, but finds it hard to stay with them. Of the forty-odd films that have been shown in the White House during his tenancy, he has managed to sit through only one—*West Side Story*. He stuck it out for five minutes of *Last Year in Marienbad*. He has given up going to public showings, because he does not want his departures to be read as the ultimate in bad notices. It is not that his attention span is short. He is capable of something approaching total concentration. Print puts him in a trance. He reads with enormous speed and seems mesmerized in the process. He moves the book around, but his eyes never leave it. He moves himself around, too, as he reads: he stands, he walks, he sits—the eyes glued to the paper but the body peripatetic. He scribbles in margins. If there is anyone else about, he discusses.

No President has been a more generous patron of amateurs than Kennedy. There is a legend that one of the things that made him so formidable a candidate in 1960 was the experience and disinterested professionalism of the group to which he entrusted his political fortunes—his brother Robert and the cluster of attractive and literate Massachusetts Hibernians sometimes spoken of as "the Irish Mafia." The legend is largely false. To the extent that these men have been with Kennedy during a large part of his career and have acquired a good deal of on-the-job training, they may be regarded as men of skill in a settled and chosen vocation, but nearly all of them began their association with the President as dilettantes and adventurers, who became involved in politics simply because life threw them together with one Kennedy or another, and because the Kennedy clan found that they met the family standards of congeniality, industry, and loyalty to Kennedy causes. Kennedy tends to regard politics as a not particularly arcane business whose operating principles can be mastered by any man of sound intelligence and nonabrasive personality. Experience, though useful, is not essential. Kennedy feels about government more or less as he feels about politics. In 1960, when he faced a particularly troublesome political situation in the Democratic

Party in New York State, his choice of a man to represent his interests there was an abstract-expressionist painter named William Walton. Walton performed his campaign mission creditably and would have been a member of the administration if his interest in politics had been more than dilettantish and if he had needed gainful employment. When Lincoln was President, he never once knew that Walt Whitman was in residence across Lafayette Square. It just could not happen that Kennedy would remain unaware of the existence of a major poet so close at hand. Kennedy's curiosity is such that he could not bear *not* to know. Had he been Lincoln, he would have known that Whitman had a government job in Washington (he was to lose it, shortly after Lincoln's death, as the author of a "filthy little book"), and this fragment of information would have led to a need for more information, which he would have been fairly certain to elicit from Whitman himself. (As it was, Lincoln and Whitman never met. "I see the President almost every day, as I happen to live near where he passes to and from his lodgings out of town," Walt Whitman wrote to the New York *Times* on August 12, 1863. Whitman lived at 394 L Street, a few blocks from the White House. President Lincoln spent the summer nights at the Soldiers' Home, about three miles north of the White House and a few degrees cooler, and the poet was accustomed to seeing the President at about eight-thirty each morning as Lincoln, either astride a gray cavalry horse or riding in an open barouche, came down Vermont Avenue, accompanied by some thirty-odd mounted troops with sabers drawn. "We have got so that we exchange bows, and very cordial ones," Whitman reported, but Lincoln probably had not the faintest idea who the man was with whom he was exchanging cordial bows each morning.) A few months after taking office, Kennedy learned—and was amazed not to have been told earlier—that the daughter of an eminent philosopher had thrown in her lot with the New Frontier. Kennedy barely knew the girl's father, and he had probably not mastered much of his work, which tends to be highly abstruse, but he knew that the man was an ornament of American culture. He invited the young woman to the White House to ask her how things were going on her job.

The Kennedys have had to the White House nearly all the leaders of the American intellectual community and a fair number of the shock troops. They come by the score, formally dressed and gowned, to the large *fêtes*—the Casals concert, the Stravinsky concert, the dinner for the Nobel laureates, the *fête champêtre* at Mount Vernon for Mohammed Ayub Khan of Pakistan, the dinner for André Malraux. They come by the dozen or the half dozen to the smaller and less widely publicized affairs—afternoon teas, informal dinner parties, after-dinner receptions—or by twos and threes and fours for luncheons with the President or Mrs. Kennedy or both. An effort has been made not to slight any of the arts, fine or lively, or the sciences, pure or applied, or the learned professions. The handful of those cultural eminences who have never been received at the White House either declined invitations or were not asked because their acceptance would have been an acute embarrassment to the host, the guest, or both. The late William Faulkner was a decliner. As a Nobel laureate, he was invited to the great roundup of his fellows in March 1961, but tendered his regrets and explained to the press that the journey from Oxford, Mississippi, to Washington, D.C., seemed a bit too long to be undertaken "just for a meal." The failure of the Kennedys to ask Norman Mailer to drop by—a failure discussed by Mailer in several thousand words in the July 1962 issue of *Esquire*—was doubtless an exercise of social and political judgment. Mailer felt that he was entitled to a place at table by virtue of his contributions to American letters, but among his contributions had been an open letter to the President calling him "rich and smug and scared of the power of the worst,

dullest, and most oppressive men of our land," and saying that
Fidel Castro was "at the moment a far greater figure than
yourself." In general, though, the guest list has included not
only severe and active critics of the administration—such as
Dr. Linus Pauling, who left a picket line outside the White
House protesting the bomb tests to put on a dinner jacket and
enter it for the Nobel reception—but people who regard the
United States today as just about beyond redemption. The
Kennedys have played host to James T. Farrell, a bitter anti-
Communist who nevertheless believes that the present social
order is so steeped in corruption that it should be destroyed; to
Edmund Wilson, who professed a total inability to distinguish
morally between the foreign policy of the United States and
that of the Soviet Union, and who was heard to mutter
"Hooey" at the Malraux dinner when the French Minister of
Culture complimented the United States for never having
sought an empire; and to the black novelist James Baldwin,
who not only regards himself as thoroughly alienated from
American society but whose novels have dealt with varieties of
erotic experience that Henry Miller has yet to hear about.

There is no doubt that Kennedy's systematic cultivation of
the intellectuals is one of the things that sets his administration
apart from all previous ones. There have been Presidents, even
in this century, whose concern for the life of the mind has
equaled his, and whose personal cultivation has perhaps exceeded his. Kennedy's essential gifts of mind are quickness,
flexibility, breadth of interest, and wit. He is far from being the
best educated of Presidents, even if one leaves out of account
those who were children of the Enlightenment—the Adamses,
Jefferson, and Madison. His background in literature does not
match that of Theodore Roosevelt, who enjoyed the company
of poets, read Dante in Renaissance Italian, could rattle off
long passages in French from the *Chanson de Roland*, made a
special study of Rumanian literature, and, while President of

the United States, was also honorary president of the Gaelic
Literature Association. In history, Kennedy is well informed on
the eighteenth and nineteenth centuries in England and on the
history of this republic, but Woodrow Wilson's knowledge was
deeper and better organized; he was a formidable historian,
though one, certainly, of narrower vision. Kennedy has no
knowledge of another civilization comparable to Herbert Hoover's knowledge of China; Hoover translated a scientific treatise
from the Latin at the age of thirty and is credited with the
authorship of thirty books. But no past President ever undertook to identify the White House with the whole range of the
country's intellectual life. None ever made it a matter of administration policy to look upon the intellectuals as a national
asset that the government should recognize and declare.

Within a fairly brief period in 1961, Arthur Schlesinger, Jr.,
arranged talks with the President for distinguished representatives of three intellectual communities—D. W. Brogan, the
historian from England; Raymond Aron, the sociologist from
France; and Alfred Kazin, the American literary critic. Each
had a White House luncheon, each questioned the President at
some length, and each went off and wrote about him—on the
whole unfavorably, a fact that let Schlesinger in for a good deal
of presidential twitting. Kazin's disappointment was fairly characteristic. In a subsequent article called "The President and
Other Intellectuals," he said that he was enormously impressed
by the President's mental agility, by his passion for learning, by
his respect for intellectual achievement, by his general good
taste in books and people and ideas. He found, he said, only
one thing lacking in the President—conviction. He, Kazin, had
wanted to know not only what Kennedy was able to do with his
mind but what his intellectual commitments were—what he
believed—and on this matter he could not seem to get anywhere.

The condition that Kazin found deplorable unquestionably exists. The President is not a man deeply committed in the sense that Kazin would like him to be. His turn of mind is eclectic, improvising, endlessly skeptical; his tradition is that of Mr. Justice Holmes, who said, "What I mean by truth is what I can't help believing." Holmes regarded fixed values as encumbrances, and one has the impression that the President feels the same way. One imagines, indeed, that Kennedy would tend to agree that he runs a bit short on convictions and beliefs—if by these terms Kazin and similarly disposed critics mean more or less settled opinions on more or less ultimate questions. No identifiable tradition contains Kennedy. He is a Roman Catholic, but his Catholicism is an inheritance and does not appear to influence his thought any more than his inheritance of wealth and Irish blood does. (This seems generally true of American Catholic politicians. It was easier by far to see the Protestant in Herbert Hoover than the Catholic in Alfred E. Smith. It was practically impossible to see the Catholic in Joseph R. McCarthy.) He never shows much interest in metaphysical questions or in abstract moral ones. The values he appears to respect the most are morally—and even, for the most part, politically—neutral: courage, learning, sophistication, taste, style. In *Profiles in Courage*, as he went to some lengths to point out, he celebrated the gallantry and doggedness of senators who exhibited these qualities, at the risk of their careers, in causes that were less defensible than those of their opponents. "I make no claim that all of those who staked their careers to speak their minds were right," he wrote. "Indeed, [Daniel] Webster, [Thomas Hart] Benton, and [Sam] Houston could not all have been right on the Compromise of 1850, for each of them, in pursuit of the same objective of preserving the Union, held wholly different views on that one omnibus measure." At the same time, Kennedy would not make an absolute value even of courage; he honors compromise almost as much—even on matters of principle—and holds that there are times when the most courageous of senators should not risk their careers, "for senators who go down to defeat in a vain defense of a single principle will not be on hand to fight for that or any other principle in the future."

There are certain clear disadvantages to the detachment and objectivity that characterize Kennedy's mind. They tend, for one thing, to make his political rhetoric rather dry, moving him to the irony of which he is a master. But any politician with a tendency to irony must suppress the tendency or risk mystifying, rather than enlightening, his audience. The Kennedy style is sometimes elegant but almost always passionless. If, in 1960, the nonstylistic endowments of Senator Hubert Humphrey, of Minnesota, had been equal to those of the then Senator Kennedy, Humphrey might well have had the nomination. Humphrey is a robust, visceral liberal with deep roots in Populism. He has a capacity for anger on the one hand and for avowal on the other, and this makes his speeches swing. Where, in 1960, Kennedy commanded respect, Humphrey commanded both respect and affection. And if Kennedy had had to compete with the Adlai Stevenson of 1952, or even of 1956, his coolness might have undone him. The affection that Humphrey is capable of arousing differs in kind from that which sustained Stevenson. Stevenson may have been no stronger on passion than Kennedy, but he seemed, in his day, full of compassion. And he was committed. Kennedy's sophisticated doctrine of courage-*cum*-compromise enabled him to get through the McCarthy years without audible protest. And it can be argued that Kennedy's lack of commitment has harmed him even in victory. On the eve of the Bay of Pigs, for example, a firm view of almost any sort would have served him better than his lack of one. Had he come into office believing that the kind of intervention the Eisenhower administration had planned was wrong in principle, he would have been spared the anguish of the fiasco, and if, on the other hand, he believed that it was terribly important to rid Cuba of Castro, Castro would no longer be. As it turned out, he got the worst of both courses.

Yet the disadvantages of Kennedy's position are ones that he has shared with the greatest of our Presidents. Washington was profoundly unideological—in a manner of speaking, mindless. Intellectually, Lincoln was one of the slipperiest creatures of his age. He believed in the American Revolution and in the Union, and he wished to preserve both, but this aim had very little moral or philosophical content. In a great piece of rhetoric, Lincoln said that the nation could not endure half slave and half free—a dubious proposition at best and one that he himself did not always adhere to. Until he issued the Emancipation Proclamation, a good bit after the war got under way, a half-slave/half-free Union was precisely what he was committed to. (If communism is slavery, as all our official verbiage holds that it is, then the United States under Kennedy, as under Eisenhower, is firmly committed to the proposition that the world *can* endure in the condition in which Lincoln said the nation could not. John Foster Dulles was the last abolitionist.) Franklin Roosevelt, too, was innocent of ideology. Indeed, he was—from the point of view represented by Kazin—by far the most unqualified of Presidents. He was an improviser who was as ready to borrow from the corporate state as he was ready to design the welfare state. Ditto Teddy Roosevelt. The ideologists who have held the presidency have done far less well than the others. Thomas Jefferson was a great statesman and a formidable philosopher, but his term as Chief Magistrate left much to be desired and much to be accomplished by others. . . .

5

Journeys and Escapes

I

Africa was where he had been happiest in the good time of his life, so he had come out here to start again.

—Ernest Hemingway,
The Snows of Kilimanjaro

I have never been to Africa and have never, at least in my riper years, given much thought to going there, but I am shortly to go, and although the initial spur was not to recover or discover anything there, the satisfaction I take in the impending journey is in some ways similar to that of Hemingway's Harry. He was, and I am, a writer in professional difficulties.* I

* EDITOR'S NOTE: In the 1960s, in the aftermath of the assassination of a President he had come to respect, in a time of urban rebellions and racial dissension and the war in Vietnam, Rovere sought escape in absorption in other cultures, traveling—"as a fugitive," in his term—to Kenya in 1966 (on an official mission to evaluate the Peace Corps), to Africa again (on a State Department tour) in 1967, to West Germany, to the mountains of northern New Mexico (to evaluate an antipoverty program for the Ford Foundation), to England, to Canada. This passage is taken from a

have not quite reached Harry's last stage—in which he "did no work at all"—but I have approached it, and I don't like the signs I see down the road ahead. Harry wanted "to work the fat off his soul." A growing obesity of mind and temper is also something of which I am very much aware. I don't expect any cures in Africa—where, I understand, corpulence is in some places much admired, and cultivated by women in "fatting parlors"—but I am hoping that leaving this country at this time will help a good deal, and that Africa will prove a good place in which to perform certain exercises I have in mind.

I have been rereading Hemingway on Africa (a disillusioning experience, by and large), because it is to his favorite part of the continent, Kenya, that I shall be going. I shall go unarmed, though it can be said that my principal occupation while there will be troubleshooting. I go to Kenya as an agent of the Peace Corps—specifically of its Evaluation Program. This is a remarkable program, without precedent, to the best of my knowledge, in the federal government, and perhaps the first of its kind in any government. Most bureaus in most bureaucracies have always had inspectors of one kind or another—employees whose job it is to check up on the work of other employees, to audit accounts, to observe the progress of bureaucratic projects, and so forth. In this government, and no doubt in others, the work is often done honestly and competently. Still, it is always a matter of government agencies checking up on government agencies, of bureaucrats appraising the work of bureaucrats. The Peace Corps is bringing in outsiders—critics of government like me—and asking them to dwell less on success than on failure. Actually, it is easier to be against the Boy Scouts (militaristic, Baden-Powell do-good) than against the Peace Corps (coeducational, pragmatic, developmental). When American reporters have taken time out from the Cold War to have a look at the Peace Corps, they have always found them-

---

1966 draft of a work to be called "Out of America," and from his report to the Peace Corps, made in the same year.

selves predisposed to admiration—to a gee-whiz, isn't it great, these splendid-ingenious-undismayed-American-kids-out-in-the-boondocks-when-they-could-be-lapping-up-cream-back-home kind of story. The journalistic scolds have either overlooked the Peace Corps or been taken in by it. Yet the PC (I am now sufficiently indoctrinated to use the initials) knows that there are, there must be, failures, goof-offs, even (God forbid) corruption. . . .

I spent a month in Kenya with Peace Corps staff and volunteers. I had extensive talks with more than seventy volunteers, mostly at their stations; a staff member accompanied me—or us, for my wife was with me most of the time—on each trip out of Nairobi. I kept no precise route or mileage records, but close scrutiny of a map discloses that I saw something of every inhabited section of the country and quite a bit of the largely uninhabited sections. I can assert that former Ambassador William Attwood didn't know what he was talking about when he told me I would never be more than fifty miles from a golf course.

I saw more of Robert Poole, the director, than of any other staff member. I have rarely encountered a public servant whose character and capabilities have impressed me so deeply. In coming to this opinion, I surprised and, in a way, disappointed myself. When I heard that he had been a football coach and a prep-school history teacher, I was appalled at the thought of having to spend many days and nights with him in the close quarters afforded by Land Rovers, small planes, and, for all I knew, pup tents. The fact is that in my adolescence and early manhood I was able to stay on excellent terms with my father only, as I see it, because I was able to discharge on football coaches and prep-school teachers all the hostilities that sons normally reserve for their fathers. Poole personified two historic enemies, and when we met in Washington, several weeks before I left for Kenya, I could see that he wore the face and exhibited the manner, as to it born, of all my oppressors. But in Kenya my bigotry dissolved in the cool, agreeable air, and although I never quite got over feeling guilty whenever I smoked in his earnest and athletic presence, I was ready, by the time I left, to lobby for him as ambassador to Kenya or just about anything else. I hope that the future, for its own sake, uses him well. . . .†

I submitted my evaluation report to the Peace Corps in 1966, but that was not the end of the matter for Eleanor and me—nor was it to be for several years. On most of our up-country trips in Kenya we had been accompanied by Sidney Pemba (not his real name), a young Tanzanian who worked on Robert Poole's staff as a jack-of-all-trades—Land Rover driver and mechanic, guide, interpreter, quartermaster, hewer of wood and drawer of water. He was the only African on the staff (there was another non-American, an Indian bookkeeper), and the only African we got to know well enough to call by his first name. He was a small, ruggedly built man of about thirty with a quick intelligence, always in high spirits, it seemed, and always enthusiastic about whatever job came to hand. Among the young American volunteers, he was easily the best-liked and least suspect figure on the Peace Corps staff in Nairobi—not excepting Poole, who, though admired and respected, represented Washington and Authority. Sidney somehow seemed American. He liked American jokes, and he could wisecrack with the sharpest of the volunteer kids, many of whom were very sharp indeed. They laughed at him as well as with him—something they were careful not to do with other Africans. In his case, there was never any question of giving offense —he laughed at himself and gave as good as he got. And he was very much at home with American artifacts—automobiles, motorcycles, transistor radios, tape recorders, guitars, cameras, and the rest. He could work them all and make them work when others couldn't

† EDITOR'S NOTE: Poole was killed in an automobile accident in Kenya not long before Rovere's own death. At the time, he was working as director of African operations for the African Wildlife Leadership Foundation.

seem to. Rare for an African, he was, like Poole, extremely interested in wildlife and vegetation, and Bob said he was the only African he'd known who liked mountain climbing. He became the first
black member of the Mount Kenya Club.

Eleanor and I were charmed by Sidney from the start. Before
leaving Nairobi, we worked out a plan with Marie Gadsden, who
supervised the Peace Corps teaching programs in Kenya and
Uganda, to try to get him the sort of education that we felt he
deserved and that, he told us, he wanted. His job with the Peace
Corps was fine as far as it went, but it didn't have much of a future.
And Sidney was already older than most of the people he was working for and with. With a little help, we thought, he could have a fine
and useful future. He had finished, or nearly finished, grade school
at a missionary (Roman Catholic) institution in Tanzania. Moreover, Sidney also seemed an uncommonly good risk from the African point of view. Too often, when Africans go to school here or in
Europe, they never see Africa again, or if they do they are miserable.
In a coastal village near Mombasa, we met a young man who had
spent two or three years at Harvard studying public health, nutri-
tion, town planning, and the like; he had returned to serve his country, and was probably doing it very well, but he was plainly wretched
—alienated by education from the people among whom he had
grown up. He was much more interested in talking about life at
Cambridge than about life in Kenya. I knew of a program in a fine
New England college to teach the economics of growth and development to thirty or forty young Africans a year; the idea, of course,
was that after receiving this training they would go home and try to
apply what they had learned, but in fact what happened was that
nearly all of them stayed in the United States, some of them selling
insurance or automobiles, some pumping gas, and some—the
brightest of the lot—teaching economic growth and development to
other young Africans, who in turn would become American salesmen or accountants or whatever. The program was more than just a
waste of time and money; it was removing from African life the kind

of talent most needed there. But this, we were confident, would not happen with Sidney. He had the Peace Corps mentality: the volunteer spirit and idealism. He loved life in Africa; he wanted to climb every mountain on the continent; he would never choose a life as a salesman in Boston or Providence over an outdoor life in the Great Rift Valley.

The scheme we worked out with Marie Gadsden was to bring Sidney to the United States (we would pay the travel expenses from Nairobi and, eventually, back) and have him live with us in Rhinebeck. Three or four years earlier, I had come to know Edward Cashin, the dean of Marist College, a young and thriving school run by the Marist Brothers in Poughkeepsie. (Unlike Vassar, Bard, and other local colleges, Marist had seized the opportunity provided by geography to become a kind of intellectual conservator of the Roosevelt heritage, and I had helped Brother Edward in organizing an annual forum where survivors of the New Deal and historians of the period met to discuss the tradition.) I told him our hopes for Sidney and asked if a scholarship could be provided. He assured me that this could be worked out; if Sidney needed extra preparation—remedial mathematics or whatever—he would arrange for help from one of the high schools in Poughkeepsie.

That seemed to be that. We paid for a Nairobi–New York air passage and wired Marie to get things moving at her end. At this point, politics and bureaucracy intervened: the Kenyan authorities could not give Sidney a passport because he was not a Kenyan. He could travel, if at all, only under a Tanzanian passport, and for that representations would have to be made to Dar es Salaam. Representations were indeed made. Weeks, months, more than a semester went by. No passport. A friend of mine, an African specialist with the Ford Foundation who was going to Dar, said he would make inquiries. He learned nothing. In the late spring of 1967, I made a second trip to Africa, this time accompanying Nicholas Katzenbach, then Under Secretary of State, on a quick tour of a dozen or so countries. In Dar, at a dinner for Katzenbach given by Julius Nyerere, the President of Tanzania, I was seated next to an English-woman who was said to be the President's principal adviser on relations with the United States and Europe. I told her Sidney's story. It seemed to me very sad, I said, that Sidney Pemba, a promising young Tanzanian who wanted to complete his education, could not get a passport. Could she help us cut through the red tape? She said she would have someone look into it. In time, I got the story, or most of it. There was no evidence that Sidney was a Tanzanian at all. He carried no papers; the school and church that he said he had attended had burned to the ground several years earlier. And, besides, the authorities reasoned, why should Tanzania, with its great need for skilled personnel, let this treasure leave the country to become someone's chauffeur in New York?

One of our reasons for wanting to help Sidney was our feeling that nothing could stop him from returning to Africa. He wasn't escaping poverty; he had done that with his Peace Corps job. I could not imagine his being satisfied with some menial job in New York. But I got the message: there would be no Tanzanian passport for Sidney, and he might grow old and gray trying to get a Kenyan one. I found this melancholy, but I was not outraged. When the Soviet Union abuses Jews and dissidents yet forbids them to live elsewhere, that is tyranny compounded. But in a poor and underdeveloped country like Tanzania, where human rights are better protected than in many more advanced countries, the control of human resources can be as defensible as the control of natural ones. We believed that bringing Sidney here for a few years would be to Africa's advantage, but we could not ask the Tanzanians to play our hunches.

I proposed to Marie that the airline tickets be redeemed for cash and the money used to send Sidney to the best school that could be found for him in Kenya. A bit later, we got a cheery letter of thanks from Sidney; he was enrolled in a technical school near the Ethiopian border, learning to drive and repair tractors and other farm machinery. Fine, we thought. But soon after—a month, perhaps two—word came that he had left the place; he simply got up one day and walked out, hiking and hitch-hiking to Nairobi, returning to the Peace Corps headquarters. I wrote for an explanation, but I should have guessed the answer. After four or five years of living and working with young Americans, Sidney had become Americanized through and through, right down to his palate. He had acquired, among other things, a taste for a varied diet—for hamburgers and hot dogs and Coca-Cola and 7-Up. In the Kenyan school in the north country, he had been fed corn and beans, beans and corn, three times a day, seven days a week. He called it quits. He had been spoiled—corrupted?—by the Peace Corps, by wisecracking American kids with their junk food. Sidney had been de-Africanized.

In, I think, 1973, seven years after we had met Sidney, a young lawyer I knew slightly—a Peace Corps veteran—turned up at my *New Yorker* office accompanied by Sidney Pemba. Sidney had arrived in this country a few weeks earlier and was going to school—he must have been forty or close to it by then—in Philadelphia. He was his brisk, smiling self. How had he managed to get here? It was a long, complicated story, he said—too long to tell. Naturally, I did not press him. I supposed he was here as an illegal alien. I like to think that he is now back in Tanzania or Kenya, an official of the Wildlife Service, driving through the highlands thwarting poachers or counting warthogs or rhinos, a six-pack of Coke on the seat beside him, stopping off now and then to swap jokes with some Peace Corps kids. (There are fewer of them now, most of them older than the ones we knew, and I imagine the jokes are less proficient.) But for all I know he is here in New York clerking for some equal-opportunity employer like Macy's or Gimbels.

Out of Africa, out of Africa. I was fifty-two when I made that second trip, and I expected then to make several more and, in time, to begin to write about what I had learned and unlearned. But now it is more than a decade later, and I sit here in *The New Yorker* office in which Sidney inexplicably turned up five years ago, and I am

ridden by pain. Even the simplest of journeys—a walk down the hall
—is painful, and I won't be seeing Africa again, perhaps not even
Europe. But the memory of that 1967 trip is a splendid one. A
friend of mine—Wayne Fredericks, a civil engineer who knew Africa well and loved it—was at the time deputy assistant secretary of
state for African affairs and doing all he could to persuade some
high-ranking official—the President, the Vice-President, the Secretary of State—to make a kind of grand tour to demonstrate and
publicize American concern. But Johnson was too busy bombing
Vietnam, Humphrey was too busy trying to hold Johnson's world
together, and Dean Rusk wasn't interested. Katzenbach was. He was
a big, hearty lawyer, jovial and articulate, an Air Force veteran and a
Rhodes scholar, a repository of what was left of New Frontier idealism. He was delighted by the assignment—anything to get out of
Washington in that awful year—and he carried it off very well.
Wayne had little luck persuading publishers to send correspondents
along, since the trip was no big deal—a ceremonial swing around
Africa by a bureaucrat with no say in policy matters. The only regular to sign up was Benjamin Welles, of the *Times*. When Wayne
told me this, I decided that the project was perfect for me. If there
was to be a large press contingent and much news to be made, I'd
have stayed home. But a small party was ideal for my purposes.
There would be plenty of time to talk and to learn.

Our small expedition was a small masterpiece of American savvy,
political and organizational. There was one minor drawback to this:
we flew all over Africa in a windowless aircraft, crossing the jungles,
the plains, the mountains, the deserts in a plane that might as well
have been a subway or a submarine. Still, we made quite a show.
The Air Force flight crew was all black. They were spit-and-polish
precision fliers; in mufti, they could have been the Harlem Globe-
trotters. Our cicerone was Irvin Hicks, a bright, fast-talking young
black Foreign Service officer—another New Frontier idealist. The
flight physician was a black dermatologist from Howard University
Medical School. The Africanologists were mostly black. Deplaning

in airports, we looked like a delegation from a perfectly integrated society. It was, of course, showmanship, but it didn't really bother me. The year 1967 was a terrible one in most respects (I was seizing every opportunity I could to get out of the country), but it was possible to feel that we were doing quite well with that nastiest of problems—race—and were on our way to licking it. I saw nothing wrong with a little display of the kind we were making in Africa.

We experienced some of the best and some of the worst of Africa. In Dakar, there was Leopold Senghor, the President of Senegal, a fine poet, the prophet of blackness, a man used by Charles de Gaulle as an arbiter of French usage and syntax. In Guinea, there was Sékou Touré, the holdout against any relationship with France—a man of great charm and forcefulness, and very suspicious of Americans. On to the Ivory Coast and Abidjan. I have never seen a city quite like Abidjan and never expect to. There must be more fine marble in the Presidential Palace than in all of Washington. Compared to that palace, the White House looks like lower-income housing. And the Intercontinental Hotel! Hilton piled on Sheraton piled on the Carlyle and the Waldorf and a Holiday Inn. Swimming pools, bowling alleys, saunas, tennis courts, squash courts, nightclubs, restaurants with recondite specialties like blintzes and enchiladas. And marble, marble everywhere, and, beyond the marble, mud, mud, mud. It rained on the marble and it rained on the mud; the marble glistened and the mud oozed. It was impossible to imagine a sharper, closer contrast between wealth so vulgarly displayed and squalor and poverty so easily accepted. "This is the African quarter," a taxi driver told us as we slithered along through the mud—an "African quarter" in a free African country in 1967! On the outskirts of Abidjan, the Peace Corps had a project that the volunteers very much wanted to show us. It was a kind of health-information center. Medical data on thousands of people in nearby communities had been gathered—things, I suppose, like blood types, chest X-rays, urinalyses, and other useful information. This was considered a very successful, well-run project. In a fleet of limousines, we drove out to look it over. Thunder, lightning, high winds, cloudburst after cloudburst. And minutes before our arrival, the fragile building that housed all these records flew apart and began sinking into the mud. The file cards were carried off in every direction by the gale—God knows how many years, how many thousands of man-hours had gone into making and organizing those records. It was desolation in the midst of desolation.

From the Ivory Coast to what a few years before had been the Gold Coast—Ghana. Accra, too, had a ritzy Intercontinental Hotel, but it was a scaled-down, almost austere version of Abidjan's. Not much marble but a riot of color—gaudy mammy wagons with fanciful graffiti and names, and slogans like American bumper stickers. Little over a year or so earlier, the military had toppled Kwame Nkrumah, at one time the quintessential African antiimperialist leader, and had installed a harsh, often bloody regime, the most powerful member of which seemed to be Inspector General J. W. K. Harlley, a handsome, swaggering man with cruel eyes and a cruel face. Merely to look at him, as Ben and I did in his office for an hour or so, was to see a man, cool and unfailingly correct in manner, who was capable of any brutality imaginable. He had lately arranged a series of executions—his coup had produced an abortive countercoup by a group of younger officers—and he planned to carry out one execution in Black Star Square, in the heart of the city. Invitations to the show had been sent out to all the embassies. Members of the diplomatic corps and other eminent personages had received engraved invitations to attend the dispatching of a young lieutenant. Despite the number of regrets received, the young officer met his death in front of a firing squad.

At a state dinner tendered to our party, I asked a leading lawyer —the wife of some high member of the government—whether she approved of the execution, and, of course, she said she did. It was a stupid question to put to a minister's wife; I should have known what she would say. The next day, I put the same question to a man I'd been told was a leading Ghanian journalist. What sort of journalist? I asked a man from the American Embassy. "Oh, he's a kind of Left-liberal," I was told. "I suppose you might say that his paper corresponds to *The New Republic* at home." That seemed to fix him fairly well in my mind. I asked him what *he* thought of the execution. "Couldn't have been better," he said.

II

The last of my CIA benefactions was a tour of West Germany in January of 1967 in the company of a dozen or so other writers.‡ We were told at the time that the bills were to be paid by the Ford Foundation and Atlantic-Brucke, an organization that got its money from German and American industrialists and financiers interested in improving relations between the two countries. Both sponsors were later revealed to have been conduits for CIA money for projects of this kind. I do not know whether CIA people planned the trip or merely paid for it, but whoever was responsible did an admirable job (at least from my viewpoint), choosing an interesting company, and working out a fine itinerary. We were led by Shepard Stone, a former New York *Times* reporter who had spent a lot of time in Germany in the postwar years and was now a Ford Foundation executive; and Irving Kristol, an ideological adversary of mine in the early 1950s, who had served in the Army's occupation forces a few years before that. Diana and Lionel Trilling, the eminent critics, were in the party; and so were Dwight Macdonald, the writer; Stanley Kauffmann, the drama critic; the writers Harvey Swados and George Elliott; Norman Podhoretz, the editor of *Commentary*, and his wife, Midge Decter, then an editor at *Harper's*. Altogether, I was eager to make the trip.

For a number of reasons, some by no means clear to me, Germany has attracted me more than any other country in Europe. As a child, I had been taught to hate it—to believe that everything about it was

‡ EDITOR'S NOTE: Rovere is here referring to the fact that *Encounter*, which had reprinted some of his articles, turned out to have been subsidized by the CIA.

vile and that but for the doughboys who fought at Verdun and on the Meuse I would have been put to death by Kaiser Wilhelm himself, a steel-helmeted symbol of evil more vivid to me than Satan with his horns and pitchfork. Just as I reached an age at which I put aside such nonsense, a truly satanic figure emerged to rule Germany; I did not revert to Hun hating, but I did feel that there had to be some dark force in the German character—some aberrant product of history and culture—that could produce a nation able to adapt itself so easily to so monstrous a leadership. For twenty-five years, one of our closest friends in Rhinebeck—our family doctor—was a German Jew from Munich who came here as a refugee in 1938. He was a charming and civilized man, liberal in instinct and with exquisite taste in many things. Yet he was often as ill at ease in a democratic society as he had been in a totalitarian one. When he saw things he did not like—mass demonstrations, unruly students, political extremism—he was puzzled as to why the government did not suppress them. He was particularly incensed when he read articles on medicine by laymen whom he regarded as uninformed. "Dick," he would say, "you are in this business. Why do they allow such things?" I would say that it's a free country, pretty much, with a free press, pretty much, and that was the difference between the United States and Germany. I would cite the Constitution and the relevant amendments and statutes, but it got me nowhere. A Jew and a victim of German authoritarianism, he died more German than Jewish. Yet I have known Germans who have seemed more American than German. Willy Brandt, the mayor of Berlin, who was Chancellor of the Federal Republic from 1969 to 1974, was a politician far closer to the American prototype than any of his counterparts in England, France, and Italy. And Germans take to American ways—the bad as well as the good, and perhaps to the bad more than to the good—far more easily than other Europeans. Nowhere else on the Continent are there cities as Americanized as Frankfurt and Düsseldorf, and not only because our investments in West Germany are far greater than anywhere else. The Germans like our

Hiltons and McDonalds just as we like their Volkswagens and Leicas.

But there has always been more than this to my fascination with things German. When I read, in the thirties, Christopher Isherwood's Herr Issyvoo stories, I felt that I knew the pre-Nazi society he described better than I knew the London of Evelyn Waugh or Aldous Huxley. And when, after the war, in the winter of 1953–54, I first saw Berlin, I felt that, ravaged as it was, it was a great, lovely, vibrant city, built and planned on a human scale, and more spirited in many ways than London and Paris. (Berlin, of course, was not Germany, any more than New York is the United States, and perhaps that was one of the things I liked about it. But then again it was German in the sense that New York *is* American, containing thesis, antithesis, and synthesis.) The place was still in ruins—a kind of Pompeii with inhabitants—and still threatened by terror, this time by the Communists. We stayed not in a hotel but in a rooming house just off the Kurfürstendamm, within sight of the Gedächtniskirche, a ghostly edifice whose steeple had been knocked galley-west; it looked like some ungainly cooking vessel, and to this day is kept that way as a kind of antimemorial of the war. Our landlady, Frau Lentz, and her house put us in mind of Herr Issyvoo's lodgings. I think it was a four-story building; the upper two had been bombed out and were open to the elements, but the lower two were cozy, and the only other tenant was a middle-class Canadian bachelor or widower who had advertised for a German wife and was interviewing applicants, of whom there were many. At the time, there was a great deal of suspicion, of cynicism, and self-delusion in that bustling city. Almost every foreigner was assumed to be an agent of one or another of the occupying powers; the Berliners' word for agent was "mister," and the most frequently put question was "Which mister do you work for?" And many of the bustlers were hustlers. There were whores and con artists everywhere, and, of course, a good many of the misters really were agents—Soviet, British, French, American. The West Berliners had managed to deceive themselves about their city. There had been enough reconstruction so that a few blocks of the Kurfürstendamm—the streets of shops, hotels, nightclubs, and restaurants—seemed, particularly at night, a busy, glittering, prosperous thoroughfare: a Broadway, a Fifth Avenue, a Rue de la Paix, a Regent Street. There were good-looking, brilliantly lighted curbside display cases of luxury goods of all kinds, and here and there a new building of clean brick or stucco, of glass and shining steel. Pointing this out, Berliners would say, "Haven't we done a remarkable job here? We never thought we'd get the place cleaned up. Did you know that more bombs fell on Berlin than on all England?" What they were pointing to were tiny islands in a sea of rubble—a rubble that covered what remained of the bodies, one kept thinking, of God only knew how many Berliners, a rubble that could not be cleaned up for years. And the reconstruction one could see was largely *trompe l'oeil*—a street-level, eye-level facade. Above the new shops and restaurants one saw gutted upper floors; it was as if a disemboweled body had been equipped with artificial legs of stainless steel.

I did not, on those first visits, learn how the East Berliners felt about *their* sector. The reconstruction there was at once more impressive and more depressing. On Stalinallee, a few blocks beyond the Brandenburger Tor, a business and residential complex had been erected that could have been the work of the architects and builders responsible for some of the most hideous apartment houses in New York and other American cities—structures that went up early in this century, some of which I had lived in as a child. Heavy, airless, sullen-looking buildings. It was proletarian housing (or so, at least, it was said), and the most adequate housing available, but it was grubby and bourgeois in its inspiration, and doubtless was occupied not by workers but by Communist bureaucrats. For all that, there was something about Berlin that could perhaps be best appreciated by a New Yorker—its planned open spaces, its lakes and rivers, its humanness of scale. And there was something about the Berliners that charmed a New Yorker; James Morris, the British journalist,

called it an "almost cockney gaiety," and I would call it the brash-
ness and insouciance of the streetwise New Yorker. At any rate, I
liked the place as I had not expected to, and, though I speak not a
word of German and have often been put off by the little German
literature I am familiar with, I have felt more at home in Berlin than
in Paris or Rome. I have felt less so in other German cities, and I am
often exasperated by the German mind—I dislike such an umbrella
term, but I think its use defensible when speaking of the products of
Teutonic culture and education—yet I am drawn to Germany and
stimulated by it for reasons not altogether clear in my own mind.

III

That summer of 1967, again a fugitive from Washington and
Vietnam, I made two tours of the mountain country of northern
New Mexico and spent most of my time in Rhinebeck learning
what I could of that distressed, depressed, and often bloody region
—actually less than a quarter of the state but very unlike the rest of
it, and unlike anything else in my experience. Not long after I got
back from my second journey to Africa, the Ford Foundation asked
me to have a look at an antipoverty project it was considering for
some substantial grants. I made it clear that in the war on poverty I
was not fit to hold the rank of corporal and that my knowledge of
New Mexico came from Hollywood Westerns, D. H. Lawrence, and
a dim recollection of a book on the exploits of Kit Carson and Billy
the Kid I had read as a boy; except for two or three one-night stands
during presidential campaigns, I had been in the state only once,
having ten years earlier driven across it with Eleanor and the children, when I was primarily occupied with resisting demands for
money to buy trinkets at the Indian souvenir shops along the highway. But the custodians of the Ford billions said that the situation
was as much political as economic—that the proposed financing by
Ford was mainly for research and education (Sargent Shriver's Office
of Economic Opportunity was taking care of operations), and that it

was foundation policy to hire amateurs like me to check the findings of their professionals. (That was the age of the amateur or, as the Kennedy people put it, the "generalist." The Peace Corps was founded on the proposition that anyone who had done well at a liberal-arts college could teach scientific poultry raising to the Punjabis, establish modern marketing organizations in the Great Rift Valley, or set up birth-control clinics in Guatemala.) If I knew next to nothing about how to combat poverty in rural areas, I knew no more about what kind of advisers the Ford Foundation should retain, and I accepted their offer.

One evening late in June, I flew to Albuquerque with one of the Ford "professionals"—William Watts, Jr., an ebullient young Ivy Leaguer who had been a Foreign Service officer in Moscow and was later to join Henry Kissinger on Nelson Rockefeller's brain trust in New York and, later still, to serve with Kissinger on Nixon's National Security Council. He resigned in 1970 in protest over the invasion of Cambodia.[1] In Santa Fe, three others arrived: Alex Mercure, the Mexican-American director of HELP (Home Education Livelihood Program), the agency for the revival of rural villages that was requesting Ford assistance; Don Devereux, an anthropologist on the staff of the State Museum of New Mexico; and Peter Nabokov, a reporter on the Santa Fe *New Mexican*.[2] For a week, the five of us, occasionally joined by others, drove through the lower Rockies—the San Juan, Jemez, and Sangre de Cristo ranges—and the fertile counties that lie south of the Colorado border between the desert on the west and the grassy plains on the east. It is a country of stunning and, at times, unsettling contrasts. Twenty-five miles northwest of Santa Fe, a city of deliberate and rather aseptic picturesqueness, lies Los Alamos, the tidy, functional, affluent, and tightly guarded enclave of the nuclear scientists, Manhattan Project West, living in

[1] In 1967, there was something of a Republican tinge to the Ford Foundation. McGeorge Bundy had become president the year before, and Watts's superior—and mine on this mission—was Malcolm Moos, a political scientist whom I had known first as an Eisenhower speechwriter.

[2] Son of Nicholas Nabokov, the composer, and nephew of Vladimir Nabokov, the novelist.

ranch houses a few miles from the site of some of the oldest cliff dwellings on the continent. And twenty miles northwest of Los Alamos is Coyote, a shantytown of pensioners and welfare recipients, a settlement as depressed and depressing as anything outside the great urban slums. The surrounding woodlands of mixed conifers, massive ponderosa pine, spruce, fir, cottonwoods, and delicate aspens are now mostly parks and public lands, well protected and tended by the United States Forest Service, and used by the public for recreation and by private interests for lumbering. Streams plentiful and pure rush down from the Colorado Rockies to water the forests and orchards and the vast green meadows—the *bolsóns,* "tablelands," used for grazing and for alfalfa growing by wealthy ranchers, mostly from outside New Mexico. The region is rich in coal, oil, natural gas, uranium, and a variety of semiprecious minerals—resources largely untapped, and even unsurveyed, although it has been inhabited by Europeans for almost four hundred years. All this grandeur we passed on our way to and from isolated villages of cracked-adobe houses (supporting vegetation on the roof), dirty concrete-block hovels, and tin shacks—hamlets inhabited by people speaking an almost archaic Spanish, barely comprehensible even to Mexican-Americans in the southern part of their state. Most of these people, one guessed, were over seventy or under seven, the middle generation having gone off to the cities. Northern New Mexico, it seemed, was populated, thinly and wretchedly, by grandparents and grandchildren.

Despite its natural wealth and its long history of civilization, Rio Arriba County, in the highlands of the north—a county somewhat larger than Connecticut—is one of the most backward, poverty-ridden, and aggrieved sections of the United States. Indeed, an observant traveler—once he leaves the paved roads over which trucks and tourists speed north to Colorado, south to Santa Fe and Albuquerque, east to Taos and Texas, west to the Apache reservations and Arizona—may be overcome by the feeling that he is not in the United States at all but in the thinly populated hinterland of some conspicuously underdeveloped country in South or Central America. Had it not been for the state and federal welfare systems, many—perhaps most—of these peasants would have been as far outside the money economy as the Indians of Peru or the pastoral tribesmen in the highlands of Kenya (which the New Mexican highlands resemble in many ways) and Uganda. The amenities of their homes were few; those without running water and electricity outnumbered those that had them, and in some places telephones were not much more than a rumor. Despite the abundance and proximity of modern fuels, wood was most commonly used for cooking and heating. Sometime in the past, most of the villages had supported a store, and perhaps a barroom, but I also noted in many villages one or two abandoned shops and numerous abandoned houses, which enhanced the general air of melancholy. The population had been slowly declining throughout this century, and the 1960 census figure for several communities in the county was zero. Though the old Spanish Trail to California was blazed across Rio Arriba in 1761, in 1967 there were few roads to connect the scattered settlements; in winter, snow made much of the road system impassable. There were no railroads—unless one counted a narrow-gauge spur of the Denver, Western & Rio Grande, which, skirting some troublesome mountains in Colorado, dips into the county for about thirty miles before reentering Colorado, neither taking on nor discharging passengers along the way. Illiteracy was widespread; unemployment was more than four times—at least—the national level. In all the county, fewer than three hundred people worked in industry, mostly in sawmills. The villagers who had anything to do were subsistence farmers, living and working on such small strips of land as had not been taken over by the federal government or bought by Anglo ranchers. The schools were among the worst in the country, and other public services almost nonexistent. There had been considerable unrest and some violence—barn burnings, destruction of fences and irrigation systems, vandalism, seizures of public property, a few kidnappings, and a shootout in a county courthouse. And, of course, many charges of police brutality. There had been mass protests in Albuquerque and a march on Santa Fe. The protests, and probably the violence, had been directed by a colorful and formidable local leader, an ex-evangelist named Reies Tijerina, who headed an organization named the Alianza Federal de Mercedes—the Federal Alliance of Land Grants, founded in 1962 and later called the Alianza Federal de los Pueblos Libres, the Federal Alliance of Free City-States—and who claimed that the government and the Anglo ranchers were illegally in possession of the land they exploited. There had been several journalistic accounts of all this, but I, like most Americans, had missed them. In any case, for the purpose of our mission all this was background. We were to look at HELP's projects, talk with the people they were supposed to benefit, and form such judgments as we could of the caliber of the personnel in charge of the agency. We met several of these last, engaged in setting up agricultural cooperatives and handicraft cottage industries. Their leader, Alex Mercure, was an energetic, articulate, politically shrewd man in his mid-thirties. I returned to New York and made a brief report of my impressions.

The requests for Ford funding were granted, and that was that, but my curiosity was aroused by what I had seen and heard. I wanted to know more about Tijerina and his Alianza. He had been in hiding during our trip—wanted on several counts, including kidnapping and attempted murder—but I read some of his harangues and met some of his lieutenants. One was Rodolfo "Corky" Gonzales, a clubhouse brawler and Golden Gloves champion, a bail bondsman and insurance salesman by trade, a poet and playwright, the first Chicano to be a Democratic Party district captain for Dewey, the head of a Chicano organization called La Cruzada para la Justicia (the Crusade for Justice) and editor of a militant Denver newspaper called *El Grito*. He was a thoroughly urban type, a product of the Denver barrios and the Colorado sugar-beet fields—jumpy, aggressive, streetwise, full of anger. He was bitter, for one thing, because he was able to write only in English—for his paper with a

Spanish name. "I don't know my own language," he said. "The stinking gringos taught me only theirs." Though he seemed out of place among the elderly, sad-faced campesinos of the mountain towns, he was for the moment Tijerina's official spokesman. The other aide I met was Jerry Noll, a bald and tubby Anglo-Saxon from Seattle, billed in Alianza leaflets as a "historian of international law" and a "judge." He had just been sprung from a Seattle jail when he read something about Tijerina and wrote to offer his services. He could be useful, he explained, because he was in fact the King of the Indies, a title that was rightfully his because it fulfilled a prophecy by Nostradamus that had something to do with a familial link between the Hapsburgs of Austria and Queen Isabella of Spain, whose regal heir he somehow was. When, a year earlier, some Alianza members, intending to "liberate" the forest, had organized a camp-in at the Echo Amphitheatre, a public campground in the Carson National Forest, Noll had held a press conference and handed out a proclamation that read, in part, "We shall commence to liberate our Kingdom, and if the aggressors [the U.S. Forest Service] shed one drop of blood of any of our soldiers during the progress of this campaign, a state of war shall exist as of that moment." It was signed "Don Barne Quino Cesar, the King Emperor." The more I was to learn of the Alianza, the more it seemed to me that the King Emperor was a more suitable spokesman for it than Corky Gonzales.

By June of 1967, though, the Alianza seemed to many people to be just another ethnic protest movement, like Cesar Chavez's United Farm Workers in California or the Congress of Racial Equality. The Republican Governor of New Mexico, David Cargo, formerly a Michigan lawyer and a protégé of George Romney's, expressed sympathy for the Alianza's aims and, indeed, may have owed his election to it. (His wife, a Spanish-American, had been a dues-paying member.) People like Dr. Benjamin Spock, Marlon Brando, Dick Gregory, and Martin Luther King, Jr., regarded it as an ally in the civil-rights movement and in the struggle against the war in Vietnam.

In July, I went back for another look, this time with Eleanor. We flew to El Paso, rented a car, and drove north through the desert to the mountains. (It was a memorable flight, the most festive one in my experience. Flights from New York to Mexico, or to towns on the Mexican border, were then booked solid, because New York State had recently announced that as of a certain date that summer divorces obtained under Mexican law would no longer be recognized in the courts. Our plane was full of happy, convivial people en route to Ciudad Trujillo, just over the Rio Grande, to have their shackles struck from them before the deadline.) In El Paso, I called on Clark Knowlton, a University of Texas sociologist who was a specialist on the region and one of the few Anglos—apart from Jerry Noll—who had Tijerina's confidence. I believe it was through Dr. Knowlton's intervention, and perhaps Peter Nabokov's, that we were permitted to attend an Alianza meeting in the Albuquerque headquarters, an abandoned freezing plant in an industrial quarter of the city. There were speeches and singing and some rather decorous, slow-paced dancing for the elderly. Tijerina was there with his young and beautiful second wife, Patsy. He was a tall man, lean and erect, with a strong-featured, mobile face that might have adorned a recruiting poster for Castro's army or Zapata's. He was not a compelling speaker; the self-styled revolutionary was by turns pedantic and sentimental. When I talked with him, briefly, he sounded like a New York social worker explaining conditions in East Harlem.

Tijerina, unlike most of his followers, was a Mexican-American, born, he said, on a pile of cotton socks in a farm worker's shack in a cotton field near Fall City, Texas, in 1927. In the thirties and forties, his parents and their nine children lived as migrant workers, mostly in the Southwestern cotton and beet fields but also in the Midwest, as far north as Iowa and Indiana. He was full of stories of his family's poverty and persecution. His mother, he said, once had to hunt jackrabbits for food with a homemade bow and arrows. He pictured his family as constant victims of persecution by Texas ranchers, Texas Rangers, and, later, employers and other authorities as far north as Michigan. By the time he got to school, both his parents were dead—his mother of natural causes, his father by judicial lynching: according to him, his father was hauled before a sheriff or a justice of the peace who accused him of some offense he had not committed and ordered him hanged on the spot. Just as the noose closed, it struck the officer of the law that he was having the wrong man hanged, and he ordered the executioner to remove the victim from the gallows. He was still alive when the rope was loosened, but his neck had already broken, and in a day or two he was dead. The story had an implausible ring, but Tijerina insisted it was true, and the Santa Fe journalists who knew him and knew something of the life of Mexican farmhands in the Southwest were inclined to take his word for it.

Tijerina was a mystic as well as a romantic. Interviewed by an Eastern academic in the state penitentiary outside Santa Fe, he was asked, "What leader—old or modern—do you consider as a model?" He replied, "Moses, above any other character. Because of the land he gave the Israelites. New Mexico is a promised land, too. We need strong faith. God is our father, the land is our mother." His accounts of his childhood were largely tales of religious dreams and visions. He said, for example, that one day before his mother died he sat down at the family table and learned that his meal was to be a half cup of a tea brewed from pecan bark. Instead of drinking it, he went off, disturbed, to bed, where he lay for twenty-four hours and appeared to his family to be dead of hunger. "They got a coffin for me," he said. "Then I woke up and told them I had been walking with Christ. And I told them about the flowers and green pastures." This greatly impressed his family, who felt that he enjoyed some special relationship with God and was destined for spiritual leadership. Picking beets in Michigan when he was about fifteen, he encountered a Baptist preacher, who fished for his soul and gave him a New Testament. "In five or six days, I read it all the way through and decided to go to Bible school," he has said. He had little education, but he was a studious youth as well as a religious one, and at eighteen he enrolled in the Assembly of God Bible School in Yeleta, Texas, and was soon on the road as an itinerant preacher. He acquired a following among migrant workers and at one point established a small commune in Arizona. But he had some brushes with the law—mostly for alleged larceny—and spent several years as a fugitive, in Texas and Mexico, riding out the Arizona statute of limitations. He gradually became more political than religious, and in 1960 or thereabouts took up the cause of the land-hungry in northern New Mexico.

Addressing the Alianza meeting in the Albuquerque freezing plant, Tijerina spoke about the glories of Spanish culture, about his visit to Don Quixote's town of La Mancha, about the noble history of the *raza*. He and the other speakers drew only perfunctory applause from the senior citizens sitting in the steamy hall on funeral-parlor chairs, downing tacos and coffee. But it was an extraordinary thing to find oneself at such a meeting in 1967—the year of the Six-Day War, of the Yippies, of Operation Junction City in Vietnam, and the March on the Pentagon. One of the speakers mentioned Lyndon Johnson, and a grizzled old man in the audience (which must have contained at least one FBI informer) rose to say, "I owe no loyalty to the President of the United States. I am loyal only to the King of Spain." Loyal to the King of Spain? But there was no King of Spain, and had not been for a quarter of a century. The old man was speaking of no one alive in the twentieth century but of Philip II (1527–98), during whose tempestuous reign the territories of which New Mexico is now a part were parceled out among the monarch's servitors and deserving subjects. And the program of the Alianza—a program soon to be approved by the leftist Conference on the New Politics, in Chicago—was essentially a demand for a return to the laws and practices that governed New Spain four hundred years earlier. An Alianza slogan was "The United States is trespassing in New Mexico." And this did not mean that the land should be returned to Mexico; it meant that it should be returned to Spain, or, if not returned, be allowed to secede and govern itself by

Philip's laws—laws that, of course, sanctioned armed conquest, wars
for the propagation of the faith, the Inquisition, the enslavement of
Indians, and the divine right of kings. The FBI was making noises
about Communist control of the Alianza; in point of fact, the organization with which the New Left and the civil-rights movement
were making common cause was royalist.

"Wetbacks, go home!" Anglos in Albuquerque used to shout
when they came upon Alianza demonstrations. But the demonstra-
tors were anything but wetbacks. And they were not and never had
been Mexicans. They were Spaniards whose ancestors had come
over in the wake of the conquistadores and had settled in the Rockies more than two centuries before there was a Mexico. The bureaucracy in Madrid had pored over the primitive maps brought them by
the explorers and by royal decree had granted huge tracts, to be held
in perpetuity, to settlers who were judged worthy of the Crown's
favor. Near the confluence of the Rio Chama and the Rio Grande is
the site of San Juan, settled by Spaniards a decade before the first
Englishmen arrived in Virginia and more than two decades before
the Mayflower dropped anchor in Massachusetts Bay; the settlers
were members of a party of four hundred Spaniards and Indians, led
by Don Juan de Oñate, the conquistador who established Spanish
rule over the territory—the second European colony in what is today the United States. (The first was St. Augustine, Florida, settled
in 1565.) In 1598 Oñate proclaimed San Juan Nuevo Bautista the
capital of the province. It remained the capital until the completion
of the Palace of the Governors in Villa Real de la Santa Fé de San
Francisco de Asis, now known as Santa Fe, in 1610. Some Spaniards
remained in New Mexico in the century that followed, but many
returned to Mexico or Spain; others were killed by Indians resisting
enslavement; others died in the brutal winters. In 1680 the Pueblo
Indians staged a mighty rebellion and for a time put an end to
Spanish rule. But then, almost a century after Oñate's triumph,
came the reconquest: a new conquistador, Don Diego de Vargas,
marched from El Paso del Norte (now Ciudad Juárez, just across the

river from El Paso) up the Rio Grande Valley to Santa Fe and reestablished Madrid's authority, and though there were times when this authority might have been struck down with a feather, it was not to be challenged again until 1821, when Mexico won its independence and undertook to exercise a tenuous sovereignty over the region. Then, in 1846, came the final thrust, when the United States annexed New Mexico and much else that had once been part of New Spain. It was after Vargas's reconquest, just at the close of the seventeenth century, that colonization began in earnest, and the chances are that the ancestors of most of today's Rio Arribans came to the territory in the early years of the eighteenth century. They came as Spaniards to lands they thought of as New Spain, and though Madrid ignored them for more than a century, they continued to think of themselves as Spaniards right into the nineteenth century. Thus, when Mexico broke away from Spain and, after a fashion, took charge in New Mexico, the New Mexicans resented Mexican sovereignty without resisting it. Mexico's tenure was brief as well as unwelcome, and the people of Rio Arriba have always taken offense when spoken of as "Mexican-Americans," preferring to be called "Spanish-Americans"—though in the mood some of them are in today, some may not be too pleased at being called Americans of any sort.

6

The Aftermath
and the End of the Line

I

In May of 1975, I attended, in Kansas City, a conference on the war that had begun in Korea a quarter century earlier. It was sponsored by the Harry S. Truman Library Institute, and among the participants were several military men and diplomats who had served President Truman, a number of young and middle-aged historians, and a few political writers, like me, who had written about the events under discussion. There was an interesting and at moments dramatic confrontation of the older Truman men by the younger historians. Among the former were W. Averell Harriman, Truman's leading adviser on national-security affairs; Clark Clifford, a Truman political adviser and, in 1968, Lyndon Johnson's Secretary of Defense; and Generals Matthew Ridgway and J. Lawton Collins, both of whom had commanded troops in South Korea and had later served on the Joint Chiefs of Staff. All four had been critics of General Douglas MacArthur's in 1951, and all four had—at least in the closing phases—been opponents of the Johnson-Nixon strategy in Vietnam, which was, as we met, drawing to its belated and ignominious end. The historians, of whom only a few could be classified as left-wing revisionists, were in general agreement that our Korean adventure had been a grave mistake, and one that prepared the way for the hideous misadventure in Southeast Asia. In Korea, as in Vietnam, we had confused the national interest with an ideological preference. In both places, we had violated the traditional American doctrine that precluded committing ground forces to the mainland of Asia. In both places, we had fought to strengthen a corrupt and tyrannical government. And so on.

Harriman, Clifford, and the generals insisted that the comparisons were without validity—that the war in Korea was as defensible as the war in Vietnam was indefensible. In Southeast Asia, they said, we had vainly sought to oppose an idea, communism, with military force; in Korea, our aim had been solely to resist aggression —a legitimate use of American power and sanctioned by the United Nations. Korea, the generals insisted, should not be considered mainland territory, because it was a peninsula, while Southeast Asia, the seat of four sovereign governments, was an integral part of the Asian mainland. We did not go into Korea to strengthen any particular regime but to preserve the independence of a state to which we had binding treaty commitments. Twenty-five years had not lessened the ardor of the Truman loyalists.

As the coauthor (with Arthur Schlesinger) of a book that was harshly critical of MacArthur but warm in its support of Truman and the actions he had ordered in Korea, I had some sympathy with the loyalists, but several years earlier I had become persuaded that the views expressed by the historians in Kansas City were essentially sound, and while I was glad that we had defended Truman against MacArthur, I wished that we had examined Truman's position as critically as we had MacArthur's. There were, of course, large differences between the two wars. In Korea there was no civil war and revolution, as there had been in Vietnam. The North Koreans were not regarded as liberators in the South; unlike the Viet Cong, they recruited no troops in the territory they were invading, and found little sympathy among civilians. It was true that we were resisting aggression in a rather simple and direct form, and that in so doing we were carrying out a mission that had United Nations approval. Still, it had to be regarded as an ideological war; that, indeed, was part of its rationale. No one could seriously believe that if the anti-Communist South had invaded the Communist North—and this could well have happened if Syngman Rhee's regime in Seoul had felt it had the power to unify the country by force of arms—we would have come to the defense of Pyongyang. As for the mainland-peninsula argument, it struck me as geopolitical nonsense. Both Korea and Southeast Asia are as much a part of the mainland as Florida is part of the continental United States; to a military man, I would have thought, intervening in Korea was somewhat more risky, because it was easily accessible to both the Chinese and the Russians, while Vietnam was inaccessible to the Russians and separated from the developed and industrialized parts of China by some very inhospitable terrain, with only the most primitive lines of communication.

But the clinching argument for me was that Korea led directly to the militarization of American foreign policy. Some of the revisionists maintained that the Truman administration saw in Korea an opportunity to use the strength we had built up in the course of the recent war against the Axis—that foreign policy was already militarized and that Washington was merely waiting for a war to happen. The fact is, however, that we had demobilized with great celerity and thoroughness in the late 1940s. True, we were trying, in NATO, to build the defenses of Western Europe, but we were having a hard time doing that, and we were quite unprepared for anything like Korea. Still, a decade earlier we had been even less well prepared for a far greater challenge, and we had met it with prodigies of industry and organization, and after the war we had mounted the Marshall Plan to strengthen our democratic allies to meet another totalitarian challenge. By 1950, we were becoming prey to what Denis Brogan was to call the illusion of American omnipotence. A year earlier, to be sure, China had succumbed to Communist might, but some Americans, chiefly those on the Right, attributed this to subversive influence in the State Department, while others, chiefly on the Left, were convinced that the Communist victory could have been averted if we had understood the true nature of the revolution and cultivated the goodwill of its leaders. Right and Left alike were agreed that events around the world could be controlled by us if we had the wisdom to understand them and the will to act.

In retrospect, I think the Truman policy was only slightly less mistaken than the policy MacArthur wanted to pursue. I now think our intervention in Korea was, if not in itself a certifiable disaster, a prelude for one. South Korea was the victim of aggression by North Korea. One tyranny sought to annex another. The aggressor was Communist, the victim anti-Communist. It was assumed—we assumed—that North Korea was a puppet of the USSR, that the attack had been ordered by Moscow, which perhaps was the case. Still, where was the American national interest in Korea? In 1941 the case against intervention, except for the pacifists, had come down to the argument that democracy would be an early casualty of war—that in fighting fascism, we would risk becoming Fascist ourselves. By 1945 it was clear that either the argument had no merit or that we had surmounted whatever risk there was; we had defeated the Fascist powers, and in only one instance—the internment of the Japanese-Americans on the West Coast—had we seriously curtailed liberty. Within two years, we had launched the Marshall Plan—an instrument of self-interest, to be sure, but one that was of huge importance in strengthening democracy in Western Europe. In other words, we had achieved the political end we sought—the death of fascism—by military means, and our democracy had emerged intact. This led us—including me, a former noninterventionist—to new heights of self-confidence and, as it turned out, self-delusion.

II

In mid-July of 1965, I spent several days with the Lippmanns at Southwest Harbor, discussing with Walter the plans for the biography I was thinking of writing. The air was full of talk of great troop commitments in Vietnam—a million, a half million, a quarter million—and it was clear then that there was in prospect something like a quantum leap in our involvement there. In the spring, General James Gavin had proposed, in newspaper articles and speeches, and in testimony before the Senate Foreign Relations Committee, that we employ ground forces only for the defense of certain designated enclaves—centers of population, strategic bases, and the more important coastal areas. Our troops should not, he said, be sent into the jungles and mountains, the villages and rice paddies, to hold territory for Saigon. Walter, though he had from the beginning opposed any commitment at all in Southeast Asia, seized on this idea and wrote a number of columns in support of Gavin's enclaves strategy. If we adopted it and stuck to it, he said, it would not really matter whether or not our strength on the ground increased; it was not the number of our troops that counted but their mission. If it took more men to defend less territory, so be it. At least the bombing would stop, we would abandon the notion that we were defending the national interest by trying to defeat the Viet Cong, and we would be far better off. I thought this a reasonable proposition and had written several articles myself explaining and defending it.

It was during my few days at the Lippmanns' that Johnson announced the first really large-scale dispatch of troops, and on the day of Johnson's announcement one of Walter's pro-Gavin columns had appeared. Sometime in the morning, he received a phone call from George Ball, then Under Secretary of State, a neighbor and a close friend, and a man often described as an opponent of administration policy in Vietnam who was kept in office by Johnson and Rusk so that they could hear the other side—or, at least, so that they could assure their critics that one of their number, and a highly articulate one, could have his day in court whenever he wished. "Well, Walter," George said, "you've won! The troops are going, but they won't be fanning out all over the place. There'll be no search-and-destroy. They'll be there only to secure Saigon and a few other places that we know can be defended without heavy casualties." Walter signaled me to get on an extension, and the conversation went on for another fifteen minutes or so. George made it sound as if the President had listened carefully to Gavin and Lippmann, had become persuaded of the soundness of their views (which implied that he had conceded the error of his own), and had told the Pentagon that we were in Vietnam not to win a war, or even to fight one, but only to secure a few very limited and defensible areas, in most of which there were American installations.

Walter, of course, was pleased. He was fond of George and considered him a thoroughly honorable man. By the time I left Maine, though, he was furious. The next day's news made it clear that George had either lied or been lied to, and the latter possibility was almost worse than the former. Those troops were going to Vietnam to broaden the war, not to narrow it. If George had lied, he had surely known that he would be believed only for a matter of hours, and that his credibility gap would be larger than the President's. It was conceivable that Johnson had said one thing to the Pentagon and another to the State Department—or that he had told the Pentagon to lie to the State Department. That Johnson could lie was not news; what was unacceptable to Walter was that George would not only fall for the lie but get on the phone to circulate it. It was all very well to have an antiwar man as Under Secretary of State, but if he was as gullible as George seemed to be, he didn't deserve the job, or any responsible job. And how, if he had let himself be lied to on so important a matter and still continued to work for Johnson and Rusk, could he be any longer regarded as honorable? In the remaining years of his life, Walter kept going back to this as an instance of how monstrously corrupt and corrupting the Johnson administration had been. I think it played a large part in his decision to back Nixon in 1968; though he did not die until 1974, he was so ill during that final year that he knew little of Watergate.

III

After that summer of 1965, whenever I met with Lippmann I could defend no aspect of the war. I felt that it would be insupportable even if—as I knew would not happen—Johnson should belatedly accept the Gavin thesis. And I was developing a highly personal stake in withdrawal. Mark became twenty that year, and it was plain to Eleanor and me that college, and the opportunity it offered for deferment, was not for him. He was a freshman at American University, in Washington, and no more comfortable in an academic setting than his father had been. He was getting an education, but not in the classroom, and both Eleanor and I knew, from our own experience, that it was idle to urge him to do what his instructors instructed him to do. Just as he was not the sort to seek a degree, neither was he the sort to seek exemption as a conscientious objector. In fact, he felt increasingly guilty at being out of service, for he knew that the underprivileged of his generation were fighting and dying in Vietnam; he regarded himself as overprivileged, as having squandered his opportunities, and he could not bear the thought that this would somehow exempt him from the fate of those who could neither seek sanctuary in a college nor know how to go about conning a draft board into accepting them as conscientious objectors. He had none of the infirmities that I had at his age, and we were sure that if the war was not over shortly our son would be in it —as, in time, he was.

In 1968 Mark enlisted. After American University, he had tried and then dropped out of Bard, and he had no plan to return to college. He had no more stomach for Vietnam than most of his contemporaries, but, as noted, he was not a conscientious objector and had not been part of any antiwar movement. He could, of course, have avoided service. We would have been delighted to have him go to Canada or Sweden or, with medical collusion, claim exemption on any ground possible. We not only didn't want him to be killed; we didn't want him to kill. But he would have none of that. We couldn't really quarrel with his decision, though God knows we wanted to, as we saw so many of his friends and so many sons of our friends dodging the draft with no qualms of any kind. At the end of 1968, just after he turned twenty-three, he signed up for Army training as a warrant officer flying helicopters. He had flown a lot and loved it, and had a private-pilot's license for small planes. He thought that he would sooner do his time in the air than on the ground. The services would not train airplane pilots who did not have a bachelor's degree, but the Army did not require any degree for those who flew its helicopters, so he applied for this service and was accepted. He spent 1969 in basic training in Louisiana and Georgia and at flight school in Camp Wolters, Texas. (We visited Camp Wolters once—a vast, appalling sprawl of barracks surrounded by used-car lots, fast-food joints, fundamentalist churches, and a network of roads through the cow country posted with signs like DANANG—22km, QUANTRI—16km, THAN SUN NUT—14km, and PLEIKU—64km.) For a time, there seemed a chance that Mark's outfit would be sent to Germany or Japan or somewhere other than Southeast Asia, but that was not to be. He spent 1970 in Vietnam, and we spent it, in dread and misery, in Rhinebeck and New York. We said good-bye to him at Kennedy a few nights before New Year's Eve. Eleanor was quite persuaded that helicopter pilots never came home alive; I juggled some figures showing that the chances of survival were about 80 percent, perhaps better, but I didn't convince her, or even myself, and anyway who wanted a son to run a 20 percent risk of dying for a bad cause in a stinking war? For a year, I went to bed with a small transistor radio under my pillow, and turned it on whenever I came awake (as I often did) at four or five in the morning, to hear a news program that for some reason specialized in telling how many choppers had been lost the day before and where they had been shot down—a service not provided by the newspapers I read. Television and newspapers supplied body counts; only that program, as far as I could learn, gave helicopter counts. Perhaps the station manager had a son flying them. Our interest in the war became increasingly selfish, centered on one participant. When, in April, American forces invaded Cambodia, I was properly outraged, but as Mark's father I was rather relieved. He was in Tayninh, on the Cambodian border, and in every letter he had been telling us of dodging shells lobbed over by the Viet Cong on the other side. Widening the war by this "incursion," as Nixon and Kissinger had done, was surely wicked, but routing the troops who were shooting at our son was all right with his parents. What was even more all right was that just as the invasion got under way Mark developed a hernia and was sent to a hospital for surgery, then to a secure place on the seacoast for recuperation. Splendid hernia! Timely surgery!

Our war came to a welcome end in the middle of a December night in 1970, when, in our apartment in the city, we got a call from Mark saying that he was at Fort Dix, in New Jersey, being mustered out, and that he would be with us in a matter of hours—as indeed he was, unscarred physically (except by the surgeon's healing knife) or, as far as were able to tell, in any other way. In fact—and this, in a way, was hard to take—the young man who came back from Vietnam was more thoughtful, more considerate, more responsible, more at ease with himself and with us than the one who had gone there a year earlier. It was not easy to acknowledge that the war we hated had done this, but there it was—Satan's benefaction, good sprung from evil, life from death.

This was a happening that, I believe, should never have happened,* not because I have any wish to deny exposure to

* EDITOR'S NOTE: The happening was a television debate on New York's Channel 13 not long before Mark Rovere's return home. The participants were, on one side, Jerry Rubin, Abbie Hoffman, and Rennie Davis—the three Yippies who had been recently convicted in the celebrated Chicago trials before Judge Julius Hoffman and were now

Rubin, Hoffman, and Davis, and not because of any discomfort caused me by my exposure to them, but because it was a put-on falsely labeled as discussion. I have never had much confidence that group discussion of any kind is of value in arriving at truth of any kind. Certain kinds of truth may emerge from certain adversary proceedings, but such truth is generally of a limited kind—e.g., the answer to "whodunit?" But nothing like this could be said in defense of this not-brief-enough encounter. I foolishly agreed about an hour before the event to participate; I should have known better. Worst of all, though, the promoters —men working in "educational" television—were pleased with themselves after the broadcast, felt that they had a solid hit on their hands, and compounded the original mistake by rebroadcasting it several times. It gives one pause about certain issues of intellectual responsibility.

Rubin and Hoffman do not believe in rational discourse. (Davis seems a somewhat different case, but not, I would gather, *very* different.) Indeed, they do not believe in rationality at all—though a disbelief in reason, as in anything else, must be the product of some process of reason. However that may be, what is the sense of setting up a debate in which half the debaters have nothing but contempt for the form and declare in advance that they are playing a different game with a different set of rules? It is rather like arranging a contest between a basketball team and a football team, with one side seeking touchdowns, the other baskets. If the principal object was—as I now believe it to have been—to give a particular public a view of some exotics who see politics as theater, why not just give them time and a stage?

I cringe at some of the observations I made—in particular, my response to the question of whether they were "right" to

out on bail—and, on the other, Norman Dorsen, professor of law at New York University Law School; James Wechsler, editor of the New York *Post;* and Rovere. This passage is taken from a draft of an article that Rovere wrote some time later but never published.

behave as they did in the Chicago trials. I meant, quite simply, that I thought their premises were all wrong, but that *if* I shared them, I would have done as they did. But nobody wanted to get on with a discussion of premises.

I suppose we can seize this opportunity to say something about the "issues," though, God knows, over the years everyone has said, time and again, just about all there is to be said on these matters. About ends and means: I have always felt that Paul Porter, one of the finest and funniest minds ever turned loose in Washington, dealt properly with the question when he said some years ago, "If the ends don't justify the means, what the hell does?" The means have a way of corrupting the ends, but this is not always the case, and I would be willing to consider traveling down any one of several roads to a better society if I had reasonable assurances that we would get there. But violence and terror in this country in the foreseeable future will lead away from, not toward, a more humane society. And if the mood of the country should change, so that postadolescents like Rubin and Hoffman could emerge as the Trotskys of the revolution, I think I would resort to prayer, for their mentality seems to me, in essence, totalitarian. I think I would about as soon seek justice before Julius Hoffman as before Abbie Hoffman. But the violence I fear is from the Right, and I fear it because it would bring repression and would in all likelihood remove from our society the freest and most humane young spirits, nearly all of them now somewhere on the Left.

Liberals and liberalism: I like to think of myself and of most of the people I admire as being liberal in temperament—that is to say, undogmatic, tolerant, receptive. But in programmatic terms, I don't think that "liberal" as a category means very much—at least at the present time. It may please Rubin and Hoffman to think that they are somehow *more* against the war than, say, Senators George McGovern and Frank Church, but it just isn't so. It may bolster their egos, which appear in need of underpinning, to think that they are fiercer enemies of Spiro Agnew's than what is generally described as the liberal press. But that isn't so, either—a fact easily documented by a study of Agnew's speeches. The political differences between most of today's liberals and most of today's radicals—and, for that matter, many of today's conservatives—are primarily tactical, rhetorical, and, as I have noted, temperamental. There is nothing liberal or conservative or radical about wanting an immediate end to the war in Vietnam. The same is true of injustice of any kind. There may be differences about the proper structure of society and the economic order, but of this one cannot really be sure—at least as between liberals and radicals—because none of these categories seems now to stand for much of anything in programmatic terms. (To a degree, this may be accounted for by the priorities that both sides accord to ending the war and establishing racial equality.)

Hoffman, Rubin, Davis, and others of their general persuasion (I write cautiously here, for I am not sure that they really share a common persuasion) base their scorn for liberals and liberalism not on ideological grounds but on grounds of character and of political effectiveness; liberals, they hold, are at once cowards and political idlers, of no help—indeed, a hindrance—in the course of political conflict. Yet liberals have played a very large part in securing the social gains that few on the left would care now to forfeit: collective bargaining, the abolition of child labor, federal aid to education and medicine, and such of our civil liberties as remain intact even today. And much more. It was demagogy of the most transparent kind that led Rubin to say that he and his codefendants were out on bail because someone burned a bank in Santa Barbara; they were out because their lawyers could invoke judicial principles established by lovers of liberty and justice—some of them conservative, many of them liberal, and a few (I think here of Mr. Justice

William Douglas) who may be described as radical in the context of today's politics.

It is also pure demagogy to generalize about the court system as these defendants did. There are God knows how many court systems in this country—thousands, anyway. Some we know to be corrupt and venal; others are corrupt without being venal. Nearly all, perhaps, deal less justly with the poor than with the well-to-do—though not necessarily because they are either corrupt or venal. It is not altogether the fault of the courts that some people know their rights and can afford to defend them with able lawyers; it is, rather, the fault of the economic order. To me, Kingman Brewster [then president of Yale University] made sense when he said that he doubted if a black revolutionary could get a fair trial in New Haven in 1970. But what would prevent a fair trial is the climate of opinion, not the structure of any particular judicial system. What, in Brewster's place, I might have gone on to say was that fairness denied (by prejudice or whatever) in the lower courts would probably be restored in the higher ones. Generally speaking, the appeals mechanism, particularly in the federal system, remedies injustice as fairly as any system ever devised. To which Rubin and Hoffman and Davis would surely reply that it's a hell of a system that lets a man rot in jail for months and years waiting for the dispensation, if any, of justice he should have been accorded in the first place. Of course it's a hell of a system— justice delayed is justice denied, in itself injustice. But the root of this problem is not to be found in the court system—there I go: *systems*—but in the reluctance of the taxpayers to put up the money needed to trim months and years back to weeks, days, and hours.

Perhaps we have all been debasing political discourse. I find this infinitely saddening, and for no one more than for the three who sat across from us in that absurd happening. Each was intelligent in his way, and each likable in his way, despite every effort to knock intelligence and to capitalize on displays of obnoxiousness. I hope they stay out of jail, for I think they were indicted and tried under an absurd law and I see no point in punishing them for their offenses (some of which may have been illegal) against civility and other values that I hold and they don't. If they avoid jail, I think they will have to turn their gifts to other fields, for they, like all of us, are aging, and plenty of others are eager to play similar roles. There are substantial numbers of young men and women who accept the notion that politics is theater and enjoy it that way. Well, it so happens that —though it has always had its show-business side—politics is not theater. Would sometimes that it were, but it isn't. Politics is Vietnam and Nixon and Agnew and Lester Maddox and Kent State and ABM and SALT and a great many things that are not—unfortunately, in most cases—works of the imagination.

IV

It is as much by chance as by choice that this place, Key West, is the place where I find myself trying to confront the chaos of experience, to fix on paper the disordered, ungainly, and furtive elements of my life. Eleanor and I came down here just a year ago, in January 1977, to escape for a week or so some brutal weather in Rhinebeck. We had no thought of becoming full- or part-time residents. I had first come here in 1951, on a brief professional visit. Harry Truman was President then, and I was to do a *New Yorker* article on him and on the town he had chosen as a retreat from Washington. The poor man needed a retreat; he was running the war in Korea and trying to get an ambitious domestic program through Congress, and he was being harassed by Senator Joe McCarthy and upstaged by General Douglas MacArthur, both of whom commanded followings larger than his. In those days, Key West was as far as you could get from

the continental United States and still be within its political boundaries, and the remoteness was more than geographical.

On that visit in 1951, I became interested in the island's history,
particularly its recent history, and I met some of the people who had
played a part in it, but I left with no desire to return. The U.S. Navy
was in charge—Truman's Southern White House was the comman-
dant's residence—and the town seemed to belong to the sailors.
Duval Street, the busy thoroughfare that runs the mile between the
Atlantic and the Gulf of Mexico, was honky-tonk from one end to
the other—bars, sleazy restaurants, tattoo parlors, verminous hostel-
ries of one sort or another, strip-tease joints, and whorehouses. Na-
tives were complaining that the Cuban coffee shops—which offered
such amenities as billiards, dominoes, and chess, along with the
bracing coffee and its stirring scents—were giving way to vendors of
Coca-Cola and hamburgers. The cigar factories had long since
moved north to Tampa and Ybor City, and the sponge trade, even
before there was competition from synthetics and from Greek divers
in Tarpon Springs, was suffering from some kind of biological blight.
The Key West of Ernest Hemingway—with its gunrunners, drunks,
brawlers, and casual killers—was, I guess, more or less intact, like
Hemingway himself, but it held no enchantment for me. But even
that Key West didn't seem likely to last. The few attractive sites not
claimed by the Navy were being grabbed up by developers, mostly
motel builders. Florida was then trying to break Nevada's grip on
the quickie-divorce trade, and the motel where the White House
press, of which I was a temporary member, was quartered also provided shelter for women no longer young but not yet old, who baked
and bleached themselves beside the swimming pool while waiting
for accommodating judges to certify their freedom from bondage.
Before long, it seemed to me, the seven square miles of the island
would be something like a cross between the Marseilles waterfront
and a cut-rate Miami Beach.

It was twenty-one years before I came down here again, and that
was largely due to circumstances beyond my control. In the spring of

1972, we had been visiting my father in Bradenton, a small city on the Gulf, where he was to die three years later, and we decided to spend a few days exploring the Everglades, with a base at the Flamingo Inn, in Everglades National Park. After a day or two there, the rains came; when they let up, the sky remained dark with heavy clouds and murderous mosquitoes. To go to the Everglades and stay indoors seemed about as absurd as going into a saloon for a glass of buttermilk. We decided to decamp, and because Eleanor had not seen Key West and had heard reports about the place that cast some doubt on the validity of my gloomy recollections, we headed down the Overseas Highway. Indeed, I had been wrong, or largely so. The motels had proliferated, but not at the expense of the town; most of the new ones were on filled-in salt marshes at the eastern end of the island. Because divorce was easier everywhere, Key West had not become another Reno. The naval personnel was much reduced. Duval Street was not so much honky-tonk as artsy-craftsy—in many ways a mixed blessing—but it was at least tidier. Thanks partly to federal funds for urban renewal and to the passion for meticulous decor on the part of the large homosexual community the town had attracted, the street had a neat, orderly look. The Cuban coffee shops were fewer in number, but the Cuban groceries and restaurants were flourishing, and the increased American appetite for seafood had brought prosperity to the fishing fleet. But we gave no thought to spending more than a few days here, nor did we when, in 1977, we returned for a short stay. The idea of spending a whole winter in Florida, or anywhere else that distant from New York, had never attracted me; I felt my age, and I did not relish coping with snow and ice, but I have something of the feeling for New York that Samuel Johnson had for London. Living in it or near it has its difficulties and its dangers, but for one as addicted as I the dangers of being cut off from the city are comparable to being cut off from air. A lamentably provincial feeling, but my own. Last year, however, I knew that some kind of change, not necessarily permanent, was imminent, almost inevitable. For one thing, I have a physical

problem of some seriousness. I am just about immobilized by arthri-
tis and (worse, I think) by what orthopedists call a "muscle deficit"
—a condition visited upon me when, in 1973, a surgeon sliced
through some neck and shoulder muscle in order to remove a malignancy fetchingly known in the trade as a "rodent ulcer" (and to
transplant some skin from my thigh to my neck). He got the rat, and
I got a pain in the neck and a cervical collar that keeps my head
from falling into my lap. I am able to sit before a typewriter and do
what I can to sort out those mixed and furtive elements, but beyond
that very little. Were it otherwise, I doubt that I would be writing
this now. I would, I like to think, be gaining new impressions of the
world rather than examining old ones. I would still be making regular trips to Washington for close looks at the follies and occasional
splendors of that awesome center of imperial power—a city I first
got to know when it seemed an outpost of empire rather than a
center. And I would be going to Africa and Europe and the American Southwest to follow through on projects I undertook many years
ago and had hoped by this time to be completing. But I now know
that I will not see Africa again—perhaps not Europe or the Southwest. The least demanding forms of travel—walking around a mid-
Manhattan block with Eleanor and our two small dogs—is almost a
torture, and a strain on my slim resources of physical energy. Whoever described pain as the absence of pleasure must have had only a
passing acquaintance with pain—and probably with pleasure, too,
which is certainly more than the mere absence of pain. Chronic
pain, I have learned, does not lessen the possibilities of pleasure; in a
way, it increases them, for the slightest measure of relief—the respite of a sound sleep, an anodyne that works, sights and sounds and
words that rivet the attention—can have an almost erotically plea-
surable effect. In general, though, pain affects the mind and spirit in
distressing ways. It heightens one's natural selfishness, one's self-
pity. It foreshortens the horizon and constricts the universe. Of all
this, the writer—and, of course, the reader—must be wary.

So, this year, in 1978, we bought a small, narrow house in Key

West and came down in the winter. Remembering my father, my thoughts raced from him to his grandson in Dutchess County, preparing (to Eleanor's and my dismay) to move to Colorado. We were saddened by this, but considerably less so than by the last time we said good-bye to Mark. That was a bit more than seven years ago, when he left for Vietnam—likely never to return, we thought that miserable December night, from that most obscene of all obscene wars. Vietnam, Vietnam. I am halfway through a book—I am halfway through several books—that is a kind of indictment of my generation for having brought our country into that wretched conflict. It is *The Best and the Brightest,* by David Halberstam, who covered much of the war for the New York *Times* and argues here that the best and the brightest among us brought out the worst and the most stupid in the national psyche. I should have read the book years ago, but I didn't, I guess because I had the impression that it wasn't very good, which in a way is true. Once Mark was home and Nixon seemed at last to have had his fill of gore, I wanted to fix my mind on something else—something far from Vietnam. But Halberstam's case has some strength. My generation has a lot to answer for, and I hope to get around to that.

In the aftermath of Vietnam, and, indeed, in the last years of the fighting there, I felt about the war there much as I had felt about the Spanish civil war when it ended. Not betrayed, of course, for who could possibly feel betrayed by Richard Nixon? It would be like saying of a bank robber that the man was dishonest. But I felt intellectually and morally spent, drained, exhausted by a controversy over what had long since ceased to be controversial. I wanted as much distance from the event as I could possibly get. I didn't want to hear about it, and I didn't want to write about it, though I had to do both. Just as I could not bear to look at Picasso's Guernica murals when I recognized the full squalor of what had gone on in Spain from 1936 to 1939—had the Stalinists destroyed the town to make propaganda, perhaps to inspire a work of art?—and could not read Hemingway's *For Whom the Bell Tolls,* so I could not read the angry books being written about Vietnam. I had spent my anger on my own book. I had had my say, belted out my screams of anguish, in *Waist Deep in the Big Muddy*, which had been published in the summer of 1968 and which had been overtaken by events even before it was on the press. When the two articles that were the bulk of it appeared in *The New Yorker*, several months earlier, they were well received, though I was rather pained to note that nearly all the approving comment came from people of about my age; the young were not listening—at least not to a middle-aged man writing in a middle-aged magazine. (I do not think the young were reading at all. When I walked among the thousands of angry young men and women in Grant Park in Chicago during the Democratic National Convention in 1968, I was struck by the absence of books, magazines, and newspapers. When I was that age, no one would have spent hours sitting or lying on the grass without reading matter of some sort. But in Chicago in that sickening week, those who weren't zonked out on dope or weren't making love were listening to transistor radios and tape recorders or creating their own music with guitars.)[1] By the time *Waist Deep* appeared, the landscape it sketched had disappeared. The Viet Cong had launched the Tet offensive. Robert Kennedy and Martin Luther King had been gunned down. Johnson was a burnt-out case, no longer in the running, driven from office by the antiwar movement, by then a great political force. The propositions I had put were now immaterial. The war was going to end one horrible way or another—if not by Richard Nixon's "secret plan," then by turmoil here or defeat in the field. In any case, there was, I felt, nothing more for me as a writer to do or say, except for taking notes on how the whole misbegotten business would wind up —or "wind down," as Nixon was putting it. There was no longer any point—or so I thought at the time—in fixing blame, in engag-

[1] Elizabeth Hardwick, who accompanied me on some of these walks, took the view that reading is a solitary activity, a pleasure or a solace rarely to be indulged in by those who are part of a movement, solitude being the antithesis of solidarity. Maybe. But I can't imagine anything less conducive to solidarity than drugs, which, like books, produce hallucinations, though I suppose of a different order and intensity.

ing in polemics with the hawks, nearly all of whom by then had taken flight, or with those doves whose reasoning seemed to me as spurious as that of their adversaries. No longer any point in asking Mary McCarthy why compassion led her to celebrate virtue and strength of character in Hanoi that she had never discerned else-where—not in Saigon, not in New York or Paris, not on Cape Cod or in the groves of academe. The point earlier had been that to have done so would have weakened the argument she was making and damaged her credibility as an observer, but now it was all beyond argument, and Mary's credibility was her affair, not mine. No longer any reason to spend hours with Dwight Macdonald—when he was agitated, which he was most of the time, his voice assaulted the eardrums like a jackhammer—saying how absurd it was for him to be writing manifestos calling Vietnam an "illegal war" when he knew damned well that it wouldn't be any better or worse if the Supreme Court handed down a unanimous opinion certifying its constitutionality. I simply didn't want to go on making a career of writing about Vietnam. I applauded when Daniel Ellsberg leaked the Pentagon Papers, but I didn't read them. Ancient history. Lies from start to finish. For a time, I found myself avoiding Washington and American politics as much as I could. Watergate seemed less a series of revelations than a fulfillment. In 1975, the year the cursed war finally did end, I put together a book, *Arrivals and Departures*, which was as nonpolitical as I could make it: reminiscences of my father, who died that year, and of schoolboy friends and antics, of travels in France and Italy with Eleanor and the children twenty-two years earlier, sketches of New York and of some exotic types I had known there in my younger days. But then on William Street in Key West, in the winter of 1978, I found myself returning to Viet-nam, trying to sort the whole thing out, once more (the Calvinist in me) fixing blame, reliving the sixties, which in an article on the period in the Sunday New York *Times Magazine*, I had airily charac-terized—borrowing a phrase of John Updike's—as a "slum of a de-cade." I knew my way around the place. I knew many of the slumlords; some were close friends, old friends, family friends, comrades, collaborators, drinking companions. In a way, I had flakked for them. I bore at least a measure of responsibility for the mess. I had prattled about the "free world," "Communist aggression," "global menace," and the like. With Arthur Schlesinger I had written a book stoutly defending American intervention in Korea, which I now saw to have been based on the very fallacies that led to Vietnam—conceiving communism to be monolithic and using military means to achieve political aims. I had been opposed to intervention in Vietnam in 1954, when Nixon and Dulles had wanted us to rescue the beleaguered French, but I had not opposed our own subsequent presence there until 1965, when Johnson Americanized the war with large contingents of combat troops. Late in 1977, shortly before Eleanor and I went to Key West, I had been deeply moved by a book called *A Rumor of War*, by Philip Caputo, a young Marine Corps lieutenant who had spent 1965 in the first wave of combat units to engage the Viet Cong in the hills and villages and rice paddies. I normally dislike reading about combat, more or less as I dislike reading detailed accounts of fires, floods, and natural disasters. Caputo's book is about combat and little else; there are bloodstains on every page. But what held my attention was not so much the killing as the killer. A restless, adventurous young man, bored with life in a Chicago suburb and with efforts to please his family, just out of the working class and upwardly mobile, he was stirred by John Kennedy's calls for service and sacrifice. After college, where he had performed indifferently, he decided that if he could serve "freedom" by fighting insurgents in Vietnam, he would do so. He joined the corps and discovered that he liked the military life, that soldiering excited him as the professions did not. He was a war lover, delighted when he learned that his mission in Vietnam would be not merely security but combat. He was at times deranged and exhilarated by it. In time, his loyalty to his men and his hatred of the "enemy" provided motives more powerful than the New Frontier ideals that had led him into the war. He killed with abandon, not only the Viet Cong but anyone, old or young, he judged to be hostile. He had his own little My Lai, for which he was punished but remained unrepentant. Yet his idealism, though twisted and dirtied, never quite left him, and toward the end of his hitch it reasserted itself. He saw the fraud and madness of it all, and when it was over he sent his campaign ribbons to the White House (which returned them with a note saying it was not authorized to keep them) and joined Vietnam Veterans Against the War.

My generation . . . A few of its literary members are settling in here at Key West. In a small compound a couple of blocks away are the poets Richard Wilbur and John Ciardi and the novelists John Hersey and Ralph Ellison. And a few blocks farther away is Joseph Lash, the political firebrand of my left-wing student days—the most influential and durable of any of the youth leaders in my time. He is still a leader of sorts, though no longer a firebrand, and the young people who come down here to open boutiques and smoke marijuana have never heard of him, except for a few, perhaps, who may recognize him as a historian and a Pulitzer Prize–winning biographer—a career he took up after many years as a United Nations correspondent and editorial writer for the New York *Post*. He and I sometimes try to sort out the chaos of experience together. Like him, I was a Stalinist forty years ago. The two of us are among the few who did not move from the far Left to the far Right, or away from politics altogether.

One of the books I am halfway through is quite distasteful—*I Gave Them a Sword*, David Frost's account of how he, a crafty and resourceful British entrepreneur and television impresario, dealt with Richard Nixon and some other sharpies in setting up and conducting interviews with the Sage of San Clemente—an enterprise that lined the pockets of the ex-President, along with those of Frost and his collaborators, and cast some heat and a little light on the Watergate scandals. I have the impression that the interviewer and the interviewee deserved each other, and I probably won't finish the book. I know all too well how it ends. I will finish Thomas McGuane's *Ninety-Two in the Shade*, a novel set in Key West. . . .

V

MAY 1979:† Where to begin? Though I have been constantly in pain since early 1975, it has lately intensified, and seems to have taken over my life. This latest stage began five or six weeks ago in Key West. It came suddenly and found me wholly unprepared. I had, in fact, been having what for me was a good season. I had written a long piece on my early days in Washington—for the book but also to show to Shawn—two Washington Letters for the magazine, and two reviews for the Sunday New York *Times*. I had done a lot of reading (mostly novels), had missed swimming only two or three days, and had had an agreeable, even lively social life. I think of Emily Dickinson:

Pain has an element of blank;
It cannot recollect
When it began, or if there were
A day when it was not.

OCTOBER 1979: On August 6, 1979, when I was sixty-four, I was admitted on my own application to this institution, the Vassar Brothers Hospital, in Poughkeepsie, New York. As of this writing, two months later, I am still here, and due to remain for a bit. When I say "here," I mean something more than the undistinguished pile of bricks and mortar in which I spend my days and nights. Except for an occasional trip to another floor for surgery, X-rays, and the like, I have been spending close to twenty-four hours a day in a two-bed unit cramped with hospital furniture and equipment. More than that, I have been con-

† EDITOR'S NOTE: These entries are from Rovere's journal.

fined to traction and orthopedic braces that restrict my field of vision to about twenty square feet directly before my eyes— white plaster ceiling when I am in bed, which is most of the time, and pastel walls when I am sitting up. The surgery I have twice undergone is to repair, in a process known as cervical fusion, a broken or, as my surgeon says, a "dislocated," neck.

Nothing so focuses the mind, Dr. Johnson said, as the knowledge that one is to be hanged the following morning. . . .

OCTOBER 1979: *Confinement.* For as long as I can remember, my greatest dread has been of confinement, of incarceration, of enforced physical restraint. The tales of suffering that gripped me most in my earliest years of reading were prison memoirs. The prison recollections of Alexander Bergman, the anarchist who killed Henry Clay Frick, moved me as few other books of my early memories ever did. While others have argued over the effectiveness of our penal system in deterring crime, I have known that in my case its effectiveness is beyond dispute. I cannot understand it when I read of some veteran criminals accepting prison sentences of five to ten years as a not unreasonable price to pay for their profitable misdeeds. To me, the thought of a sentence of five to ten days is quite sufficient to deter the smallest of my larcenous instincts, and I can think of no prize on earth that would be worth a year in anyone's lockup. . . .

NOVEMBER 1979: *Boredom.* My strategies for fighting it are, I suppose, as ancient as the affliction. I say to myself, lips moving, all that I have ever committed to memory. Scraps of poetry, mostly doggerel—Kipling, Macaulay, Longfellow, etc.— and a few moderns: Eliot, Yeats, Frost, and some of the Southern agrarians for whom I once had, inexplicably, a strong taste. I also have some bits and pieces of the New Testament, passages from the likes of the *Communist Manifesto*, the Dec-

laration of Independence, and various other documents. And I
go through lists of names—people I knew as a boy in Brooklyn
and Stony Brook, and on down through what will soon be four
decades on *The New Yorker* and in Dutchess County. I pose
myself arithmetical problems, adding, say, five or six four-digit
figures without writing anything down. Also I have been making a study of the alphabet, and have come to the conclusion
that the letter *q* is one—and I think the only one—for which
we have no need. I can think of no word in which its place
could not adequately be taken by *k*, though this might cause
some kwite serious visual offenses. . . .

NOVEMBER 1979: *Sleep.* I probably sleep about as much as I did
before coming here, but in unaccustomed and largely unsatisfy-
ing patterns—fifteen minutes, a half hour at a time, in daylight
segments—possibly as much as two unbroken hours just before
dawn. My waking hours have been transformed into a narrow,
almost fixed, pattern for avoiding death. Six times a day, I'm
connected to complex and shiny machines that lend power to
my apparently misguided efforts to breathe in a proper fashion.
Sessions with these simulators of what should be an easy and
natural bodily function last perhaps half an hour each, though
some of this time goes into endless connecting and discon-
necting. Then there are the interminable dealings with people
who draw blood and chart and diagram various of my func-
tions. If I were applying for employment, I would have to describe myself as having spent the last year staving off death as a
fireman puts down flames.

Oh, but I hate it, hate it, hate it. I hate it and fear it and can
find few words that reach the depths of my feeling. The truth
is that my character is being altered in ways I find unbearable
to record. I seem to myself to become pettier and meaner and
more selfish by the hour . . .

In ten weeks I must have shared my room with close to

twenty other patients, two of whom have died in this period, the second only yesterday. The experience suggests certain generalizations about American marriage among people of my approximate age. The wives seemed in splendid health and were devoted spouses. I overheard much intimate conversation, but there seemed to be no trace of rancor or resentment in any of them; the children and grandchildren appeared to be uniformly devoted and respectful. Socially and economically, the range has been from the world of the skilled industrial worker to the middle levels of corporate management—meaning, in this case, a large number drawn from high-technology companies like IBM, whose presence comes close to dominating the life of our era. Put another way, the range is from John O'Hara's hardhats to his upper crust, which isn't very different today from what it was when he died, ten years ago. In the lives of these people whom I see and hear at such close range and in so defenseless a posture, there must be great tangles of corrosive desires and ambitions—greed, the lust for dominion, the betrayals and deceptions, the pettiness—that are now accepted as the "realities" of Middle American life not only in the works of writers like O'Hara but in the scripts of the most popular daytime serials. Surely, as I eavesdrop on the whisperings of those Middle Americans who move in and out of my room as they face fate's cruelty (never, in my experience, its splendors), there should be evidence of this. Yet what I see and hear are responsible, well-adjusted men and women, like those my parents used to read about in *The Saturday Evening Post,* as this century moves toward what must be its squalid end. . . .

NOVEMBER 1979

Dear Mr. Balz,

After fifteen weeks at Vassar Brothers Hospital, I have become a close and, I hope, accurate observer of the institution. There is much in it that I have found disappointing and much that I think could and should be changed. But this is not why I write you now. My purpose is simply to say that the members of the nursing staff (particularly on the second floor, where I have spent nearly all my time) have almost without exception seemed to me able, generous, and a pleasure to be with in difficult times—times when overwork has often been the rule. Obviously, I can name names and cite some striking incidents. I would be happy to do so in a more private form of communication. But for the moment I will content myself with the generalization that the level seemed high—admirably so.

Sincerely,
Richard H. Rovere‡

‡ EDITOR'S NOTE: Richard Rovere died at about 1 A.M. Thanksgiving night, November 23, 1979.

Index

NOTE

Many people helped in assembling this book. I should like to thank, especially, Eleanor Rovere for her confidence and encouragement; Betsy Rovere for aiding in the search of closets and attics for lost manuscript pages; Mark Rovere, Ann Rovere, William Shawn, Arthur M. Schlesinger, Jr., Robert Bendiner, Andy Logan, Ann Malamud, and Daniel Aaron for their useful suggestions; and Janice O'Connell and others of the staff of the State Historical Society of Wisconsin, in Madison, Wisconsin, to which Mr. Rovere gave his files, for their ready assistance in locating and copying certain memoranda and notebooks. The book was designed by Wilma Robin; the index was prepared by Sydney Cohen. Janis Langsdorf typed the manuscript.

I am grateful, finally, to the author for his personal and professional trust, on which I have relied in preparing this book for him.

—JEANNETTE HOPKINS